Personal Witness
A Biblical Spirituality

Personal Witness
A Biblical Spirituality

by JOHN J. NAVONE, S.J.

with a Foreword by Eugene H. Maly

SHEED AND WARD · NEW YORK

© *Sheed and Ward, Inc., 1967*

Library of Congress Catalog Card Number 67-13761

9389

Imprimi potest:
  Johannes J. Kelley, S.J.
  Praep. Prov. Oregoniensis

Nihil obstat:
  Thomas J. Beary
  Censor Librorum

Imprimatur:
  †Robert F. Joyce
  Bishop of Burlington
  November 3, 1966

Manufactured in the United States of America

To My Professors

Roderick A. F. MacKenzie · David M. Stanley · Jean-Louis D'Aragon

Acknowledgments

The author wishes to thank his former Scripture professors without whose instruction and inspiration this work would have been impossible. By far the greatest debt is due to R. A. F. MacKenzie and David M. Stanley who taught the author Old and New Testament respectively during his four years of theological study at Regis College in Toronto, Canada. Insights culled from R. A. F. MacKenzie's lectures pervade all the essays on the Old Testament in varying degrees. Apart from their regular responsibilities and lectures, both of these Scripture professors graciously rendered much assistance and enlightenment in countless informal discussions during this period.

It is a pleasure to recall and to acknowledge the professors for my courses at the Pontifical Biblical Institute in Rome: Ignace de la Potterie, Louis Alonso-Schökel and Francis McCool—three most stimulating scholars. And for his splendid seminar and constant helpfulness, I am deeply indebted to Donatien Mollat of the Gregorian University.

The author is especially indebted to his former professor of

Johannine studies, Jean-Louis D'Aragon, S.J., and to the editors of *Sciences Ecclésiastiques* for their kind permission to incorporate the greater part of Father's article, "La notion johannique de l'Unité," into the tenth chapter of this book. Father D'Aragon's remarkably thorough scholarship and helpfulness outside the classroom made the period of his guest lectureship at Regis College a most welcome experience.

The following versions of Scripture are quoted in the text: *The Complete Bible: An American Translation* (The Old Testament, translated by J. M. Powis Smith and a group of scholars; The Apocrypha and The New Testament, translated by Edgar J. Goodspeed). Copyright 1939 by the University of Chicago; *The Holy Bible.* Confraternity Edition. Copyright 1962 The Confraternity of Christian Doctrine; *The Holy Bible,* translated by Ronald Knox. Copyright 1944, 1948 and 1950, Sheed and Ward, Inc., New York; *The New English Bible.* Copyright The Delegates of the Oxford University Press and the Syndics of the Cambridge University Press, 1961; *The Holy Bible, Revised Standard Version* (New York, Nelson, 1953). Copyright 1946 and 1952 by the Division of Christian Education of the National Council of the Churches of Christ in the U.S.A.

Finally, to the editors of *Bible Today, Review for Religious,* and *Worship,* my gratitude for permission to use, in this book, articles which earlier appeared in their publications. Chapters 1, 3, 4, 7 and 8 appeared originally in *Bible Today;* Chapters 2, 5 and 6 were published in *Review for Religious;* and Chapter 16 originally appeared in the pages of *Worship.*

Foreword

So much has been said and written about the advances made in biblical scholarship that almost anyone who has done any listening or reading could itemize the theological breakthroughs occasioned by the advances. In most cases, we realize, it is a question of a new insight, a new emphasis rather than the discovery of a new truth. But, as a result of recent studies, we have grown accustomed now to emphasize the dynamic and historical character of Revelation rather than its propositional content; faith as a movement of person to person rather than, primarily, as an intellectual assent to abstract truths; grace as the divine presence rather than as an entitative habit; Christian morality as a love-inspired way of life rather than as a list of commandments; all of theology as anthropocentrically orientated rather than abstractly theocentric.

Behind all of this there stands the unconditioned adoption by the Church of the scientific method of biblical exegesis. While many are quite aware that there have been advances made and are willing to accept them singly, the failure to recognize this basis for the advances still occasions a doubtful and even re-

strictive attitude with regard to the future. "How far are you going
to go?" is a question still asked of the biblical scholar by the one
who feels that *he,* at least, has gone about as far as he cares to
go. It is a question to which the Catholic scholar can only answer,
"As far as honest Christian scholarship leads me." It must be
honest scholarship inasmuch as it is thoroughly dedicated to scientific principles; it must be Christian scholarship inasmuch as it
recognizes the Church as the ultimately supreme interpreter of
God's word. And the true Christian scholar has no fears that the
supreme interpretation (proferred, in any case, extremely rarely in
an infallible manner) will ever contradict or even limit his scientific investigation.

Once this road of scientific exegesis has been taken, there can
be no turning back. There can be no hesitation with regard to
some "sacrosanct" passage that could be claimed to possess the
charism of inspiration in some unique way. The words of institution of the Eucharist are no more inspired than are those that tell
of David's sin with Bathsheba. Both can and must be subjected
to the same rigorous methods of interpretation if we would know
what God is saying to us.

This road has not always been accessible to scholars. Indeed,
in an earlier age there was not even the awareness that such a
road existed, at least as it is understood in contemporary thought.
Before the Reformation, the understanding of the meaning of
Scripture was heavily dependent on traditional interpretation and
on authoritative statements. As a consequence, tradition and authority were deeply ingrained in the Christian consciousness as
the sole reliable guides to God's word. Whether the Reformation
opened the door to a more scientific approach, as is often said,
can be debated. (It is still keenly disputed whether the Reformation was medieval or modern in spirit; *cf.* the article by H. Rückert
in *Journal for Theology and the Church,* 1965 [vol. 2], pp. 1–19.)
W. Neil more properly traces the origins of biblical criticism back

to the Renaissance when "The liberation of men's minds from the dead weight of authority and tradition made it inevitable that, sooner or later, the Bible would cease to be treated, as it had been throughout the Middle Ages, as a supernaturally guaranteed revelation beyond the scope of rational inquiry" ("The Criticism and Theological Use of the Bible, 1700–1950," in *The Cambridge History of the Bible, The West from the Reformation to the Present Day,* ed. S. L. Greenslade, Cambridge, 1963, p. 238). While we might hesitate to characterize authority and tradition wholly as "dead weight," the substance of this judgment seems accurate enough.

The liberation achieved by the Renaissance, however, was not an overnight experience of *uhurru.* On both the Catholic and the Protestant sides the restrictions imposed by tradition and, in the case of the former, also by an authority that, justifiably, feared the results of an undeveloped and frequently undisciplined rational approach kept scientific exegesis from gaining maturity for a long time. A classic illustration is the case of the French Oratorian, Richard Simon, whose trail-blazing *Critical History of the Old Testament* (1678) was condemned by Rome almost as soon as it appeared. The Catholic scholar had many hurdles to master, not all of them occasioned by his particular religious profession, before he could embark freely on the way of scientific exegesis.

It is not my purpose here to trace the history of this development. I merely wish to indicate the very deep roots that the present-day breakthrough had to contend with before it could become what it is. The more thoroughly these historical roots are appreciated, the more profound will the breakthrough appear. It received its official authorization, of course, in Pius XII's encyclical *Divino Afflante Spiritu* (1943), where the scientific door was swung wide open for the Catholic scholar. This was then canonized in several of the documents of the Second Vatican Council, notably in that on divine revelation. There is little doubt that some undue restrictions will still be experienced from time to time, but these cannot dim the trust of the biblical scholar that the continued plying of his trade will bring about an ever richer understanding of God's word.

The essays contained in this book are the result of such trade-plying, and, despite the comparative youth of the author, are an enviable result. Our association through *The Bible Today,* to which he has made several fine contributions, has given me an appreciation of his tireless energy, his concern for accuracy and his ability to write a clear sentence. These are all indispensable attributes of the "compleat" Scripture scholar.

From the biblical essays presented here the reader will gain deeper insights into the basis of the "new theology" mentioned at the beginning. Above all, he will gain an appreciation of the dynamic development that characterizes the Christian's life in Christ. It is such an appreciation that we Catholics are so sorely in need of today. The "putting on of Christ" is no once-for-all action that terminates wholly in a state of soul, but a continuing action that keeps the soul constantly in ferment. Perhaps, as Catholics, we can appreciate more thoroughly the Protestant emphasis on the evolutionary aspects of justification, while they, in turn, can come to share the Catholic stress on the existing union with Christ more profoundly. These are the sentiments once expressed to me in a letter from the author; they will be illustrated more clearly in the studies that follow.

EUGENE H. MALY

Mt. St. Mary's of the West
Norwood, Ohio

Contents

Foreword by Eugene H. Maly   ix

Introduction   3

1   The Patriarchs of Faith, Hope, Love   6

2   God's Gifts to Our Old Testament Fathers   19

3   "In Our Image and Likeness"   27

4   "We Have Seen His Glory"   41

5   Jeremiah: Man of God   52

6   The Humanity of Christ in St. Mark   70

7   The Parable of the Banquet   78

8   Leading Ideas in St. John's Gospel   89

9   Signs of an Authentic Christian Witness   99

10 On Giving Christian Witness in John 13:35   114

11 On Remembering: Divine Gift and Human Obligation   128

12 On Returning: The Process of Conversion   144

13 On Showing Mercy: The Good Samaritan   166

14   On Creation and History   *184*

15   On Being Lord and Servant: "I Never Knew You"   204

16   Love in the Message of Paul   226

Index   237

Personal Witness
A Biblical Spirituality

Introduction

These essays seek to reflect the dynamic personal nature of the relationship between God and man. The mutual freedom of the divine initiative and the human response define the essentially personal character of this relationship, established and maintained in liberty. The patriarchs are constituted by the self-giving action of God to which they have responded in faith, hope, and love. The first two essays on the patriarchs assert that the basic relationship of the chosen people to the God who had chosen them is itself a divine gift whose many aspects are personified by the historical individuals, Abraham, Jacob and Joseph. God is where he acts, and, whenever he acts, he communicates himself. The divine intervention in history is not to be relegated to sporadic events; it appears in the process whereby man is in some way identified with his Lord as his image and likeness, realizing his unity and conformity with God whose dominion he shares in ruling over creatures in holiness and righteousness.

"We Have Seen His Glory" considers how God comes to material man in love and condescension by his real presence in time and space. "Jeremiah" is an outstanding embodiment of the appropriate human response to the call of God in history. Jeremiah realized that the rejection of God's gracious initiative was not only an act of base ingratitude, but also a quasi-suicidal refusal to accept the continuation of the creation which God had already initiated in his personal life and in that of his people.

"The Humanity of Christ in St. Mark" studies the responsiveness of God in Christ's humanity. In the humanity of Christ we discover how intensely responsive God is to the human condition in its innumerable aspects; we see he is never detached from or disinterested in men, their problems and aspirations. "The Parable of the Banquet" reveals how Jesus re-establishes the community of friendship between God and man; how re-entry into the human community symbolizes re-entrance into community with God. The two Johannine essays are somewhat complementary. The essay on John's "Leading Ideas" explains concepts which are used in development of his notion of Christian witness, which, in turn, is one of his leading ideas. John gives us the most articulate expression of all that is involved in communion with God.

The divine initiative and human response which characterize the dynamic aspect of communion with God can be understood in terms of remembering, returning, showing mercy, creating and serving. It is only in virtue of God's remembering that man remembers God; it is in virtue of God's turning toward man that man returns to God. Because God shows mercy, those who live by his Spirit are also impelled to show mercy; in fact, they are merciful in virtue of the same mercy whereby God is merciful. Similarly, the history of the people of God is the history created by the Lord of history, whose activity introduces a meaning into human life that emerges with time and attains its ultimate fulfillment in the resurrection of the just. The Christian's service of his Lord is at bottom a personal response to the Lord who serves him. It is only in virtue of Christ's service that the Christian is capable of serving Christ as Lord. Because he has been and is in our midst as one who serves, authentic communion with Christ is manifested by the same spirit of service. Thus, Christ is Lord where he serves.

Authentic Christian witness is essentially a free, personal response to the divine initiative in Christ, manifesting his presence in time and space, and therefore a manifestation of the glory of God in which Christ shows himself to men as he really is.

1
The Patriarchs
of Faith, Hope, Love

The stories of Abraham, Jacob, and Joseph had been handed down by word of mouth in Israel for generations. Before their written formulation, these stories went through a process of selection and interpretation, which aimed at setting in the clearest possible light the essential truth of the events through which God worked out His plan in human history. The traditional stories of the patriarchs are more than mere biographies; rather, they articulate the faith of the people of God, they personify the basic relationship of the chosen people to the God who had chosen them.

If Abraham is an historical individual, he is also the personification of faith. His faith stands as a constant reminder to the people of God that faith establishes them in their most basic relationship to God. St. Paul views Abraham in this way when he calls him the father of all those who believe in God (Rom 4:16). Jacob, on the other hand, symbolizes Israel's consciousness of her own moral shortcomings, which play a constant counterpoint to her comforting realization of God's patient forbearance and saving goodness. In Joseph, finally, the people of God express what they think the love of God is like. Abraham, Jacob and Joseph thus personify man's basic relationship to God. (Joseph, however, also personifies God's saving covenant love for His people.)

The call of Abraham is an event of supreme importance in both Old and New Testament history. Just how the relationship between Abraham and his personal God began, and in what it consisted, remains mysterious. But the Bible leaves no doubt that it was personal and not shared by his kindred (Jos 24:2). Genesis does not present us with a distillation of the heroic exploits of Abraham, but rather stresses the initiative, the actions and the purpose of God in His choice of the patriarch. It is God who calls and God who makes the covenant. It is Abraham who responds in faith to the divine initiative. But this relationship of election, covenant and responsive faith is remembered not only for what it *was,* but also for what it *continued to be.* The people of God read of themselves in the stories of the patriarchs. They understand the terms of their own existence, and its essential meaning, in the relationship between God and Abraham.

Faith and Promise

To Abraham is made the promise: "I will make of you a great nation, and I will bless you . . . and through you all the peoples of the earth shall be blessed" (Gen 12:2-3). To possess a land, to become a great nation, to be a blessing to all the peoples of the earth is the threefold promise which runs like a golden thread through the tapestry of the Genesis epic, from Abraham to the conquest.

The divine promise is a challenge to Abraham's faith by the very vagueness with which the goal is indicated and by the magnitude of God's demands, which appears in the simple enumeration of what Abraham must voluntarily surrender: "Go from your *country,* your *kindred,* and your *father's house* to the land *that I*

will show you" (Gen 12:1). Abraham's first step must be a gesture
of renunciation of all the support and security normally provided
by a man's kinsfolk and neighbors. The very essence of this vocation, as of every other, is trust in God (Mt 10:37).

The promised destiny, though still vague, is stated with equal
emphasis: "I will make your name great." A "great name" was
the very thing that motivated the builders of Babel: "Let us make
a name for ourselves" (Gen 11:14). God now grants that which
men had tried to gain by their own resources, but to the man of
His choice and on *His* terms. Abraham will be the instrument and
means of blessing, not for himself and his descendants alone, but
for "all the peoples of the earth." "So Abram went as the Lord had
told him" (Gen 12:4), obedient to the word of God as were the
elements at the time of creation. Such is the faith which makes
possible the fulfillment of the promise.

Abraham's call and response initiate salvation-history for all
mankind. From the story of the creation and the first man, Genesis
had constantly narrowed the center of its interest until it focused
on the solitary figure of Abraham, the father of the people whom
God had chosen for His universal redemptive plan. Coming almost
immediately after the Babel story, which presents the total denial
of God in the absolute assumption of self-sufficiency and the dark
picture of divine judgment on mankind, the story of Abraham's
call is like a burst of light that illumines the whole landscape.
The people of God realize that Abraham's response must be their
own appropriate response to the divine initiative in their regard.

Faith in Trial

In episode after episode, Genesis shows how Abraham's faith
is severely tested. Yet, when everything seems lost, God intervenes.
In Egypt, for example, Sarah is in danger of being taken into
Pharaoh's harem. Had this mishap befallen the ancestress of Israel,

the promise of a great progeny would not have been fulfilled. But the divine plan, so solemnly initiated, is not to be thwarted, and God's hand intervenes. The God of Abraham is Lord in Egypt; the protection of His chosen ones is not circumscribed by space.

Again, when it is necessary for Lot and Abraham to part, Lot is given the freedom to choose where to go. The future of Israel depends upon his decision. Lot chooses, not the land of promise, but the Jordan Valley that would later know the Moabites and Ammonites. The promise of the one land, made to Abraham, has been safeguarded and the promise is now renewed (Gen 13:14).

The totality of Abraham's response of faith is demanded when God tells Abraham: "Take your son, your only son Isaac whom you love . . . and offer him there [in the land of Moriah] as a burnt offering upon one of the mountains of which I shall tell you" (Gen 22:2). It seems that God is asking him to destroy in faith the only concrete evidence that that faith could be fulfilled. Isaac is the only visible hope for the ultimate fulfillment of God's promise. Although Abraham realizes that God has the right to demand this sacrifice, the test to his faith is unimaginable. God is satisfied with his readiness to obey; a ram is substituted.

The near-sacrifice of Isaac is understood by Abraham and the people of God to mean that, unless we are willing to lose our life for God's sake, we shall neither find nor save our life. This total demand of faith expects a complete, unqualified response, a total commitment. We find a strong echo of this in the succinct statement of Isaias: "If you will not believe, surely you shall not be established" (7:9b). For thus said the Lord God, the Holy One of Israel, "In returning and rest you shall be saved; in quietness and in trust shall be your strength." And you would not . . . (30:15). Just as the history of the people of God begins with Abraham, so, too, the spiritual life of this people begins with faith. Salvation comes to him who believes in God's promise and accepts life on His terms. Only thus can the promise be fulfilled.

Jacob—Patriarch of Hope

Genesis tells us little about Isaac who seems to be a replica of his father; but it has much to say about his son Jacob-Israel. Jacob is a most dislikeable character—treacherous, deceitful, acquisitive, proud and self-centered. The disreputable Jacob tricks his brother Esau out of his birthright and his father's blessing. Although Esau is magnanimous, forgiving and noble in character, God, in His supreme and unfathomable liberty, has made Jacob the object of His special providence. Jacob may cheat his brother and outsmart his father-in-law Laban, but dishonest as he is, he is still the object of God's loving covenant-promise. Jacob's morality is like that of any Middle-Bronze-Age sheik, but God takes him as he is, working with him and slowly educating him.

At a time of despair Jacob has a dream at Bethel (Gen 28:10ff). God appears to him and renews the threefold promise made to Abraham. Now Jacob can hope in the goodness of God. Assured of the divine Presence, he journeys to his kinsmen in Haran where, through the providence of God, he acquires great wealth and two wives, and is enabled to return in safety to his own land. Again at Bethel, but now at a time of prosperity, he has another dream. He wrestles with the angel of God until daybreak, when he receives the angel's blessing and a new name, "Israel," indicating his new mission in life as the father of the chosen people.

For this chosen people Jacob is both an historical individual and a symbol of their own relationship to God. In Jacob-Israel they recognize their own wayward nature, through him they realize that their own election is neither ethically nor morally merited. Election, the call, God's favor is not theirs because of any intrinsic nobility and goodness of their own, but rather, as it would appear, despite the deviousness of their ways, in the grace and purpose of God. They have no claims on God; they cannot "force

His hand" with human efforts. The people of God realize that the righteous man is not he who conforms his conduct to what is right but he whom God recognizes as righteous. It is for him whom God loves to learn to love. Jacob was not chosen because he was righteous. He is righteous because he is chosen. Jacob eventually receives his comeuppance for his sins and becomes a wise and mellow old man.

Jacob expresses the tension between human perversity and divine love. In Jacob the people of God read the shame of their own sinfulness, and the hope offered by God's eternal goodness and saving love. Jacob grew in faith at Bethel, "Surely God is in this place; *and I did not know it.*" The history of the people of God, too, is one in which they understand themselves to be supported only by the grace of God, a story of sustained hope and confidence in a beneficent, life-giving Providence communicating His goodness to all. The people of God live in the light of His countenance, humbly realizing that God has not chosen them because of their own qualities or goodness. God's act of saving love is for "His name's sake"; the reason for His choice and deliverance of His people is to be found in God alone. This is the mystery of election and grace. God loved Jacob, and the ground of His love lies solely in His own goodness, not in the lovableness of Jacob. God's love is *agape* for those who have nothing to offer in return, as opposed to *eros* which is based on the attractiveness of the object loved. God has not chosen them because they are righteous; rather, because God has chosen them they must be righteous.

Mindful of His covenant with Abraham to bless all the nations of the earth, God elects Jacob-Israel, not to privilege, but to service, to further His saving purpose among the nations. Israel, too, is appointed to be "a kingdom of priests," a kingdom set apart to represent God to the world and the needs of the world to God. She is to be a dedicated nation, a light for the Gentiles (Is 42:6).

Above all, Jacob is the symbol of Israel's own humble hope.

And because he continues to hope, he (and the people of God) becomes the hope of all the nations who would receive God's blessing through him. Everything is against Jacob, except the mysterious ways of God, and these eventually triumph in him. He is the youngest brother in a land where pre-eminence is naturally given to the oldest son. In contrast with Esau, Jacob is clearly the lesser vehicle; yet he bears the promise and the blessing. Israel, too, the "least of all the nations," is the most unlikely candidate for God's election. And yet, like her ancestor, Jacob-Israel, she is chosen by God to be the instrument of salvation.[1]

Joseph—Patriarch of Love

Joseph is very different from his father. He is Jacob's first and favorite son by Rachel, a master of dream, sold into slavery by jealous brothers. He becomes a lord of Egypt who saves the nations in time of famine, leads his brothers to repentance before revealing his identity in a magnanimous act of reconciliation, and fulfills his father's last wish by burying his remains in the land of promise. He is the consolation of his father's old age, after having been the indirect cause of his broken heart.[2]

The Joseph-saga (Gen 37–50) is a superb presentation of the biblical doctrine of vicarious suffering, for Joseph, when triumphant, saves his brothers who had cruelly wronged him. Salvation comes through suffering; God makes the moment of Joseph's apparent destruction the starting point of his ascent to glory. The whole story of how God overrides men's evil purposes and out of their misdeeds works their salvation is found in both the Joseph-saga and in the passion and death of Jesus Christ. The wickedness of Joseph's brothers is overcome by the goodness of Joseph. The act whereby they attempted to destroy him, eventually leads to their salvation in time of famine. Through love Joseph and Christ "destroy" their enemies by converting them into friends, and in this remarkable way show how the psalmist's frequent prayer for the "destruction" of God's enemies is actually accomplished. Love is the way God "destroys" His enemies, when the very crucifixion of the Messiah is turned by divine wisdom into the means of salvation for all mankind.[3]

No tension between nature and grace, disbelief and faith is found in Joseph. He suffers patiently when treated with malice because his is the peace of a true friend of God, "Yahweh was with Joseph and was kind to him" (Gen 39:21). Thus God's loving friendship sustains him in prison, and enables him to accept ill-fortune as well as good. There is no wrestling with the deity (Jacob 32). No tensions between faith and unfaith (Abraham) or sinfulness and grace (Jacob) appear in Joseph, but rather in his brothers.

Joseph's first dream is fulfilled when his brothers, seeking grain in Egypt, bow to him as the sheaths of wheat had done. When Joseph jails them for three days, his brothers begin to repent because their harsh treatment reminds them of their past cruelty to Joseph (42:24). Joseph insists on the presence of Benjamin for his own purposes. The old crime against Joseph is still on their consciences when, accused of stealing the silver cup, they throw themselves down in guilt and penance. Joseph leads his brothers to an effective penance and conversion of heart. By re-enacting the first scene (and setting up the very same circumstances) Joseph wishes to see whether his brothers will for a second time abandon the other son of Rachel, their youngest brother, Benjamin, and return home to their father telling him that his son is lost. If they refuse to abandon Benjamin, their moral renewal and penitence will be proven. If their hearts are changed, they are forgiven. This is their judgment in which Joseph identifies himself with Benjamin to test his brothers, just as Christ identifies Himself with the least of men when He comes to judge at the Final Judgment. In each case the judge determines his relationship to the judged by their freely chosen relationship to others. Only when they have shown their love of Benjamin in their refusal to depart without him does Joseph reveal himself as their brother, and restores their friendship.

While his brothers recover from their shock, Joseph (45:4ff.) explains the divine plan behind all these incidents. Despite famine and their sins God has been looking after the family of Jacob-Israel to insure their survival. Salvation is bestowed on the group because of the suffering of one just man. Salvation for both criminal and victim is seen in this amazing insight into Providence.

Joseph is seen as a type of philosopher-king, the ideal of Israel's wisdom teaching. He is the type of the Messiah in whom the people of God believe and hope. With Joseph, the people of God easily make the transition from the historical individual to the corporate personality. Joseph saves his brothers. He is the loving, beneficent ruler who not only cares for the physical needs of his people, feeding them in famine, but also for their moral rebirth, leading them to a change of heart and reconciliation.

In Joseph there is a fulfillment, in a certain sense, of the divine promise made to Abraham: "In you all the families of the earth will be blessed." Against fantastic odds, God preserves his life and brings him to a position in which he is responsible for saving, not only the life of the family of Jacob, but of the whole world. The universal nature of the original promise made to Abraham is recalled in the statement: "Moreover, *all the earth* came to Egypt *to Joseph* to buy grain, because the famine was severe over all the earth" (Gen 41:57).

Because the Joseph-saga comes out of Israel's ancient past and was for centuries transmitted orally before its written formulation, it is possible that the germ of the later development of messianism was found in these early traditions. Perhaps the people of God came to see in Joseph the salvation motif which, after the fall of the nation, was expressed in the Servant of God: "It is too light a thing that you should be my servant to raise up the tribes of Jacob and to restore the survivors of Israel; so I will make you a light for the nations, that my salvation may reach to the end of the earth" (Is 49:6).

In any case, Joseph is everything Israel loves most. Joseph is the living personification of covenant love: the gracious, saving love of God for those whom He rules, and the steadfast love of the people of God for their Lord. Because Joseph expresses Israel's concept of the perfect ruler, he also expresses, in human terms, what Israel thinks of its Lord with whom she is bound in the mutual adhesion of covenant love.

God had taken the initiative in establishing the covenant alliance with His people. He has conferred His benefits upon them and requires their loving obedience and undivided loyalty in return for His continued support and protection, "you shall not have other gods besides me" (Ex 20:3). His chosen people bound themselves to "love, honor and obey" only the Lord. Because the Lord is a Person, His worshippers are bound to a personal response of loyalty, service and devotion that is summed up in love; and because His covenant is with the people as such, individuals are bound in similar loyalty to each other. For example, Deuteronomy 4–11 repeatedly exhorts the people to grateful love toward the divine Benefactor, insisting that the motive underlying the Covenant was not any merit on Israel's part (7:7; 9:6), nor the Lord's advantage (10:14) but simply the overwhelming mystery of His arbitrary love (7:8). This is the meaning of Joseph for the people of God.

Today we tend to express our basic relationship to God in terms of faith, hope and love, whereas the men of the Bible preferred to express these same concepts in the concrete terms of a corporate personality. Instead of "I have faith," they would say "I am a son of Abraham." Faith, for them, is the way Abraham lived; hope is the way Jacob lived; love is the way Joseph lived.

The living God was the sole source of life and to depart from Him was death. The various aspects of this covenant life, which they had received as a gift of God, were understood in terms of their patriarchs.

Conclusion

Each patriarch lived his covenant-life with God in a personal way that was peculiar to him and shed new light on man's fundamental relations to God, on his life with God. When Israel, the people of God, made a total commitment of faith in God's promise (Abraham); when they lived in the awareness of their sinfulness, recognizing that the fulfillment of the promise transcended them and depended entirely on the gracious love and power of God (Jacob); when they lived lives of steadfast covenant-love with God in solidarity with their brothers (Joseph)—then were they incorporated into the lives of their fathers. Then they truly became "sons of Abraham, Jacob and Joseph." The patriarchs became corporate personalities unifying the people of God.[4]

The solidarity of the people of God in their corporate relationship to God through their fathers foreshadows the revelation of our relation to God through Jesus Christ, who is at once a person and a corporate personality. Through baptism we are incorporated into Christ the Redeemer who is the fulfillment of the promise made to Abraham: "For you are all sons of God by faith in Christ Jesus. All of you who have been baptised into Christ have put on Christ . . . all of you are one in Christ. Now if you are Christ's, then you are Abraham's seed, heirs to the promise" (Gal 3:26–29). The men of the Bible, in expressing their solidarity with God and with one another in terms of a person, have helped us to understand the nature of our solidarity with Jesus, through whom, with whom, and in whom we are united with God and with all mankind.[5]

Notes

[1] Pre-eminence is also the lot of Joseph, Gideon, David and Solomon all younger sons. The mysterious ways of God in electing those who are, humanly speaking, the least eligible finds an echo in Paul: "God chose what is foolish in the world to shame the wise, God chose what is weak in the world to shame the strong. God chose what is low and despised in the world, even things that are not, to bring to nought the things that are, so that no human being might boast in His sight" (1 Cor 1:27:29).

[2] Jacob had cheated his father in his old age by acquiring the birthright. The law of talion is seen operating when Jacob is cheated by the loss of his favorite son, Joseph.

[3] The Joseph-typology may very well appear in the Marcan passion story: as Joseph the Patriarch buries the old Israel (Gen 50:4–6), so Joseph of Arimathaea buries the new Israel (Mk 15:42). (The NT does not explicitly set forth Joseph as a type of Christ.)

[4] What had been the characteristically personal mark of Abraham's, Jacob's and Joseph's relationship to God, now became the universal hallmark for all the people of God living the same lives of faith, hope and covenant-love. Their father's way of life with God was now *incorporated* and extended among his numerous progeny according to the spirit, if not also the flesh. The patriarchs in this way became truly *corporate* personalities unifying the people of God.

[5] Thus the Old Testament patriarchs were but dim shadows of the reality to come, for in the humanity and Person of Jesus, God has shown and given to his people the Way, the Truth, the Life. We have seen the Wisdom and Glory of God which force us to declare the good news of St. John that "God is love." Our Israelite fathers have prepared us for understanding the profound truth that love, wisdom, life, and truth are ultimately, not mere empty concepts, but are found in a Person: Jesus Christ, the Son of God.

We hope to have shown the need for understanding how the men of the Bible thought of their patriarchs in order to grasp the significance of both the Old Testament and the context of the New Testament teaching about Jesus as an individual and as Head of the Mystical Body. We have shown how people of God personified their consciousness of their solidarity with their fathers in their basic relation to God.

Jacob-Israel not only represents an historical person, but what is vastly more important, Israel (the people of God) itself. Therefore, when we read that Joseph was the son whom "Jacob–Israel loved . . . more than any other of his children" (Gen 37:3), we must employ the same principle: Joseph, too, is not only an historical individual, but the people of God's (Jacob's) idealized, personal representation of what their life of covenant love with God should be. Joseph is everything the people of God (Jacob) love most. Joseph expresses the hunger of their souls for the idealized fulfillment of covenant love in his perfect obedience and fidelity to God, his redemptive suffering which is turned to the good of his people, his merciful forgiveness, his solidarity with his brothers, the children of Jacob–Israel (the people of God), his providential care for them, feeding them in famine, leading them to repentance, his fulfillment of his father's last wish to be buried in the Promised Land. If we recall that Jacob–Israel is also the people of God, then Joseph is the fulfillment of the people of God's last wish, too; he is their ultimate hope for a Messiah. Thus, in Joseph, the people of God are not only looking back to the meaning of covenant love as expressed in one of their fathers; they are also looking forward to the type of a person who could save them. Joseph is their last wish. Joseph will bring them to eternal repose in the Land of Promise. Joseph *does* bury Jacob-Israel in the Promised Land. But this Joseph only reveals himself to the sons of Israel (people of God) after they have repented of their past wickedness. From Moses to the last of the prophets, John the Baptist, Israel is always being called to repentance. Only when they have been converted from their infidelity, will the Messiah (Joseph) become known to them, reveal himself. Only after reconciliation will Israel's (Jacob) last wish be granted.

Jesus Christ is the fulfillment of Israel's messianic hope. We cannot fully appreciate our relation to Him unless we understand the corporate aspects of this relationship foreshadowed in the Old Testament. Just as the men of the Bible expressed their solidarity with God and one another in terms of Abraham, Isaac, Jacob and Joseph, we find the fulfillment of ours in Christ Jesus.

2
God's Gifts to Our Old Testament Fathers

The Bible is the story of God's gift to man; its heroes are those who have graciously accepted the generosity of God. Reading the Bible can be very helpful in suggesting the special gifts of God that we might pray for; and because God is His own best gift, every particular gift will be some special way in which He ultimately gives Himself to us. Each gift is some particular way in which we are made capable of reacting to, thinking of, and loving God who always communicates Himself in His gifts. A sketchy consideration of God's gifts to our Old Testament fathers will reveal some particular attitude toward God for which we might pray, some particular way in which we might become more receptive of the three divine Persons in our lives.

Abraham has a place all his own. The Bible does not say that all things religious began with Abraham; but if Abraham was not the beginning, he was certainly a very important milestone. What was it that raised him above his own generation and those that followed? The answer is indicated by two major facts. First, Abraham made a number of decisions which altered the whole

future of his people. He decided to leave Ur and seek a land some-
where in the south. This was the resolve to be a homeless nomad
no longer and the ambition to become a people. Secondly, Abraham's vision was not of his own devising, but God's. The urge to
go out from Haran, the conviction of ultimately establishing a
people were respectively the divine call and the divine promise.
Abraham "believed Yahweh and he reckoned it to him as righteousness." His belief is remarkable in a world populated with demons,
goddesses, and godlings. God's gift of faith enabled him to risk
all, even if it meant the surrender of his hopes in Isaac. His was
the simplicity that could say perfect obedience to and reverence
for God is the one all-important attitude to life, despite the
humanly incomprehensible ways in which God fulfils his promises:
the sacrifice of Isaac involved a terrible contradiction of apparently
having to destroy the very means whereby the promise of establishing a nation was to be fulfilled. Abraham is the answer to those
who refuse to believe unless they understand all, who refuse to
accept God on His own terms, demanding that His ways be our
ways. Against all odds, Abraham believed in the wisdom of God
transcending, and often appearing painfully to contradict, human
reason; through the gift of faith Abraham was able to surmount
the limitations of human reason and accept that transcendent
Wisdom which is "foolishness to the Greeks and a stumbling-
block to the Jews."

What gift had Jacob received? Jacob had cheated his brother,
deceived his father, outwitted his father-in-law, and yet this scoun-
drel whose exploits often suggest Shakespeare's scenes of comic
relief had successfully managed to keep ahead of his past until it
caught up with him on returning to his homeland. Fearful of
Esau's reception, Jacob arrives at the ford and broods over the
future. As night comes on, suddenly the spirit is upon him, and
he must wrestle for his life until the dawn. But this is no ford-
demon; it is Yahweh himself, forcing Jacob to confront his own

past. How can he come to terms with his own former self? And in that long night of struggle, Jacob comes to see that this is just what a man cannot do. It is only as he abandons his own cleverness, only as he ceases to be "Jacob," the Usurper, the one that catches by the heel (Gn 25:26) and overtakes and supplants his rival, and becomes "Israel," the one who has struggled with God and learned his own weakness and surrendered his all into the hands of God, that he can learn the real name of God and find Him to be forgiving and redeeming love. But such wrestling is costly; Jacob limps away, the old cleverness, the old self-confidence is gone, but it is replaced by a new peace of mind, a new humility, a new sense of serving not his own plans but God's austere and mighty purposes in history and for the human race. Thus, Jacob no longer, Israel goes forward in the morning to meet Esau with a penitence and a humility which disarm his brother's wrath. Jacob is a symbol of hope. Despite the fact that Esau was a better man than his brother, God had chosen the lesser brother to work out His purpose, perhaps that "no man might glory in His sight." God accepts men as they are and patiently educates them. God's hand is not forced by the goodness of Esau, nor is it put off by the sinfulness of Jacob. This is the mystery of the divine election; He chooses whomever He pleases, apparently contradicting human wisdom according to which Esau, rather than Jacob, would have been the better choice. (This is not to say Esau was rejected.) Jacob is the answer to those who trust in their own self-righteousness rather than in the goodness of God. Jacob is the answer to those who think they have claims on God, that He owes them something and is indebted to them because of their "good behavior."

Joseph represents the Hebrew ideal. Perhaps no character of the Old Testament is such an excellent prototype of Christ. His love of God and neighbor is unswerving despite his apparent abandonment by God who permits him to be made a slave in pagan

Egypt, and his betrayal at the hands of murderous brothers. Joseph remains faithful to God and his family: "Do not be distressed, or angry with yourselves, because you sold me here; for God sent me before you to preserve life . . . so it was not you who sent me here, but God" (Gn 45:5,8). The Joseph story is one of God's providential care for the man who loves Him. In the desert pit, the slave market, the prison, and in high office, God is with Joseph, to watch over, guide, and protect him. He forgives his brothers and heals the broken relationships with generosity and affection, insisting that his family share in his good fortune. And although nomads were objects of scorn and distaste to the sophisticated Egyptians, Joseph takes his old shepherd father by the hand and brings him before Pharaoh and says with love and pride: "This is my father." Joseph, who had been left to die of starvation in the pit, is the refuge of his brothers in time of famine. Joseph is the story of how a loving providence cannot be thwarted by the most heinous deeds of men, of how all things work unto the good of those who love God, of how providence effects the conversion of sinners through the suffering of the just man.

Moses was a giant among men. Whereas Abraham had only one clan, Moses' achievement consisted in binding disparate elements into a fraternal community, a people held together by family feeling. Abraham and the patriarchs did not settle in Palestine, which remained a land "in which they dwelt as strangers" (Gn 17:8). They wandered as nomads. Egyptian oppression aroused in these half-settled nomads a longing for the desert which became incarnate in Moses who led Jacob's descendants out of the "house of slavery," followed by tribes of various origins (Ex 12:38). This was the Exodus which would lead to the formation of the people of Israel through the creative activity of Moses in the desert of Sinai. Under the leadership of Moses, this federation of twelve tribes, united by religion, successfully resisted the centrifugal tendencies which tested its strength for forty years. Under Moses they became the people of the covenant, the people of Yahweh whose name means "He who is truly and really there," the God who intervenes and acts, the living God who is always close at hand and who would tolerate no other gods and imposed moral demands. Because Yahweh was righteous he demanded righteousness from those who followed Him: religion and morality were bound together. Yahweh saved His people from the Egyptians and revealed His name to Moses in the wilderness. Moses is always displayed as a man of humility, understanding, and patience: "Now the man Moses was very meek" (Nm 12:3). Even when his anger blazed out against his people worshiping the golden calf, he pleads, rather than that he alone should survive and become another Abraham, God should blot him out of the book of life and let his people go free of their fault. Greatness of heart won him the strong affection of his people. Moses lived in the tradition of his people because he also lived in their hearts. Moses had received the grace of an ideal leader: mildness, intelligence, a passionate love and identification with his subjects, an infinite forebearance and patience, a keen sense of responsibility for uniting and leading his people to Yahweh along the paths of righteousness in accordance with the covenant. As a great leader, Moses wished his people to achieve the maturity of wise decision. Thus he speaks across the centuries to us: "As I have chosen, so you may choose— and so you must choose. See, I have set before you this day life and good, death and evil . . . therefore choose life, that you and your descendants may live" (Dt 30:15, 19).

Joshua appears in close association with Moses (Ex 23 and 24). He is a commanding figure solemnly commissioned to lead the people into Canaan; yet he has not received the title of king, priest, prophet, or judge. He is merely the successor of Moses. His best known role was the military one; his main achievement was the conquest of Palestine. Joshua completes Moses' work bringing divine prophecies to fulfilment and renews the loyalty of the people to the Mosaic covenant. Joshua is the ideal servant of God as envisioned by deuteronomic historians. His perfect devotion to Yahweh and the covenant wins the respect of Israel. He is also an agent of God's redemptive activity in history, a savior, leading his people into the land of promise, conquering it, giving them rest from their enemies. His name means "Yahweh is Salvation." Joshua shows how God brings about the salvation of mankind through His faithful servants. By the very fact of Joshua's faithful following of the covenant, he became a reliable leader of his people in their quest for salvation.

The transcendence of the supernatural, the power of man to do that which utterly transcends his natural powers, characterizes the Samson stories. When the "Spirit of God" takes possession of a man, it gives him the ability to do the extraordinary. Samson's feats of strength were attributed to divine possession and illustrate the uniqueness of God's gifts. Samson symbolizes the power of grace which enables its recipients to do what would otherwise transcend them, such as the power to believe, the power to hope, the power to love, the power to pray.

Samuel appears as the priest. He is the great intercessor whose ministry of prayer arises out of his pastoral concern for the people. Samuel pleads on their behalf in their danger and repentance at Mizpah; he brings their request for a king before Yahweh, and their subsequent penitence and fear before the offended deity. His continued intercession averts the divine wrath (1 S 12:19–23). As priest Samuel stands before God on behalf of the people and before the people on behalf of God (1 S 12:7). Samuel offered sacrifices of expiation and reconciliation whereby friendship with Yahweh was renewed. Samuel thus helps us to appreciate the priesthood of Christ who never ceases to intercede for us before His Father and win His favor through His loving obedience which Samuel prefigured with his "Speak, for thy servant is listening!"

It is precisely this "listening," this receptivity and loving attention to the Word of God which makes a great priest.

The Jews rarely enjoyed the privilege of wielding the rod of empire; and it was natural that they should think of David, who had established his throne in Jerusalem and exercised wide and effective rule, as the ideal king. David's eating of the holy bread in the sanctuary of Ahimelech, his dancing before the Ark reveal that David was no religious formalist whose "religion" is primarily a matter of rules and juridical proprieties. David's was a deep personal commitment to God. Everything else was useless without this sense of personal attachment at the center of one's life. David grew with experience. The nineteenth-century scholar Benjamin Jowett once said: "I hate to meet a man whom I have known ten years before and find that he is precisely at the same point; neither moderated, nor quickened, nor experienced, but simply stiffened." There was a great difference between the young warrior here offering to take on the Philistine giant and the man who had to suffer the agony of seeing his favorite son, Absalom, die. In David we see the struggle between good and evil, order and chaos, light and darkness. We see the slow but steady disintegration of his character, as the "wholeness" and "integrity" of a man whose life had once been rooted in Yahweh breaks up and crumbles into chaos (*tohu*). Sin for the Hebrew mind was seen as a type of creation in reverse, a return to the primordial chaos. *Shalom* is its opposite ("peace," "integrity," "integration") and characterized the right order of things before Adam's sin. David's adultery and instigation of murder bring the consequent judgment of God upon him but also the gracious "reintegrating" action of the saving God. And when peace (*shalom*) had been restored to his soul, after many tears and tragedies following upon his sins, a much wiser David would realize it was a "peace that is not of this world," but one that was the gift of God alone. The David story helps us to appreciate the gift of forgiveness (a word which seems much too passive and negative!), or, better, "reintegration" and reconciliation with God. So perfect is God's forgiveness that God will make Himself present to us through David's offspring and reestablish the kingdom of His peace in the hearts of all those, who like His ancestor David, humbly admit their sins and graciously accept the gift of His forgiveness. St. Peter is David's New Testament counterpart: after the forgiveness of his sins, he is made the head of Christ's kingdom on earth.

Abraham, Jacob, Joseph, Moses, Joshua, Samson, Samuel, and David are only a few of the great men of the Old Testament. Others, such as Solomon, Elijah, Isaiah, and Jeremiah might also have been considered. The eight whose gifts we have admired, undoubtedly could be contemplated from many other interesting aspects; however, the main purpose of this study has been merely that of suggesting a spiritually profitable approach to our reading of the Scriptures; namely that of discovering the gifts that God has given to our spiritual fathers, the many ways in which He enters the human mind and heart.

3

"In Our Image and Likeness"

The sacred writer of Genesis (1:26) fills us with wonder when he puts into God's mouth the words: "Let us make mankind in our image, after our likeness, and let them have dominion. . . ." The sacred writer affirms that man enjoys a transcendence over the rest of creation somewhat analogous to that which is proper to God.

The Meaning of "Image"

The Hebrew word for "image" (*selem*) is a concrete term which implies a strictly physical resemblance; but the second phrase, "after our likeness" (*kidmuthenu*) qualifies and considerably weakens its force. *Selem* alone suggests the carving of a statue. Man is like a statue of God, so that, looking at man, you know what God is like. By the fact that the sacred author toned down the concrete term *selem* with *kidmuthenu*, he implies that we should not take *selem* literally. Secondly, the Israelite's conception of the supremacy and transcendence of God excludes every idea of a physical resemblance from the phrase "image and like-ness." Man is "flesh" (*basar*), and for the Israelite "flesh" is a visible and concrete stamp of man's weakness. Therefore, the writer does not see in man a strict resemblance to God in a physical shape that implied weakness. This would have implied a notion most alien to Israel's theological and moral tenets. Man was God's "*graven image.*"

Nor is man's likeness to God found in anything so purely spiritual as intellect or will, in our sense. For the Israelite, what we would call "will, knowledge, soul" would be expressed by the word *nephesh* and includes outward appearances and inward attitudes, the visible and the invisible, the totality of elements that make this man a distinct individual. The Israelite did not consider the body as distinct from the soul. The systematic Greek precision which characterizes our thought about the soul, reason, will and the other human faculties was foreign to him; neverthe-less, the sacred writer's theological value in no way depends on our systematic precisions. Consequently, he neither conceived nor expressed any purely spiritual resemblance between God and man.

The sacred writer of *Genesis* 1:26 affirms that man is somehow a special reflection of God, and that man has been given dominion over the rest of creation. It is man's dominion that explains what is meant by "image and likeness." The statement that man is God's image is first palliated by calling it a likeness, and then developed in terms of dominion over lower creation.

Man has dominion and consequently is God's image: he is God's image precisely because he rules over the animal kingdom and lower creation, thus sharing God's universal dominion. For the Israelite, man does not rule because he is God's image; rather, he is God's image because he rules. Although this rule and dominion is reductively spiritual, the sacred writer, for reasons seen above, was incapable of making the precision explicit with his concrete, crude and inexact categories. Although he lacked a metaphysics on which to base his thought-structures, he could still manage to express himself quite well. He could perceive a similitude, with regard to man's dominion, analogous to that existing between an Oriental autocrat and the vassal representatives to whom local rule is delegated. Functionally, man imaged God in that man was to act on earth as God acts in the universe. Man represented God among creatures. (Implicit is the notion that when man no longer images God in this way, he no longer enjoys perfect dominion over creation.)

From the moment of creation man enjoys this dominion and is consequently God's image. That man could have been created without this dominion seems implicit by the solemn deliberation which precedes his creation and by the exultant hymn following his creation, which stresses not so much man's creation as his creation in the image of God.

The Meaning of Dominion

At man's creation, God breathes the spirit (*ruah*) of life into his nostrils (Gen 2), giving man a share in God's vital, dynamic efficiency. *Ruah* makes man a divine image empowered to control lower creation.[1] A most significant omission occurs in the fact that this same *ruah* is not breathed into the nostrils of other living things at their creation.

Ruah (spirit, breath), *nephesh* (soul, person) and *lebh* (heart, will) imply various aspects of the complex human totality and are not adequately distinct. *Lebh* is the *nephesh* as an operating force; *ruah* is the strength emanating from the *nephesh,* or its motive power. These aspects of man distinguish him from all creation, enable man to have dominion over creation and thereby ground his imaging forth of God.

The Israelite did not distinguish between existence and activity. Activity is the person (*nephesh*) manifesting his strength and dominion. Man's perfection and happiness lie in his controlling creation. This is the dynamic expression of his whole person (*nephesh*) in an activity of free self-determination in the exercise of dominion in which he resembles his Creator, the living, acting God who watches over the work of His hands, instructing, commanding, consoling, promising, threatening, proving His power in the effective fruition of His every word, controlling the course of human history, causing everything to exist at each moment of its existence. If Israel's God is primarily a God who acts, His image will mirror Him primarily in activity in a relationship whereby man is the image of God as the supreme underlord of creation, subject only to the supreme Lord of creation.

Israel's image-of-God theology is especially remarkable when considered against the background of polytheism, by reason of which the pagans were subservient to the rest of creation, placating the gods in nature.

An ideal state of idyllic peace (*shalom*) in which all creation was subservient to man, under his control, was envisaged by the sacred writer as the primordial order of things. The prophets and psalmists lived with the golden hope that God would eventually restore that *shalom* which had been lost by the fall of man. Only then would lower creation and all nations be subject to Israel's rule and, therefore, to her God. The Kingdom of Israel was destined to rule the rest of creation as God's chosen race. Had Adam kept his primitive implicit covenant with God, there would have been no need for a new creation. Peace without effort or the need for conquest would have lasted forever. But now, because of sin, Israel was selected, as Adam, to form a covenant with God and creation for the re-establishment of the kingdom of God's perfect dominion upon earth. From the chaos of sin and disorder a re-creation was in progress. The re-establishment of subjection to man's dominion was taking place in the person of Israel, a new Adam. All mankind must submit to the universal dominion of God, and therefore to His people, Israel, who had been chosen to re-establish the primordial *shalom*.

Not because man has an intellect and will is he God's image, but because he was created with potentialities in the dynamic order above the grasp of unaided human nature, the state of grace. Man is the image of God when he is perfectly subject to the dominion of God. Only then does man enjoy peace (*shalom*) with God and all creation in the sense which St. Paul expressed so well when he said that for those who love God everything is a grace.

Man is the image of God in his dominion over lower creation, but not with regard to his own existence. In *Genesis,* chapters 2 and 3, man, as a free agent, attempts to reach out and assume control (dominion) of his own nature completely, by determining what is good and what is evil for himself, at the terrible cost of denying his subordination to the dominion God reserves over him. His eating from the "tree of knowledge of good and evil" is the symbolic expression of man's setting for himself a norm of moral action contrary to God's plan for human nature. Not satisfied to be master of the rest of creation, man assumes complete self-mastery, usurping God's prerogative of determining the terms of human existence.

For the Semite, knowledge was always to some extent experimental, connoting control, dominion, power over the object known. The knowledge of the tree of good and evil had been in some way reserved to God alone and concerned His effective dominion, power and control of the moral order. God alone knows good and evil in an effective way, by determining them and naming them and imposing them as norms to guide the tendency of the human *nephesh*. To depart from the living God's dominion will be to "die the death," for the very nature of sin is to reject the Source of all life.

With sin, everything within and around man that constituted him the image of God is destroyed or marred. Only an entirely new creation will ever be able to repair or restore this image. Shame drives man to cover his nakedness (Gen 3:14ff.) when through sin he loses mastery over his own lower nature. His irrational attempt at complete self-mastery and self-sufficiency has destroyed the primordial equilibrium with himself. No longer will lower creation peacefully cooperate with man's efforts, but the soil will bear him thorns and thistles and his daily work will bring sweat to his brow. He is surrounded by enemies and a hostile nature after having shattered his ideal *shalom* by his deliberate refusal to accept life on God's terms, to accept his role as the underlord of creation. The "image and likeness" of God wished to become God. The very wish implied the desire of self-destruction, self-rejection as "image" in the mad attempt for a new, unlimited, divine existence. Divinity, of course, was impossible, but the desire for self-rejection as God's "image" was fulfilled.

The sacred author affirms that man is God's image not because of what he is, but because of what he is given: a share in the divine sovereignty over creation. God is the Lord of the universe; man is the underlord of the universe who represents God among all creatures. The subjection of all things to man, and of man to God, was the primordial order of things in an idyllic peace (*shalom*) which involved implicit covenants between man and God, man and creatures. The absence of Greek philosophy prevented the sacred writer from considering man's "image-and-likeness" quality as purely natural (physical or spiritual) or purely supernatural. The author conceived this quality in an operative dynamic way. Man was "image and likeness" when he shared dominion with the Dynamism, Governing Force, Divine Will, Supreme Lord that was the living, acting God of Israel.

"Image" in the Old Testament

After the fall, man is deprived of his secure control over creation. He is deprived of the intimate relationship with his Creator, symbolized by the ideal life of paradise; but he is still God's "image and likeness." Though man does not have the power of creating, he does have the capacity of procreating living beings in God's image (Gen 1:27; 5:5; Luke 3:38). Ordinarily, the theme of dominion is developed in Old Testament texts on the "image and likeness" (Ps 8; Sir 17) and enriched with precisions and additions, where the "image" seems to be identified with a state of "glory and splendor," and to have been created "but a little lower than God" (Ps 8).

Throughout the Old Testament the weight of the expression "image and likeness," which had already been employed by Egyptian and Babylonian poets in describing the creation, comes from its religious context. For, unlike the Egyptian and Babylonian polytheists, the Israelites do not conceive man as the "image and likeness" of a god which is itself conceived in the image and likeness of man, but of an entirely transcendent God of whom image-making is strictly forbidden. In Israel only man can claim the title "image and likeness of God," which expresses his greatest dignity (Gen 9:6).

The best translation, then, of "image and likeness" is "according to a more or less similar representation." This formula contains in a nutshell the full religious meaning of the analogy of being. Man is an image of God, yet he remains always at a distance from Him who is perfect and totally other. The resemblance is not physical, but rather dynamic, in the sense that man, in his personal relationship with other creatures, becomes God's representative. "God of my fathers . . . you who . . . in your wisdom have established man to rule the creatures produced by you, to govern the world in holiness and justice" (Wis 9:2).

In this functional conception of the image of God, man appears as the delegate of his Creator in the sacred mission of co-regency. Man's duty is to bring out the values of civilization. Thus, every act of authority constitutes an order imposed in the name of God Himself. Man is in some way identified with his Lord, because he rules the world in His name. When man obeys God's command, "Let him have dominion," in the use of the creatures of this earth, he realizes his unity and conformity with God.

The book of *Wisdom* also calls man the image of God: "God created man for immortality, and made him the image of his own eternity" (Wis 2:23). *Wisdom* is bolder than *Genesis* in affirming that man *is* the image of God, rather than "*in* the image and likeness" of God. Secondly, man's resemblance to God in the book of *Wisdom* is primarily in man's immortality, whereas in *Genesis* the resemblance was rooted in dominion.

Man, according to the Book of *Wisdom,* is an imperfect image, but wisdom is the "spotless mirror of the activity of God, and a likeness of his goodness" (7:26). Man's dominion and his imaging of God are seen as effects of wisdom: "God of my forefathers and merciful Lord, who created all things by your word, and by your wisdom formed man to rule over the creatures you had made, and manage the world in holiness and uprightness, and pass judgment in rectitude of soul, give me the wisdom that sits by your throne, and do not reject me as unfit to be one of your servants" (9:1–4).

Preparation for Christ's Image of God

The doctrine of a transcendent and quasi-personal Wisdom in God, "the pure emanation of his glory" and the "image of his excellence" (7:25ff.), paved the way for the fulness of revelation made through the perfect image of God, Jesus Christ. The forbidding of images in Israel's worship also prepared man for Christ by expressing the seriousness of man's title, and in a negative way anticipated the coming of the God-man, the only image in which the Father fully reveals Himself.

Christ, the Image of God, in St. Paul

Man no longer must address his obedience and homage directly to God, nor to the Law which had been graciously given to sinners, but to Him who has assumed our humanity (Rom 10:5–13); for Jesus Christ is the sole mediator between God and man (1 Tim 2:5). Only through Jesus Christ, the Son of God, are men led to the Father that they may possess the fulness of life for eternity.

If Jesus communicates His Father's life, it is because He is the principle, the first-born of the dead, through whom all creation has been reconciled with God (Col 1:18ff.). The risen Christ has surmounted the divisions that separated a sinful humanity, and in Him "there is neither Jew nor Greek" (Gal 3:28). Through the revelation of God's image, man can now dominate human situations: liberty or slavery; marriage or virginity (1 Cor 7); each has its value in Christ.

The confusion of languages symbolizing the dispersion and divisions of mankind has been surmounted by the language of the Spirit of love through whom Christ continually communicates Himself to man in a love expressed by a variety of charisms glorifying the Father.

Christ is *the* new man, and through Him all believers are new men (Eph 2:15). The continual dominion of the spirit over the flesh has been restored (Gal 5:16–25; Rom 8:5–13). United to Christ, who has assumed our humanity (Col 1:22), the body of the Christian is dead to sin (Rom 8:10) through the assimilation of baptism in the death of Christ (Rom 6:5). His body of suffering has become a body of glory (Phil 3:21), a "spiritual body"

(1 Cor 15:44) to which the Christian is assimilated. Because of this renewal, metamorphosis, restoration of dominion and the perfection of the image of God (Rom 12:2; Eph 4:23), man's understanding is illuminated by the Spirit who enables him to judge (Rom 14:5) according to the ways of God (1 Cor 2:16) and, thus, the irrationality of the *Genesis* desire for equality with God is reversed when man now sees and lovingly accepts his place of submission to the Spirit of God.

In union with Christ who has died once for all, the new man continually dies to the "old man" so that "reflecting the glory of the Lord in our unveiled faces, (we) are being transformed into his very image, ever more glorious, as befits the action of the Lord who is a Spirit" (2 Cor 3:18). The new man must continually progress in putting on the image of Christ, the glorious image of God replacing the disfigured image of God reflected by the old man. Thus the new man "is renewed in the image of his Creator" (Col 3:10).

Creation, which despite itself has been subjected to the consequences of the Fall and human vanity, finds its hope of liberation from the slavery of corruption and the possibility of a glorious liberty of the sons of God in Jesus Christ. If the effects of suffering, pain, and other consequences of sin perdure, they have been given a value, a new dimension by the Christian's hope of their being transfigured in final glory (Rom 8:18–30). And when the last enemy of man, death, shall have been destroyed, the Son will turn over His kingdom to God His Father and all creation will be under the gracious dominion of God who will be everything for everyone (1 Cor 15:24–28).

As Adam lost God's many preternatural gifts by his abortive attempt to extend his dominion, Christ restored man to the perfect image and likeness of God by "emptying himself" of His divinity (Phil 2:6–11) and, in a sense even of His humanity, for "he no

longer has a human appearance" (Is 52:14), becoming "a worm
and no man" (Ps 22:7). The effects of Adam's irrational and ungrateful disobedience are reversed by Christ's loving obedience
to His Father, even to the death of the Cross. Before the disfigured
image of God could be restored, the Son of God would have to
become sin, "He made him who knew nothing of sin to become
sin for our sake that through him we might become God's justice"
(2 Cor 5:21).

Paul's Sources

St. Paul used the *Genesis* doctrine (1 Cor 11:7) as well as the
rabbinic and Philonian interpretations of the two Adams (1 Cor
15:49) in his "image of God" teaching. According to the speculations of Alexandrian Judaism, echoed by Philo, the image of
God was the Word, the instrument which God used for creation,
the archetype, the principle, the exemplar, the eldest son after
whose image God created man. This was the "heavenly" man, as
opposed to Adam, the "earthly" man.

But it is finally in the teaching of Wisdom, the perfect image,
that Paul sees the grounds for applying the title "image of God"
to Christ (2 Cor 3:18; 4:4). Paul employs various sources of
inspiration for fathoming the mystery of Christ. Christ is the image
of God by filiation (Rom 8:29); as image of God He presides at
the creation of the new man (Col 3:10). The concept is complex
and rich; especially in Col 1:15: Christ's resemblance to God as
image is spiritual and perfect, by a filiation prior to creation; He
is *the* representation of the Father whom no man has ever seen;
He enjoys cosmic sovereignty and immortality, being the first-
born of the dead; the only image which assures the unity of all
creation and the unity of the divine plan—the principle of creation
and the principle of its restoration by a new creation.

The Christian and the Image of God

All these elements found in Christ Jesus, *the* image of God, attract man, the sinful and imperfect image of God, who so desperately needs *the* image of God, Jesus Christ, before he can ever hope to rediscover and accomplish his original destiny. Under the attraction of *the* image of God, the Christian is transformed into the image of the Son, the first-born of many brothers (2 Cor 3:18; Rom 8:29), who, when lifted up, has drawn all men to Himself.

Through baptism the Christian "has put on that new man, constantly being renewed in view of perfect knowledge *in the image of his Creator,* where there is no Greek and Jew . . . but Christ, all in all (Col 3:10–11). Through baptism man enters the new solidarity of grace with *the* image of God; he puts on the new self by his union with the new Adam and is "constantly renewed." The union of man with God, in Christ, God's image, is initiated by baptism and is dependent for its growth upon the faithful practice of the Christian life.

"Perfect knowledge" is "true moral knowledge" when Paul alludes to Gen 3:1–22, where Adam attempts to "be like God" by eating from the tree giving the knowledge of "good and evil." Disobedience brings Adam death, whereas the wholehearted acceptance of and submission to Christ brings man eternal life. The Christian advances towards "perfect knowledge" in his total self-giving to Christ, in whom is found the "perfect knowledge" of God. The Christian grows in his likeness to Christ, the image of God, "in the image of his Creator" (2 Cor 3:18).

In the glorified humanity of the risen Christ, "the image of his Creator" has, in one sense, been perfectly realized. He is the "first-born before all creatures" (Col 1:15), as "image of the unseen God" (Col 1:15). But, in another sense, the completion of the glorification of Christ's humanity includes the perfect assimilation of all Christians, who must pass through death and resurrection before they can be *fully* one with Christ. The working out of this process gives true significance to the period of salvation-history between Christ's resurrection and the glorious resurrection of the just. If considered as a struggle waged until "the last enemy," death, is overcome (1 Cor 15:25–28), Christ's reign is not fully established, the Father is not yet "all in all," the Son has not reached the state of perfect subjection to the Father which demands the glorification of the entire Christian people. The ultimate goal of salvation-history is reached only when the Father is "all in all." In this sense, man considers himself more as *becoming* Christian than *being* Christian. In another sense, Christ is already "all in all"; for baptism has already united Christians with Christ, permitting them to share in the death and resurrection of the Lord (Rom 6:15). The victory is basically, though only initially, won.

In Pauline thought, Christ, not man, is *the* image of God. Men are being created, at last, in Christ's image. Not by looking to the past and to something intrinsic to the nature of man, which suggests a likeness to God, does Paul base his hope for the transformation into the image of God, but on the historic action of God which has at last culminated in the revelation of *the* perfect image. By virtue of his wholehearted acceptance of this revelation man may be transformed into what he has not been as yet, a new creation, a member of the Body of Christ, a son of God. Man will come to bear the image of Christ as he is transformed by the presence of the Spirit.

Jesus is the perfect image of God (Col 1:15; Heb 1:3). Original sin obscured the image, impaired man's dominion over all creation; but in the humanity of Christ a man is the perfect image of God and enjoys absolute dominion over all creation. The promise of Gen 1:26–28 is fulfilled in the Last Adam, through whom God reconciles the world to Himself (2 Cor 5:19); and man enjoys the solidarity of Christ when God sends "his own Son in the likeness of sinful humanity" (Rom 8:3), that all mankind may be restored through Christ Jesus to the perfect image and likeness of God. The true character of God becomes known in Christ, the perfect image of God; and, through the agency of the Holy Spirit, the transformation of all believers into the perfection of God's image and likeness has already begun.

Notes

[1] James D. Smart observes in his book, *The Old Testament in Dialogue with Modern Man* (Philadelphia: Westminster Press, 1964), p. 41, that man's unique destiny is to maintain order in the creation on God's behalf. Man is to rule for God. Man must act as the agent of the divine purpose in history; this occurs only on condition that the nature of God is reflected or participated in by man's nature. Smart asserts that to rule for God man must be just, as God is just; holy, as God is holy; true, as God is true; faithful, as God is faithful. For man to be unjust, unholy, untrue, unfaithful, would be for him to cease to reflect God's nature and so to become the cause of disorder, rather than of order, upon the earth. The likeness, Smart continues, exists in man only insofar as he is what God created him to be, the partner of his purpose, the bearer of his word, a creature responding in love to the love that has chosen him for such a glorious destiny. If he is cut off from that destiny by his own willfulness and separated from God, man will cease to reflect or share in the nature of God, but nothing he can do, Smart concludes, will make him other than a creature who was created for such a destiny as that.

4

"We Have Seen His Glory"

The Incarnation may be described in many terms. One of the most beautiful expressions found in the New Testament is the term "glory." The inspired authors speak of the glory of Christ in the sense of divine majesty. Luke acknowledges that Christ is the glory of Yahweh's people Israel (2:32), and Paul hails him as the Lord of glory (1 Cor 2:8). This glory belonged to Christ from all eternity before the creation of the world (Jn 17:5). His miracles are signs of this glory (2:11).

Glory may mean the appearance of a radiant light which mediates the nearness of God: "Now in this same district there were shepherds keeping watch through the night over their flock, when suddenly there stood before them an angel of the Lord and the glory of the Lord shone around them (Lk 2:9).

Glory is also associated with the places where God reigns: the Temple (Apoc 15:8) and the New Jerusalem which "shone with the glory of God" and had "the radiance of some priceless jewel, like a jasper, clear as crystal" (Apoc 20:10). It is also connected with the messianic age: "Then they will see the Son of Man coming in the clouds with great power and glory" (Mk 13:26; Mt 23:31–46).

St. Paul's expression, "an eternal weight of glory" (2 Cor 4:17) is essentially Semitic and recalls the original meaning of *kabod*. This is the theme that we are about to trace.

Human Glory and Divine

Kabod, the Hebrew word for "glory," originally implied the idea of weight or mass. Weight determined an object's importance, the respect it inspired, its glory. "Glory" did not originally mean fame, but the real value and worth of an object estimated by its weight. The basis for glory could be found in riches. Abraham had glory in his great property and possessions (Gen 13:2). High social status and great authority were the glory of Joseph (Gen 45:13): "Tell my father of my great glory in Egypt." With the loss of his possessions, Job was stripped of his glory (Job 19:9).

The glory of power (Is 8:7; 16:14) always implied brilliance and radiant light, dazzling splendor. There was glory in the army of Assyria (Is 8:7), in the cedars of Lebanon (Is 60:13), in Aaron's vestments (Ex 28:2), in the Temple (Hg 2:3), in Jerusalem (Is 62:2). But glory *par excellence* was ascribed to kingship. Glory was attributed a *king's* wealth, power and grandeur (1 Chr 29:28). Like no other king, Solomon received his glory from God, who has also "crowned with glory" man, the king of creation (Ps 8:6).

The glory of Yahweh designates God himself in so far as he reveals his majesty, his power, his radiant holiness, the dynamism of his being. The glory of Yahweh has the character of a disclosure, a revelation, an epiphany. The two chief manifestations of divine glory in the Old Testament are found in the great deeds of Yahweh and in the apparitions of the glory of God.

God manifests his glory in his awe-inspiring interventions, judgments and signs (Nm 14:22). The people of God saw his glory in the breathtaking miracles of the Red Sea crossing and the manna in the desert (Exod 16:7): "In the morning you shall see the glory of God." In God's wondrous care for his people, glory is almost a synonym for "salvation" (Is 35:1–4; 44:23). The glory of the covenant God is in saving and helping his people. His glory is his power at the service of his faithful covenant-love: "When Yahweh shall rebuild Sion, we shall see his glory" (Ps 102:17; Ex 39:21–29).

The Apparition of God's Glory

In the second type of divine manifestation, glory is a visible reality seen in the wilderness by the Israelites who have murmured against Yahweh (Exod 16:10). The radiance of the divinity, the glory of God, abides upon Mount Sinai and its appearance is like a devouring fire (Ex 24:16). The glory of God fills the tabernacle (Ex 40:34) and the Temple (1 K 8:11). When the cult is initiated and Aaron, with his sons, has prepared the first sacrifices, all the congregation stands before the Lord in order that his glory may appear to them. The people are blessed and then, in this festive moment, the glory of the Lord appears to them when fire comes forth from the Lord and consumes the offering; with this the sacred cult (worship) is inaugurated (Lv 9:6, 23, 24). When the congregation wants to stone Moses and Aaron, the glory of God appears—apparently as a warning and a defense—to all in the tent of meeting (Nm 14:10). It appears when Korah and his faction gather at the tent of meeting with the forbidden cult fire (Nm 16:19) and when the congregation rebels against Moses and Aaron (Nm 17:7). Again, when Solomon completes the Temple and the first sacrifices are ready, fire from heaven consumes the sacrifices and the glory of God fills the Temple (2 Chr 7:1–3).

After Sinai the glory of God dwells in the tent of meeting (Ex 29:43):

> I will meet the Israelites there, and it shall be consecrated by my glory; I will consecrate the tent of meeting and the altar, and I will also consecrate Aaron and his sons to serve as priests to me; I will dwell in the midst of the Israelites, and will be their God.

The priestly theology of the Old Testament connected the glory of God with particular places. The glory of God comes to dwell among men when God in his goodness allows his presence to be manifested in Israel. At first the transcendent glory dwells in the privileged tent of meeting: ". . . the cloud covered the tent of meeting and the glory of the Lord filled the tabernacle" (Ex 40:34; 16:10; 29:43; Lv 9:6, 23; Nm 14:10). To escape the gaze of the sacrilegious and any possible profanation, this glory is veiled in a cloud.

Within the tent of meeting was kept the ark of the covenant, which served as the throne of the invisible Lord of Israel and thus provided a visible token of God's presence among his people. The ark was called the "footstool" of God (Ps 98:5). It also served as a lasting testimonial of the solemn covenant between God and his people made on Sinai. For this purpose the two stone tablets on which were inscribed the ten commandments, the obligations imposed upon the Israelites by the covenant, were kept in the ark. Thus God made good his promise to Moses that he would go before the Israelites and be with them, ever faithful to his pact, his covenant with Israel witnessed by the tables of the law.

Israel was in the service of this glory (Lv 9:6). Israel lived, walked and triumphed under its radiance (Nm 16:1–17, 15; 20:1–13; 40:36). David brought the ark into the tabernacle (2 S

6:1–15). Solomon placed it in his magnificent temple (1 K 8:1–11).

There is a close connection between the local, cultic concept of glory and the dynamic, active concept. In both, God reveals his presence to his people to save them, to sanctify them, to rule them (Exod 29:46).

It is under the aspect of kingship that Isaiah contemplates the glory of God. When Isaiah sees Yahweh sitting upon a lofty throne, the seraphs cry one to another that the whole earth is full of his glory (Is 6:3). The glory of God fills the whole earth in what is a cosmic phenomenon. Isaiah does not attempt to describe the appearance of the King; he mentions only the throne and "the skirts of his robe," as though he had instantly lowered his eyes.

Isaiah's vision was to be the theme of his preaching and spiritual life—the holiness of God. The glory which fills the universe is that holiness made manifest. At the thunder of the angelic acclamation, Isaiah feels the solid foundations of the temple tremble under his feet. The smoke, or cloud, is another symbol of the divine presence, or glory, which marks the end of his *vision* of God; the *audition* lasts somewhat longer.

Man's Reaction to God's Glory

The religious reaction of the prophet Isaiah is typical of man's reaction to the glory of God. The glory of God is "wholly other." In it the numinous presents itself as basically and totally different. At first, in Isaiah's case, there is a shuddering, the specifically religious dread that man feels before a tremendous mystery; but there is also a moral reaction, the sense of unworthiness and guilt. Uncleanness of the lips is stressed, apparently because Isaiah feels impelled to pray, to appeal to the divine mercy. But no prayer he can utter would be tolerable to the Holy One. His unholiness is not merely personal—he is a member of an unholy race. How can he ward off the annihilation that must befall him? "For the King, the Lord of hosts, have my eyes beheld" (Is 6:5).

The overwhelming majesty of God is like nothing human or cosmic. With a feeling of terror before the sacred, man feels that he is, in the words of Abraham addressing God, "but dust and ashes" (Gen 18:27). But the Lord of glory who appears in regal splendor does not triumph to destroy but to purify, to regenerate and to permeate the universe with his glory. Though an infinite distance separates the holiness of God from the impurity of creatures, the creative love of Israel's King cannot be impeded.

The "sacrament" which effects Isaiah's purification is a live coal from the incense-altar in the Holy Place. Through the glory of God divine holiness is imparted to Isaiah, specifically to his organs of speech. His impurity is removed. He is made capable of speaking in God's name. A prophet is created through the dynamic glory of God, in a process characterized by divine activity and human passivity.

Eschatological Glory of the Glory Teaching

In the last part of the book of *Isaiah* are united the two fundamental aspects of the Old Testment teaching on the divine glory, glory in the great deeds of Yahweh and the visible, apparitional aspect. God reigns in his holy city, which is both regenerated by his power and illuminated by his presence:

> Arise, shine; for your light has come, and the glory of the
>   Lord has risen upon you.
> For lo, darkness shall cover the earth, and thick darkness the
>   peoples;
> but upon you his glory shall appear, and nations shall walk
>   by your light, and kings by the brightness of your rising
>   (Is 60:1–3).

Jerusalem sees itself "raised in glory at the center of the earth" (62:7). From Jerusalem the glory of God radiates upon all nations which come to it, overwhelmed by its dazzling glory.

With the prophets of the exile, the royal psalms, and the apocalyptic literature, glory attains a universal dimension, an eschatological character (Is 66:18): "I am coming to gather all nations and tongues; they shall come, and see my glory." But at the very heart of Isaiah's glory is the detached personage "without beauty or comeliness" (52:14) sent to accomplish the radiation of divine glory to the ends of the earth: "You are my servant, and through you shall I show forth my glory" (49:3).

Although Jerusalem is the accustomed and true habitation of the divine glory (Ez 8:4; 9:3), Ezekiel experiences the reflection of God's glory in a land of exile (Ezek 1:4–28). The actual spiritual reality which the prophet Ezekiel apprehended was the indescribable, ineffable, manifest holiness and glory of the Divinity. He labors to convey some idea of the transcendence and majesty of this glory in the traditional setting of the divine theophany: fire, lightning, thunder and storm-clouds. The concept of God "throned upon the Cherubim" in heaven or in the Temple is also present. Nevertheless, even the most sublime symbols are inadequate to describe his vision of glory, as is clear from the frequency of phrases such as "something like," "resembling" and "appearance of."

Others had seen Yahweh on his throne, but the novelty of Ezekiel's vision of divine glory is its affirmation that the glory of God can appear wherever it pleases. Just as Nebuchadnezzar had a portable throne (3 K 22:19) on which he would sit to give judgment in any part of his dominions, God in his glory can appear in an infinitely more sublime manner in sovereign majesty wherever he pleases. He is God everywhere.

Ezekiel's sense of the holiness of God was accompanied by the realization that nothing unholy or profane could stand in his presence. In his extraordinary vision (chapters 8–11), he was

carried from Babylonia to the Temple of Jerusalem, where he saw
the abominations practiced there: the women weeping for Tam-
muz, the god of fertility, men worshipping the sun, the secret
chamber depicting beasts and idols, and the princes making evil
plans. Then the prophet saw the glory of God, the divine presence
that was accustomed to inhabit the Holy of Holies, depart from the
defiled Temple. So great was the idolatry of the people that even
if the three proverbially righteous men, Noah, Daniel and Job,
were to be found in the city, it would not escape destruction
(14:12–20).

For Ezekiel the greatest human abomination was to insult the
sanctity of God with the introduction of foreign cults into the very
house where his glory dwelled. When the glory departs, the supposed protection and immunity from destruction have also ceased.
This is the judgment aspect of God's glory. For the worst crime
merits the worst of all punishments: the departure of God's
glorious presence.

Ezekiel, however, ends on a message of hope when he foretells
the return of the divine glory to a purified Jerusalem after the
time of desolation (43:1–7; 44:1–4). The departure and return of
God's glory is a dominant theme of Old Testament history.

The Glory of God in the Liturgy of Israel

The glory of God had appeared in all the wondrous events of
salvation-history: at the covenant and giving of the Law at Sinai;
at the inauguration of sacrifice; when the cult and guidance of
the people were threatened; before sacrilege in the Temple; and
at the world theophany of Isaiah's eschatological vision. The festivals of Israel celebrated the mighty works of God on behalf of his
people. The Pasch, for example, the most important feast of the
Jewish calendar, celebrated from the fourteenth of Nisan until the
twenty-first of Nisan (March–April) obliged every male Israelite

to appear in Jerusalem to commemorate the glory of God, in the mighty work of his deliverance from Egypt. Every Israelite family gathered together for the ritual eating of the paschal lamb to commemorate the departure from the land of bondage, Yahweh's merciful liberation.

The glory of God, both in his mighty work, the historical event commemorated, and in his presence in the Temple of Jerusalem where these events were celebrated, found its perfection in the Temple liturgy. The glory of God transcended time in the liturgical worship where past glory, present love and future confidence were manifested in the Temple glory. The God who had miraculously delivered his people was still delivering them and would always deliver them.

The Feast of Tabernacles, for example, was a memorial of the old nomadic life, the blessed "golden age" of Israel's history. It was not the commemoration of a particular event so much as the celebration of God's glory or presence among them symbolized by the tent of meeting. In the glory of God's presence within the Temple, Israel rejoiced in the celebration of a past event, a present realization and a future confidence in God's presence (*kabod Yahweh*). This presence made the people of God, and were it to disappear, the people would cease to be. The glory of God was their security, strength, and happiness. Throughout the Old Testament the idea, the desire, the love of God's presence or glory was localized in some privileged spot where he manifested his holiness and power, where the people celebrated and rejoiced in it, and because of it.

The Temple liturgy celebrated the active presence of the Holy God in the midst of the men he had chosen. Here the people met God, served him and prayed. It was the tent of reunion (Ex 33:7) where God's people rejoiced in his glory and covenant-love. It was a kind of permanent theophany, a continuation of God's wondrous intervention at Sinai. Thus the Temple was the object of the cult, of fervent covenant-love where pilgrimages converged and sacrifices were celebrated that corresponded to the great moments in the life of God's people. The psalms, the collection of the songs that accompanied the feasts and divine services, were largely a reflection of the Temple liturgy praising the glory of God in their midst and of their past. Psalms 120–134 describe the joy of catching the first glimpse of the Holy City from a distance and approaching, in slow cortege, the Temple of God's glory.

But this enthusiasm was not without danger. The prophets sounded another note—not that they were opposed to worship and Temple liturgy, not that they preached a religion divorced from the Temple, but they recalled with vehemence that the presence or glory of God is not bound to a building of stone or gold (Amos 5:21–24; Hos 6:6; Is 1:11–17; and especially Jer 7). The Temple is the sign of the covenant and a great favor, but conduct must be shaped according to the demands of God's covenant. Without the fidelity of covenant-love and the worship of every instant, the Temple would lose its meaning.

Granted the transcendence of God, the divine *kabod Yahweh* (glory of God) as a material presence is possible. The ancient rabbis saw this, even though they refused to see the glory of God in Jesus. *Kabod* is a word that tells that God in love transcends even his transcendence. The human figure of Jesus was the divine glory just as the cloud of Sinai. The Christ-glory is prolonged and extended in time and space in the form of the people of God, the Church. The cloud on Sinai foreshadowed the Christ to come, and the Church prolongs the historical Christ until he comes again at the end of time.

Is God in glory? We answer both yes and no. It is his real presence in time and space. It is not, however, God's pure essence, but it is God coming to material man in love and condescension. In the glory, God is there, and only where he is can he be met. Only in the encounter with him in his glory can man be saved.

The Church, the glory of Christ in the world, is the *locus* of God in history. It is Christ prolonged, all-holy and yet, paradoxically, made up of sinners who must be built up to the stature of the full Christ. The people of God are the saints, not because of their sinlessness, but because they live, act, think and pray in Christ, who certainly is sinless, the glory of God, the true "King of glory."

5
Jeremiah: Man of God

Jeremiah's prophetic activity spanned forty fateful years (626–587 B.C.) in the history of Judah.[1] Our word "jeremiad" for a doleful lament or complaint derives from a later tradition which portrayed him as a "weeping prophet."[2] This portrait is overdrawn, for Jeremiah's message had in it all the severity of Amos and Isaiah. Like his prophetic predecessors Jeremiah announced that the Day of Yahweh for which the people waited expectantly would not be a day of victory and rejoicing but a bitter day of gloom and doom. On the other hand, Jeremiah identified himself with his message in a more personal way than any other prophet. This helps to explain why we know more about Jeremiah the man than about any other Old Testament figure, with the possible exception of David.

Jeremiah's generous response to his vocation, his intimacy with God whom he found in all things, his courageous utterance of God's word at his own personal risk and despite his natural aversion to violence, his deep interiority, humility, and heroic suffering, his meaningful celibacy and profound sense of dependence on God make him an awe-inspiring archetype of the genuine man of God.

Jeremiah's Sense of Vocation

Seldom has a man been less naturally inclined to his vocation than Jeremiah. Genial and sociable, peace-loving and even retiring by nature, he had to engage in a bitter and prolonged struggle with kings, priests, prophets, politicians, relatives, friends, and even himself. His celibacy, which was a most remarkable state in his time and place, his exclusion from ordinary social life, his role of "skeleton at the feast," always crying "Violence and spoil!" (20:8), and his perpetually ineffective preaching made for a life-long frustration and agony of soul which cannot but arouse our wonder and admiration.

The prophets have told us about their vocation: God speaks, calls, consecrates, and sends (Amos 7:15; 3:7–8; Is 6; Jer 20:7; 1:4–10). Jeremiah vividly presented the story of his call in the form of a dialogue with Yahweh in which we are told how irresistibly Yahweh's word came to him (Jer 5:14; 23:29). Throughout his career he had to struggle with the mighty power of Yahweh's word, but he could not refrain from speaking it. In retrospect, he saw that his entire life was part of Yahweh's plan. From the time when he was still in his mother's womb, his life was to have a special meaning: to be Yahweh's prophet, set aside for a special task. His vocation was but the expression of a previous election for which he had been brought into the world. Creation itself was connected with his election (1:5):

> Before I formed you in the womb I knew you,
> And before you were born I set you apart,
> I appointed you a prophet to the nations.

Despite many tribulations, Jeremiah never doubted the reality of his vocation. He could never forget that dramatic moment of interior illumination when the consciousness of his lifelong vocation to the service of Yahweh had been so vividly impressed on his mind. To Isaiah the Lord had appeared in grandeur and majesty. But the Lord came to Jeremiah in an experience that was probably rooted in the pieties of home and early life and which consisted in a growing knowledge of self and of God which finally culminated in the awareness of a special mission.[3] The mystery of a divine call is a theme found in the Bible from Abraham to the Annunciation.[4]

Jeremiah realized that vocations, prepared in eternity and inscribed at birth, are made known by Yahweh in His own hour. They are an invitation to serve Him humbly and faithfully. The one called should not be filled with fear or vanity because the call comes from God and is part of His immense plan born of His immense love. Consequently, in what was far more than a mere act of self-discovery, Jeremiah surrendered himself to the service of Yahweh who intimately knew him with a knowledge of his most individual particularities and the intimate secrets of his soul, a divine knowledge which had created him in the fullness of his singularity and individuality for this special mission "to the nations." The intimacy of Yahweh and Jeremiah is perhaps without parallel in the entire Old Testment, for this is the only prophet whom Yahweh addresses by name: "What do you see, Jeremiah?" (1:11).

Like Moses (Ex 3 and 4), Jeremiah naturally shrank from his great task, not only because of his youth but also because of his deep sense of personal inadequacy. From a purely natural viewpoint, his lack of self-confidence was well grounded in his knowledge of what the prophetic vocation implied. He realized that although messages from the gods were usually welcomed in pagan cultures, such was not the case in Israel where the task of a messenger was dangerous. The burden of all true prophets' preaching was made up of rebukes and threats of judgment (28:8). He would have to campaign for the true knowledge of the covenant God of Israel, for the observance of the First and Second Commandments in particular. He would have to attack blasphemous infidelity to Yahweh. He would have to tell his countrymen that Yahweh was not satisfied with their lavish gifts and the pomp of their temple ceremonials but wished to be served in spirit and truth, which is true religion. Jeremiah realized that he would have to strive for the moral and social reformation of his people, because Yahweh was a moral God, demanding ethical righteousness of His children. A naturally repugnant task for his sensitive nature would be that of denouncing his people for their injustice and immorality, which he clearly saw would lead to terrible chastisements and annihilation unless they amended their lives. He would have to dissuade the rulers of Judah from trusting in political alliances, which usually involved some admission of foreign cults.[5] The rulers must trust in Yahweh's power and goodness as sufficient protection for His people. Cognizant of his all but overwhelming duties, this youth—probably in his late teens—humbly protested (1:6): "Ah, Lord Yahweh! I cannot speak; for I am only a youth."

But Jeremiah's hesitation was overridden by Yahweh's promise to be with him. This situation prefigures that at the end of Matthew's Gospel in which there is also a command to preach, and to preach only what they are told to preach. In both cases God promises to be with them. Jeremiah is warned that there will be opposition to his message, whereas the apostles are left to presume it. Jeremiah is promised sufficient strength and power so that his enemies will not overcome him. His success, like that of the apostles, is guaranteed by the fact that God will be with him. His strength, after all, did not lie in his natural endowments but in the power of Yahweh who spoke through him and sent him forth.

He was to serve the history-making word of Yahweh which is filled with power to destroy and to rebuild (1:10). In their frantic efforts to gain control of history, the nations would have to learn that Yahweh controls human affairs. Thus Jeremiah depicts Yahweh as stretching forth His hand and touching the prophet's mouth to empower him to speak:

> And Yahweh said to me,
> "See! I put my words in your mouth;
> This day I give you authority over the nations and kingdoms,
> To root up and to pull down, to root up and to pull down,
>   to wreck and to ruin, to build and to plant" (1:10).

The exalted nature of Jeremiah's vocation is clearly stated. The prophet is no longer a mere legislator for his people but something like a lord of history under God. The prophet is set over the nations for their good or their evil as they respond to the appeal. Yet Jeremiah humbly realizes that Yahweh's word is sovereign not only over the nations but also over his own interior life as well.

The Suffering Man of God

The message which Jeremiah delivered aroused the hostility of his people. From the first this quiet, sensitive man had recoiled from the task to which he had felt predestined even before birth. Now he had set himself against everyone because Yahweh's judgment was against the whole land of Judah. "They will fight against you," he had been warned. But in his loneliness Jeremiah found a deeper resource than human approval: "I am with you," says Yahweh, "to deliver you."

Even if he was as staunch as "a fortified city, an iron pillar, and bronze walls" (Jer 1:18), he was also as sensitive as a mother bereft of her children. The bitter tragedy of Jerusalem and his people was intensified by the very words he felt compelled to speak in the name of Yahweh.

The moral blindness and spiritual insensitivity of his people cut deeply into his own heart prompting him to mix his prophecies of doom with outcries of agony and grief (8:18–22). His feeling for the fundamental order of things and the sacred source from which it comes, his feelings for the right and righteous order of things which constitutes the true pattern of life, was intensely acute and, consequently, was violently jarred by the moral and religious disorder of his contemporaries. For Jeremiah, moral disorder was a type of chaos which extends itself even into the physical order. Sin is a return to chaos. It eradicates the image of God from man. In one of his finest images, Jeremiah depicted sin as a type of pre-Genesis creation in reverse (4:23 ff.): "I looked at the earth, and lo! it was chaos; at the heavens, and their light was gone." Moral disorder has thrown the physical world into chaos: "It is because my people are stupid, and know me not; they are sottish children, and have no understanding; they have skill to do evil, but know not how to do good" (4:22).

Unlike Amos and Isaiah, who are on Yahweh's side, and Hosea, who is caught in the middle, Jeremiah is on his people's side. He grieved more for the people than any other prophet (8:21–22; 9:1). He agonized over their incurable sickness.[6] Jeremiah's life was so filled with sorrows that, not without reason, some of Jesus' contemporaries thought that perhaps He was another Jeremiah. Both Jeremiah and Jesus suffered intensely because of the sinfulness of their people whom they loved so much.

Jeremiah's horror for sin was concretely expressed in his account of his terrifying vision of a sinful world returning to its primordial chaos (4:23 ff.). Yahweh's wrath would not consist so much in His active intervention and punishment but rather in the withdrawal of a rebellious people from the merciful and salvific governance of Yahweh into the outer darkness. God's punishment would consist in allowing this recalcitrant people to suffer the destructive consequences of their own actions and attitudes. Yahweh's love had gone out into the chaos of non-being to establish His order and peace in the act of creation. By departing from the order and laws of Yahweh, Jeremiah's people were committing an act of self-destruction. Jeremiah did not view the order and laws of Yahweh as an arbitrary imposition of authority on rebellious subjects but rather as an act of the divine Wisdom providing a way for His people to rise above mere animality to the rational, noble, and good life to which they had been especially committed by the covenant. Jeremiah's understanding of Yahweh's laws and order should not be represented by the figure of a prison or a chain but rather as a beacon light to the sailor, as the road the lost jungle-traveler stumbles upon as the way of escape from prison. Yahweh's laws offered the solution for the soul striving upward, showing the direction of ascent; for the ruler pondering the good of his people, it would be the flash of understanding that enables him to legislate wisely. Even on the natural level, good laws were a lamp to one's feet and a light to one's paths.

The "Confessions" of Jeremiah tell the story of his anguish and misery. Similar in type to the *Confessions* of St. Augustine, these intimate outpourings came from several occasions in his career. They may originally have been a type of diary. Clearly, they are not in their original sequence. The following passages contain fragments of his dialogues with God in prayer and constitute the "Confessions": [7]

> Like a gentle lamb led to the slaughter (11:18–23).
> Why does the way of the wicked prosper? (12:1–6).
> I sat alone, because thy hand was upon me (15:10–21).
> Thou art my refuge in the day of evil (17:14–18).
> Is evil a recompense for good? (18:18–23).
> A burning fire shut up in my bones (20:7–12, 14–18).

The first two confessions may belong to the time of the Deuteronomic reformation and may reveal the hatred of the people of his village, Anathoth, who were infuriated, perhaps, by his advocacy of a reform program which threatened to deprive the local priests of their positions. The villagers plotted against his life and threatened him with death if he were to continue preaching the word of Yahweh (11:21). Even his family joined his persecutors (12:6). The fifth confession reveals plots against his life undertaken by the religious leaders of Jerusalem (18:18).

At the very brink of despair, Jeremiah accuses Yahweh of having deceived him (17:18), of making him a laughing stock (20:7-9). His words, often the result of bitter brooding, would be blasphemous on the lips of anyone less assured than he of the right to talk back to God. Yet Jeremiah realizes that he has gone too far and that he has spoken rashly. Enlightened by Yahweh, he realizes the danger of becoming like one of the rebellious people against whom he had been set. Jeremiah, much wiser for his suffering, recognizes that he stood in need of this inward purification (15:19): " 'Therefore,' thus says Yahweh: 'If you return, I will restore you, and you shall stand before me. If you utter what is precious, and not what is worthless, you shall be as my mouth.' "

Jeremiah's Celibacy

Jeremiah was the first biblical character to embrace celibacy as a state of life. Although others before him may have abstained from marriage, Jeremiah is the first to whom Scripture explicitly attributes celibacy. His confessions provide the most ancient reflection on an explanation of this subject as well as the beginnings of the biblical doctrine of virginity. His insight into the significance of celibacy derived from an introspective cast of mind which was rare in ancient Israel.

We do not know whether Yahweh had ordered Jeremiah to be a celibate or whether this state was progressively imposed by the circumstances of his isolation and the persecutions that made him a pariah. Jeremiah would eventually have understood that beneath those circumstances there was a divine ordinance and with typical Semitic disregard for secondary causes would have expressed it in the literary form of an order. In any case, Jeremiah clearly gives his celibacy a symbolic value. The loneliness of his unmarried life adumbrates the desolation of Israel. His forlorn celibacy is an enacted prophecy of the imminent doom and death that is about to sweep the country and make meaningless matrimony and procreation.

As Isaiah had walked naked in the streets of Jerusalem to announce the imminent captivity of the Egyptians (Is 20:1–6), as Jeremiah had broken a jug to symbolize the destruction of Jerusalem (Jer 19:1–11), as Ezekiel had cut his beard and scattered it to the four winds as the people of Judah would be dispersed (Ez 5:4), so too was Jeremiah's celibacy a type of prophecy in action. Yahweh often gave the very life of a prophet a symbolic significance, as when Hosea's unhappy marriage symbolized the relations between Yahweh and His unfaithful spouse, Israel (Hos 1:3).

With prophetic insight Jeremiah could already see the shadow of death covering the land. It was his bitter task to announce the imminent desolation by his own life. The temple and the kingship were the two institutions of the covenant through which God's graces had come to His people. Within a few years Israel would witness the Day of Yahweh when these two signs of Yahweh's dwelling in the land of His choice would disappear; when Nebuchadnezzar would invade the land, burn the sanctuary, enslave the king, and kill his children. The people of Israel would disappear; there would be no more heirs of the promises and children of the covenant unless Yahweh assembled a new people and repeated the exodus. A testament was over; Yahweh's plan had seemingly failed. Death would reign.

Having already been barred from the Temple (36:5), driven from his village (11:8; 12:6; 11:19) and from the community (20:2; 36:25), Jeremiah learned before the exile what it would mean to live rejected within his own country and away from Yahweh's sanctuary. He experienced proleptically what his people would later suffer. His celibacy became a sign or an enacted word with an ominous significance which portrayed what Yahweh was about to do: imminent doom and God's judgment which would find its final expression in the cross.

> The solitude of the lonely prophet of Anathoth announces the dereliction of the crucified victim of Calvary. It has the same significance: it signifies the end of an economy in which God's promises and graces were entrusted to Israel *secundum carnem* and communicated by way of generation. This order disappears. When God will raise a new Israel, it will be an Israel *secundum spiritum* in which one will have access not by right of birth but by direct reception of the Spirit (Jer 31:31–35). In such a people the fecundity of the flesh will have lost its value.[8]

Jeremiah, Man of Contemplation and Insight

Few men have ever been more intensely alive than this reluctant prophet. Whereas his contemporaries were people who simply lived in an oblong hum, Jeremiah achieved a type of apotheosis, as if a blast of divine light and sound had flung him into a new speed, a further orbit of existence. Jeremiah's happiness was something that took place within the alert core of his perceptive mind. His uncanny awareness of reality on so many levels reveals an intense activity of soul in which the highest potentialities of his being achieved their fullest realization. True, his happiness was a gift of God rooted in the many exceptional graces he had received; nevertheless, although always a gift, his happiness was his own. If sight were given to a blind man, he would nevertheless see with his own sense of sight.[9]

Jeremiah could discover cosmic significance in a twig. In Hebrew the word for almond also meant "waker" or "watcher," because it is the first tree to blossom. Once, while gazing at an almond twig, Jeremiah was impelled to pronounce its name which suggested to him that Yahweh is the "watcher" who neither slumbers nor sleeps but proceeds to judgment. In the almond twig he sees Yahweh "watching over" His word, bringing His plan into historical reality (1:12), for the word of Yahweh was the power that shaped human events.

Jeremiah's appreciation for concrete reality was kindled by his contemplative impulse which sought the divine meaning underlying all beings. An insight into Yahweh's historical purpose for Judah, indicating that an ominous judgment was at hand, was occasioned by an ordinary cooking pot. While gazing at the steam being wafted southwards from this boiling pot, he foresaw the desolation which would be let loose on Israel from the north (4:5–6). Again, the instinctive flight of migratory birds made him aware of man's instinctive yearning for God.

Enlightened by Yahweh, Jeremiah discovered a mystical significance in the ordinary objects of everyday experience. In the eternal snows of Lebanon he found a symbol for the unfailing source of Israel's true religion (18:14): "Does white snow vanish from the crest of Sirion? Does the cold flowing water of the mountains run dry?" In another vision (Jer 24) he saw two baskets of figs placed before the Temple. The basket of good figs represented the exiles with whom the future lay. Yahweh would restore to the land those whom Nebuchadnezzar had carried away and make them His covenant people. The bad figs represented the king Zedekiah and his people. They would be driven from Judah and chastised as an example to all the nations.

Jeremiah's whole mind, heart, and soul were so much *en rapport* with the spirit of Yahweh that he reacted to things much the way Yahweh would have reacted if He were a man. This intimacy would be both the cause of joy and sorrow, of his profound insights into good and evil. Jeremiah's insights into reality and the right order of things were strongly influenced by his affinity and rapport with the spirit of Yahweh. Centuries later, St. Thomas was to explain this type of wisdom when he stated that there pertains to wisdom a twofold mode of judgment: one after the mode of inclination, somewhat as a husband may know that his wife will not like a certain dress simply by his affinity to her; the other after the mode of knowledge, in which the reasons for the judgment are set forth explicitly. Theology pertains to the second mode of judgment, where, from the truths of faith, conclusions are logically deduced. Mysticism such as Jeremiah's insights into the ways of Yahweh pertains to the first mode of judgment, where the man of God judges through his experience of and consequent affinity with God.

In the solitude of his heart, Jeremiah has come to realize that the ways of Yahweh are kindness, justice, and righteousness. These are the things that Yahweh does and takes pleasure in; consequently, His sons must act thus and Yahweh will delight in their actions. Jeremiah knew that these were the matters that counted in Yahweh's eyes and not human vanity, strength, and riches (9:23–24):

> Thus says Yahweh:
> Let not the wise man boast of his wisdom,
> Nor the strong man boast of his strength,
> Nor the rich man boast of his riches!
> But if one must boast, let him boast of this,

That he understands and knows me—
How I, Yahweh, am he who practices kindness,
Justice, and righteousness on the earth;
For in these things I delight, is the oracle of Yahweh.

Again: "I have loved thee with an everlasting love: therefore have I drawn thee, taking pity on thee" (31:3). Like Jesus later, Jeremiah wept over the fate of Jerusalem for rejecting her God (8:18–9:3). St. Paul, perhaps, gave us one of the best clues to understanding Jeremiah's remarkable ability to find God in all things when he explained that everything is a grace because God is love (Rom 8:28–35):

> Now we know that for those who love God all things work together unto good, for those who, according to his purpose, are saints through his call. For those whom he has foreknown he has also predestined to become conformed to the image of his Son, that he should be the firstborn among many brethren. And those whom he has predestined, them he has also called; and those whom he has justified, them he has also glorified. What then shall we say to these things? If God is for us, who is against us? . . . Who shall make accusation against the elect of God? It is God who justifies! . . . Who shall separate us from the love of Christ?

Who, indeed, ever separated Jeremiah from the love of Yahweh? The rhythm of Yahweh's love had become the rhythm of Jeremiah's life. Yahweh was everywhere. Yahweh never ceased revealing Himself to those who loved Him. In every event and being, at each moment, Yahweh communicated His secrets and love.

Through his own conscious effort and the grace of God his contemplative soul alertly grasped and comprehended in daily experience that all reality never ceased to offer a fertile set of images out of which new ideas of Yahweh could come to birth, new reasons for loving Yahweh and marveling at His overwhelming magnificence. Each new insight and judgment offered an occasion for falling in love with God again. Jeremiah was a see-er. He could see God in all things, anticipating St. John's realization that "Eternal life is in knowing thee. . . ." (Jn 17:3).

Jeremiah's Message of Hope

God's messengers to men are usually other men. A man of God is a man with a message from God incarnated in his own existence: "God is love." If he is really a man of God, this message will come through to his contemporaries even though it is never verbally expressed. The man possessed by God possesses the message of God and conveys it to all by his very existence. He *is* God's existing message. To know him is to know, in some way, that God is love, mercy, justice, and forgiveness. This was the primary and fundamental way in which Jeremiah bore Yahweh's message, and it cannot be overlooked.

Jeremiah's preaching was not only a series of rebukes, menaces, and threats of judgment (28:8), but also a message of hope. Even when Yahweh punished His people, His purpose was to bring them to their senses. Jeremiah also bore a message of hope, of Yahweh's loving providence and gracious purpose towards His people. The goodness of Yahweh would not be thwarted by the stubbornness of men. Jeremiah saw Yahweh's loving plan for man's happiness in a further perspective in which Israel would be converted. Once Yahweh had swept the ground clean of false foundations, He would build and plant anew (Jer 24:6; 42:10; 45:4). This was Jeremiah's theme of hope: the message of a new people and a new age when men would be in a position to correspond unreservedly with Yahweh's gifts. Though he did not deny the covenant of Sinai, he looked on it as a preliminary phase or a promise that was only beginning to be fulfilled. Thus Jeremiah, the witness to imminent catastrophes, was the first to announce the new covenant (31:31–34).

The new covenant would rest upon the merciful initiative and authority of Yahweh and would surpass the old economy established on Sinai. Yet it would fulfill the intention of the Sinai covenant by the divine gift which would make possible a personal knowledge of Yahweh's ways and permit man's unreserved service: an inner, unreserved adhesion, and henceforth an ineffable and loving knowledge of Yahweh. It would effect a new community of Yahweh's people: "I will be their God and they shall be my people" (31:33). Thus, even the destruction of Judah offered grounds for hope, for Yahweh was like the potter that shattered the imperfect vessel in order to create another of better clay (19).

Conclusion

Men of God of Jeremiah's stature are as rare today as they were 2,500 years ago, and yet the world needs such men desperately. It was not only in Judah of the seventh century before Christ that human dignity had fallen on all fours and that kings and priests betrayed their calling through neglect or malice or cowardice. Jeremiah might well reproach us today just as he reproached his contemporaries, and for the same reasons. The word of God still falls on deaf ears; and like the words of Jeremiah (6:10) they become an object of scorn to the people. Even "practicing" Christians have that "stubborn and rebellious heart" (5:23) which remains insensitive to racial and social injustice.

Jeremiah's "Temple Sermon" (Chapters 7 and 26) is just as relevant today as then, yet how many "men of God" would have the courage to give it? Who would dare to preach that external cult without an interior spirit is worthless; that mere attendance at Sunday Mass, a Catholic education, membership in Church organizations, the fact of being a cleric and other externals are too often accepted as infallible signs of having found favor with God? Jeremiah would still inveigh against the blind spirit of self-righteousness, the presumptuous belief that men have a claim on God because of their virtues and Church membership. He would still rebuke us for our spirit of self-sufficiency whereby we forget that "life" is not something we control but is a gift received only by those who acknowledge their constant and loving dependence on God.

The message of Jeremiah was the living word of the living God and it continues to have meaning for us.[10] It was a message which Jeremiah lived in his generous acceptance of and courageous fidelity to the ideals of his vocation, in his purifying anguish of spirit, in his meaningful celibacy,[11] and in his painful yet voluntary surrender to the spirit of Yahweh which, even today, speaks to us through this lonely prophet, telling us that "God is love."

Notes

[1] *Hearken unto the Voice,* a splendid novel about Jeremiah by Franz Werfel, tells the prophet's story in a more orderly fashion than we find in the Book of Jeremiah.

[2] A few dates in the life of Jeremiah: birth, c. 645 B.C.; his call, c. 626 B.C.; the Deuteronomic reformation, c. 621 B.C.; the Temple Sermon, c. 608 B.C.; exile and death in Egypt at the age of 60.

[3] John Skinner, *Prophecy and Religion* (4th ed.; Cambridge: Cambridge University, 1936), Chapter 2: "Predestination and Vocation." See also Alexander Jones, *Unless Some Man Show Me* (New York: Sheed and Ward, 1951), pp. 36–37. This author makes several distinctions which help explain the nature of prophecy and of inspiration:

"1. *Scriptural inspiration* is God's movement of the human author's will and practical judgment; this movement is directed to the production of a written work. Thus, for instance, when Isaias uses the terms of Phoenician myth he pronounces no judgment on their truth or falsity. His speculative judgment is not involved. It is his practical judgment that has been at work in choosing this form for his message; it is the practical judgment, therefore, which receives the influx of inspiration. The effect of inspiration in this case is not to produce a true speculative judgment but to ensure a sound practical judgment on the means well suited to secure his end.

"2. *Prophetic inspiration* is God's illumination of the speculative judgment of a writer or speaker. The raw material for the judgment has been gathered, perhaps, by unaided human effort and the judgment itself already made by the unaided human subject but prophetical inspiration confers a new formality upon this judgment. The judgment is, as it were, born again in the human mind by the power of the Spirit. Being God's judgment now, as well as man's, it is not only true but inevitably true. Luke's "fifteenth year of Tiberius Caesar," for example, has more backing than that of historical research; it is not only Luke's judgment but God's.

"3. *Prophetic revelation* is God's communication of a new truth. Normally, of course, this is accompanied by a divine illumination of the speculative judgment enabling the recipient to comprehend that truth (i.e. accompanied by "prophetic inspiration"). But it need not be. Baltasar received the revelation (Dan 5) but he needed Daniel's inspiration to explain it to him.

"Now in the sacred books what we have numbered '1' is always present, usually '2,' sometimes '3' also. When all three are present the sacred writer has received a revelation, understood it and committed it to writing in a suitable form."

[4] Albert Gelin, *Jérémie* (Paris: Cerf, 1951), p. 16.

[5] Skinner, *Prophecy and Religion,* p. 71. Jeremiah, according to Skinner, condemns the unreality of Baal worship: ". . . The Baals are not real deities, but figments of the imagination. Israel has foolishly 'exchanged its glory for that which does not profit' (2:11). And where the object of religion is unreal the subject becomes unreal also: 'They followed after vanity and became vain' (2:5). They neither worshipped a real God, nor worshipped with their real selves. That is the most distinctive point in Jeremiah's analysis of religious experience. The principle that the worshipper is assimilated to that which he worships had been enunciated by Hosea in a more obvious fashion when he wrote 'They became an abomination, like that which they loved' (Hos 9:10)."

[6] H. Wheeler Robinson remarks on Jeremiah's sympathy for others in his book *The Cross in the Old Testament* (Philadelphia: Westminster, 1955), p. 162: ". . . the prophet's desire to intercede with Yahweh for His people was sternly checked by the divine command: 'As for thee, pray not for this people, nor lift up for them a ringing cry and prayer;

and do not make intercession with me, for I hear thee not' (7:16), a warning repeated more than once (11:14; 14:11). . . . It was not that the element in his nature which made him struggle against his office was in itself wrong; on the contrary, it was natural that with such a temperament he should shrink from the task, and right that he should feel the sorrow of a great sympathy with those whose coming suffering he must proclaim. But for him there was a higher duty—obedience, and an obedience which of necessity was crowned with thorns."

7 Bernhard W. Anderson, *Understanding the Old Testament* (Englewood Cliffs: Prentice-Hall, 1958), pp. 339–40.

8 L. Legrand, "The Prophetical Meaning of Celibacy," *Review for Religious,* v. 20 (1961), pp. 331–34.

9 I believe that Jeremiah possessed that freshness of vision which, according to Thornton Wilder's description, saw that: "Every action which has ever taken place—every thought, every emotion—has taken place only once, at one moment in time and place. 'I love you,' 'I rejoice,' 'I suffer,' have been said and felt many billions of times and never twice the same. Every person who has ever lived has lived an unbroken succession of unique occasions." From his preface to *Three Plays* (New York: Bantam, 1958), pp. ix–x.

10 Bruce Vawter, C.M., *The Conscience of Israel* (New York: Sheed and Ward, 1961). See especially "Conclusion: The Endurance of Prophecy."

11 L. Legrand, "Prophetical Meaning," p. 338. Legrand asserts that Paul understood virginity exactly as Jeremiah. Paul did not know the date of the end, but he knew that the world had condemned itself by condemning Christ.

6
The Humanity of Christ in St. Mark

A correct idea of the personality of Jesus is supremely important for the attainment of Christian perfection. This knowledge enlightens our understanding of the role of the emotions in the approach to God. Pope John XXIII told seminarians that they must have the natural virtues to an outstanding degree, "for you cannot find a Christian or a priest worthy of his calling who does not possess the natural virtues."[1] Now, these natural virtues, wrote St. Thomas, will be accompanied by a certain degree of emotion: "What is good is determined for every being according to the condition of its nature. Consequently good human action [*virtus*] is accompanied by emotion and the service of the body" (1-2, q. 59, a.5 and 3).[2]

In Jesus, St. Mark found humanity in its absolute perfection. St. Mark's Gospel offers a rich harvest of rewarding insights into the emotions of Jesus. More vividly than any other evangelist, St. Mark depicts the emotions of Christ in all their variety and intensity. He shows us that Jesus can become sharp in His rebukes, angry, sad, sensitive to His hearers' reactions, and surprised at the turn of events.

Jesus, as viewed by St. Mark, never leaves His audience in doubt as to how He feels about things: He is never inhibited or awkward in the presence of others but expresses Himself freely and naturally. He even makes a violent scene. He drives buyers and sellers from the temple and upsets the money-changers' tables and the pigeon-dealers' chairs. He forbids these profiteers to carry anything through the temple and excoriates them for turning a house of prayer into a robbers' den.

In the very first chapter of this Gospel, we see Jesus reprehending an unclean spirit and ordering it to be silent. Jesus is indignant (1:25). Shortly afterwards, He has healed a leper and is "moved with pity" (1:41). He manifests His typically intense compassion for the outcast, the sufferer, who, by his sin or by his suffering, had put himself outside respectable Jewish society. Then, His attitude suddenly changes when He brusquely sends the leper away and warns him to say nothing to anyone (1:44).

With a knowledge arrived at by the close attention He pays to particular persons, Jesus is able to perceive the thoughts of His opponents and gauge His audience (2:8). With one sweeping glance of His anger, He silences the Pharisees and is "hurt by their obstinacy" (3:5). The swift, searching glance of Jesus upon His friends and His enemies is a human characteristic to which St. Mark frequently alludes. His anger is not that of personal animosity, but rather an anger which is justly provoked by the spectacle of men whose narrow legalistic literalism is matched only by their blindness to moral values and insensibility to the spirit of God.

On the Sea of Galilee, Jesus is awakened by a storm and scolds the wind just as He rebuked the demons (4:39): "Hush! Silence!" He recognizes nature as a vehicle of divine power. The effect is

instantaneous. He turns to reproach His disciples for their cowardice and lack of trust in the power of God. He frequently rebukes them for their lack of faith and understanding (7:18; 8:17;
21:32 ff.; 9:19). This display of emotion has a good effect: something akin to faith is born of their great fear. They immediately
see that His word is effective and that they are faced with a reality
of another order.

Jesus becomes immediately conscious of His healing power at
work, when the hemorrhaging woman touches Him (5:30); and
His question, "Who touched my garments?" reveals His human
knowledge, since an answer is sought. The unbelief of His fellow
Nazarenes surprises Him (6:7) who appears to have thought of
faith as a natural attitude.

Just before feeding the five thousand, His heart is "moved to
pity" when He sees a crowd reminding Him of "shepherdless
sheep" (6:34).[3] When the hostile Pharisees demand a sign from
Him, He reacts in a most human way: "with a sigh from the
depths of his heart" (8:12). Jesus excoriates Peter for judging by
human and not divine standards (8:33).

Jesus "looked with love" upon the wealthy young man who had
kept the commandments faithfully from his youth (10:21). The
man's claim of fidelity is genuine and Jesus loves him for it. Some
exegetes suggest the translation "caressed him"; but despite the
possibility of this meaning, most of the authorities agree that
admiring affection is more precise. Jesus felt instinctively attracted
to this good man and did not conceal His feelings of love and
friendliness. It is a highly distinctive phrase recalling "the disciple
whom Jesus loved." In both cases, Jesus shows no reluctance to
display an overt affection for those whom He loves.

Jesus loves some men more than others. At His transfiguration
He has three witnesses, the same who accompanied Him when He
raised up the daughter of Jairus (5:37), the same, also, who were
to be the privileged witnesses of His agony (14:33).

His human reactions and emotions clearly underscore His ideals and attitudes, revealing that He is anything but a detached spectator from another world. He is so human, so much a part of His people and His times, that no contemporary calls His humanity into question. On the other hand, had He suppressed His emotions and feelings, His contemporaries might well have suspected His humanity and found it easier to accept His divinity.[4]

The Jesus of St. Mark is neither shy nor aloof. He moves with great ease among crowds of people He has never seen before (2:15), and He speaks to them with facility, friendliness, and authority (10:17–22). Free of that ghetto mentality which avoids every form of dialogue with those holding diverse and conflicting views, He converses openly with non-believers and Gentiles (who are generally referred to as "sinners" in the English translations of the Gospels). He argues with the Pharisees about the Sabbath observance (2:23–28); He asks his adversaries whether they prefer his curing the man with the withered hand (3:1–6) or the evil of omitting it; when certain hostile men of learning come from Jerusalem and attribute His powers to Beelzebub (3:22), He explains to them the untenability of their position.

In his dialogue with both friends and foes, He understands the demands of a rational and flexible consistency of thought, purpose, action, and evaluation. He knows where to insist stubbornly: "If thy hand is an occasion of sin to thee, cut it off!" (9:42). On the other hand, He also knows when to cease and desist: "But Jesus made no further answer, so that Pilate wondered" (15:5).[5]

Sensitive to and keenly interested in other people, Jesus delays his departure from Jericho (10:46–52) to attend to a blind beggar who calls him by name. This incident typifies the close attention He pays to others, as well as his sympathy, concern, and apparent eagerness to help those who call upon Him. No evangelist has ever recorded his final refusal to help anyone.

Intensely alive and responsive,[6] He is always reacting to the

Spirit, individuals, crowds, foreigners, non-believers, sinners, saints, authorities (priestly and Roman), friends, enemies, young and old, suffering and dying, injustice, persecution, betrayal, "wasteful extravagance," poverty, intellectuals, and common folk. Responding in a great variety of ways, He is never detached from or disinterested in men, their problems and aspirations.

He so loved little children that He promises himself as a reward to those who would welcome a child for his sake (9:35–36). It is also remarkable that in the two episodes St. Mark recounts about children, Jesus is described as putting his arms around them. Yet this same Jesus, magnificently displaying strong emotion in the service of Divine Wisdom, does not hesitate to make a public "scene" in driving money-changers from the temple (11:15–19). Disrespectful behavior in a sacred place provokes a violent emotional reaction which brilliantly and dramatically underscores thoughts and judgment on this subject.

Finally, in the Garden of Gethsemani (14:33–34), Jesus begins to feel dread at the thought of his passion: "My soul is sad even unto death." In this gigantic conflict where the master of life and the emperor of death meet each other, the flesh cannot remain serene and without emotion when the spirit of man keeps watch, attacks, and defends itself. In Jesus, as later in his disciples, the whole being of man is mobilized. But victory soon comes with the Resurrection.

Thus the Gospel of St. Mark provides us with ample evidence of the role Jesus thought the emotions should have in the approach to God. His emotions were not only an intregal part of his perfect human nature, but they also helped his contemporaries to see clearly what He thought and loved. They were visible indications, to all who believed in Him, of a divine mind and a divine will expressing itself in human terms.

The emotions of Jesus, so vividly displayed on frequent occasions, require no apology. Consequently, the mistaken notion that the emotions should be all but extinguished in those striving for Christian perfection calls for an ascetical reorientation and a careful rereading of the Gospels. The example of Christ; the great commandment to love God with our whole heart, mind, and soul; the injunction of St. Paul to rejoice with those who rejoice and to weep with those who weep, clearly demonstrate the importance of the emotions in the approach to God. Lethargic, aloof, irritable, and unkind religious may be grievously remiss in failing to *show* that "God is love."[7] This obligation is especially serious in a society where so many feel rejected and where so many have made the inevitable transfer from feeling rejected by society to feeling rejected by God, from seeing the angry face of society to seeing the angry face of God. It is important that our horror for sin should not cloud our love for the sinner, who may already feel overwhelmed by the "wrath" of God. If the grace of God is ever to come to these broken, tormented souls, the chances are that it will come through the instrumentality of an understanding priest or religious. If these unfortunates have never seen anything but the angry face of God, it may be only through us that they will ever see the loving face of God.

Notes

[1] It should not be forgotten that the natural virtues include the intellectual virtues. Pope John XXIII in his address to Italian seminarians (November 22, 1959) takes this aspect into account when he urges them to cultivate a taste for studies along with their practice of charity and affability.

[2] St. Thomas' teaching on the role of the emotions in our lives can be summarized by the following texts:

a) Moral virtue does not exclude the emotions (1–2, q.59, a.2, *sed contra*).

b) Since human nature is made up of body and soul, of an intellectual and a sensitive part, human good demands that man surrender himself in his totality to virtue; that is to say, both in his intellectual and sensitive (emotional) part, and with his body. Hence, for human virtue it is necessary that the desire for just vengeance should reside not only in the rational part of the soul but also in the sensitive part and in the body, and that the body should be moved to serve virtue (*De Malo,* q.12, a.1).

c) The emotions are in themselves neither good nor bad, since in man good and evil are determined according to reason. Hence the emotions, considered in themselves, can be good as well as evil, according as they can correspond with reason or be contrary to it (1–2, q.59, a.1).

d) It is true that to act from emotion lessens both praise and blame, but to act with emotion can increase both (*De Veritate,* q.26, a.7, ad 1).

e) He who is angry or afraid is not praised or blamed, but only he who, while in this state, behaves either properly or improperly (2–2, q.125, a.1, ad 1).

f) There are four basic emotions of the soul—sadness, joy, hope, and fear (*De Veritate,* q.26, a.5).

g) Of all the emotions, sadness causes the most injury to the soul (1–2, q.37, a.4).

h) Every virtue by which an emotion is ordered also gives order to the body (*De Virtutibus in Communi,* q.12, ad 2).

[3] Many persons in the pagan, non-Jewish world believed that God had a mind; however, it was only with the Incarnation and Christianity that they discovered God had a heart and that "God is love." There is a danger of taking for granted the humanity of Christ through which for the first time in history man could visibly see God's love for him. This realization prompted John to write "God has *shown* his love towards us." It is also the basis for the Sacred Heart devotion.

[4] Karl Stern, *The Third Revolution* (New York: Harcourt, Brace, 1954), p. 282: "Vigilance in the face of evil may give rise to preoccupation with evil. And, as the Fathers of the Church taught, if we are unduly preoccupied by evil, we become evil. There is danger in giving more thought to the things we are *against* than the things we are *for*. It is easier to have distrust than to have faith. The story of the early Church shows clearly that it is the *positive* in faith which conquers the world."

[5] A. M. Henry, O.P., *The Holy Spirit* (London: Burns and Oates, 1960), p. 51. The following passage of Father Henry helps to round out this study with examples from the other Gospels: "This force of the Breath in and through which he acts does not leave Jesus humanly indifferent. On many occasions the Gospel draws our attention to the effects of the Holy Breath in his humanity. When the disciples return rejoicing from their apostolic errand, Jesus 'was filled with gladness by the Spirit' (Lk 10:21). When Mary, the sister of Lazarus, throws herself at the feet

of Jesus and weeps over the death of her brother, Jesus 'sighed deeply' (Jn 11:33)." In this same episode we read "And Jesus wept" (Jn 11:35).

6 Jesus was never bored. The state of being bored is subjective. Life is not boring, *you* are bored. But Jesus is Life itself. No man has ever been more alive: He loves, thinks, and prays as a man but with the facility and the intensity of a God-man. The great source of boredom is the loss of the sense of wonder and awe which has proceeded from the partial loss of the Christian image of man. Wonder at his own marvelous origin and nature and the worship of the Creator which this wonder impels are what nourish the psyche of man. The whole man is a wondering and worshipping man, grateful to his Creator for the existence and promise that he has received from Him. When men have lost their sense of mystery, when awe and wonder depart from their awareness, despair may ensue or the quest for more violent and bizarre emotional outlets begins. The loss of wonder at the mysterious presence of God and at existence itself is a condition leading to the death of the soul. There is no more withering state than that which takes all things for granted, whether with respect to human beings or the rest of the natural and supernatural order. The blasé attitude means spiritual, emotional, intellectual, and creative death. Jesus, however, apprehended the deepest aspects of reality in the ordinary things of everyday life.

7 Gabriel Marcel, *The Philosophy of Existence* (New York: Philosophical Library, 1949), p. 27. The kindness and humanity of the beautiful soul can provide the apt conditions for an unbeliever's encounter with God, overturning one's habitually naturalistic perspectives. "In this connection, the study of sanctity with all its *concrete* [italics mine] attributes seems to me to offer an immense speculative value; indeed, I am not far from saying that it is the true introduction to ontology."

7

The Parable of the Banquet

It is not by accident that St. Luke should refer to the "poor, the cripples, the blind and the lame" as those invited to the great banquet (14:21). He had just cited this same fourfold category as those whom Jesus had advised His Pharisee host and dinner companions to invite to their tables whenever they would give a dinner party (14:13): "But when you give a party, ask the poor, the cripples, the lame and the blind." The advice which Jesus gives at a banquet both helps to explain and is explained by the parable of the great banquet which immediately follows. Both represent complementary aspects of the same Christian revelation.

Immediate Context

An appreciation of what Luke is presenting in 14:12–24 presumes an understanding of the entire context in which the passage is found. It is part of a larger unity, embracing the entire first part of the chapter, 14:1–24. Moreover, the entire passage is based on the banquet theme. This is a traditional biblical symbol expressing the Messiah's fulfillment of all Old Testament aspirations in the achievement of perfect happiness with God at the end of time. The banquet is an essentially eschatological symbol expressing the ideal of happiness and loving union among all men and between man and God. The literary and didactic unity of 14:1–24 manifests the genius of St. Luke, who has so intelligently organized historical data into a meaningful presentation of Jesus, in the context of actual banquet situations, as the Messiah who fulfills the messianic banquet prophecies of *Isaiah*.

We can divide the passage into three principal sections:

I. Jesus is the Messiah (14:1–6). We have here the story of a miracle, the curing of the man with dropsy on the Sabbath; it is an adequate sign for men of faith that Jesus is the Lord of the Sabbath, the Messiah. The miracle occurs at a banquet.

II. The Messiah teaches men how to live among themselves in the present life if they wish to attain future happiness (14:7–14). This section is subdivided into two parts, the first of which treats of humble self-acceptance without self-seeking (vv. 7–11), and the second of which treats of the loving acceptance of all men without self-seeking (vv, 12–14).

III. The Messiah teaches man the proper attitude towards himself if he wishes to attain future happiness (14:15–24). No human good should assume such importance in men's lives that the Messiah's loving invitation is rejected. Self-seeking, self-satisfaction, self-righteousness do not attain eternal happiness. This is attained only on the Messiah's terms. Self-seeking is presented as the greatest obstacle to happiness.

The transition from the present to the future end-time is made with the promise of happiness at the resurrection of the just (14:14) to all those whose charity is universal. This transitional note is re-emphasized in the dinner guest's remark: "Happy the man who shall sit at the banquet in the kingdom of God!" (14:15). This in turn occasions Jesus' parable of the great banquet. In it He clarifies the remark, or better, brings out all that is meant by it. Eternal happiness does not come automatically by the fact that a man is a son of Abraham. Nor does salvation come to the self-righteous who have worked out their salvation on their own terms. It is Jesus who declares the terms of eternal happiness, because He is the Messiah through whom it is achieved.

The story of the great banquet is a parable. Unlike the allegory, the parable belongs to a literary genre in which only one point or idea is intended. Already the immediate literary context of the banquet parable is an argument that the one point or idea of it is universal charity, God's universal salvific will. The parable's point, then, would be that no one is excluded from the kingdom and loving friendship of God except by his own choice. This can be stated positively by saying that God invites all men through Jesus to enter into the community of His friends. Jesus had already stated that the Christian should invite all men to his dinner (14:12-14). This parable complements that statement by giving it its proper motivation: the genuine Christian invites (loves) everyone because God invites (loves) everyone. No one is excluded in either case except by his own free choice.

The verbal unity of repeated, interlocking words is another literary device used by Luke to indicate clearly the doctrinal unity between the two. The key verb whereby Luke interlocks the pericope with the parable is "invite." In each case those who are invited are the same: "the poor, the cripples, the blind and the lame" (14:13 and 14:21). Finally, in both cases the word "happy" is used, once by Jesus (14:14) and once by the dinner guest (14:15); in each case its significance is eschatological.

Diptych Development

Parallelism by means of comparison or contrast is another literary device which Luke employs and which manifests his didactic method.

In his balanced literary structure the evangelist presents one truth which complements and explains another; he thereby creates a didactic unity. This has been called Luke's "diptych development." It is illustrated by the parallelism in the infancy narratives of John the Baptist and of Jesus. The angel Gabriel appears to both Zachary and Mary to announce an extraordinary act of God. They both celebrate the announcement with a hymn of praise, the *Benedictus* and the *Magnificat*. In the case of each child, Luke relates the circumcision, hidden life, growth and development before God and man, as well as prophecies of future greatness.

Another illustration of Luke's "diptych development" is had in the parable of the Good Samaritan and in the story of Martha and Mary which immediately follows. The two form a diptych and complement each other. The Good Samaritan story (10:30–37) teaches that man's fundamental relationship with his fellow man should be one of *giving*. This is counterbalanced by the Martha and Mary episode (10:38–42), which suggests that man's fundamental relationship to God is one of *receiving*. Mary's receptivity in listening is preferred to Martha's wish to do something for Christ. A loving receptivity and response in faith mark the human relationship to God, whereas, in relation to other men, the primacy is given to an active generosity. Men can only give to others what they have received from God.

Luke employs the same "diptych development" when he balances the passage dealing with Jesus' advice to the dinner guests (14:12–14) with the parable of the great banquet (14:15–24). In the former, Christians are told that they should do something for others who cannot repay them: "When you give a banquet, *invite* the poor. . . ." Among men, giving is better than receiving. On the other hand, this advice is counterbalanced by the banquet parable, which presents the responsiveness of those who accept God's invitation as the preferable attitude in man's relationship to God. Thus universal charity is seen from two points of view: it is seen as the way in which God acts when He invites *all* men through Jesus to become His friends in the banquet community; it is seen as the way in which the sons of God act when they invite the poor and others living on the periphery of society to their banquets. The authenticity of the sons is manifested when they act as their Father acts in the spirit of universal charity.

The Lucan balance is also maintained by the reference to the "poor, the cripples, the blind and the lame" who are the recipients, in the one case, of a universal human charity, and in the other case, of a universal divine charity. In both cases, again, there are those who have no means of repaying their benefactors; they are open to and in need of the overtures made to them by charitable persons.

The same balance is maintained, though more subtly, in the matter of attaining the happiness. In both an eschatological note is present. In the first case it is struck by the reference to the reward to be given "at the resurrection of the just" (14:14). In the second case, that of the parable, it is struck by the very theme of the banquet, which is eschatological in its development. We might say that St. Luke has emphasized this by implying that those who accepted the spirit of Jesus' charity and did invite the poor to their banquet will, "at the resurrection of the just," become the poor who are invited and actually participate in the great eschatological banquet. The roles are then reversed: the banquet-giver becomes the banquet-guest, and the happiness promised becomes the happiness fulfilled "at the resurrection of the just."

While this eschatological note does seem to be emphasized by the evangelist, we would not exclude all reference to the present time of the Church. Even now the banquet-giver is the banquet-guest. Inasmuch as he has accepted Jesus' invitation and lives according to His spirit of universal charity, he is an authentic member of the banquet community, the Church. The promise of happiness, therefore, is actually in the process of fulfillment.

Banquet Theology

The consideration of the general context of Lucan doctrine is also necessary for an understanding of a passage such as ours. A banquet theology, a poverty theology and a happiness theology are all part of this doctrinal context. And all of these have their roots in the eschatological prophecies of *Isaiah*. We shall first consider the banquet theology.

Luke, like the other synoptic writers, is concerned to exhibit the historical events of Jesus' life as fulfilling the eschatological figures of the Old Testament. His banquet theology has its roots deep in the old Testament messianic tradition (Is 25:6f.; 55:1f.; 65:11f.; Deut 12:4), according to which perfect happiness is established by the Messiah among the poor and afflicted and between them and God. He is to inaugurate the community of the blessed. Lucan banquet situations are to be understood against this Old Testament background. The banquet is an eschatological messianic-community concept expressing the harmonious new order established by the Messiah among men and between them and God.

Accordingly, in *Luke* the meals or banquets at which Jesus is present represent the fulfillment of that which was prefigured in the Old Testament banquet prophecies. The fact of His presence is interpreted by Luke as an expression of the rejoicing foretold in the prophetic books. The days of John, which were the period of waiting, are superseded by the days of Jesus, which are the period of presence and fulfillment: "When John came, he would neither eat nor drink, and you say 'He is possessed.' When the Son of Man came, he ate and drank with you, and of him you say, 'Here is a glutton; he loves wine; he is a friend of publicans and sinners'" (7:33–34).

This quotation reveals a second characteristic of the Lucan banquet theology. The banquets at which Jesus was present attracted attention. The Pharisees disapproved of them because Jesus ate with publicans and sinners. In the passage that follows, Luke describes the banquet at the home of Simon the Pharisee, where Jesus allowed the sinful woman to touch Him. By accepting this intimacy of a common life with sinners, Jesus shows that He has come to break down the barrier that separates sinful men from God. For Luke this is a properly religious sign revealing the essence of the Messiah's mission.

Luke's banquet theology, therefore, expresses the universal charity of Jesus as opposed to Pharisaic exclusivism: "When they found all the publicans and sinners coming to hear him, the Pharisees and Scribes were indignant: 'Here is a man that welcomes sinners and eats with them'" (15:1–2). Luke consistently attacks the self-righteousness and exclusivism of the Pharisees, who seem more eager to see men excluded from the kingdom of God than admitted to it. Jesus' story of the Pharisee and the publican, Luke relates (18:9f.), is a rebuke to "some who had confidence in themselves, thinking they had won acceptance with God" and who despised "the rest of men, who steal and cheat and commit adultery."

Jesus, on the other hand, is the Messiah who re-establishes the community of friendship between God and man. Giving Himself to those who will accept Him, to "the poor, the cripples, the blind, the lame," He forgives their sins, reuniting fallen man with God. These are the same ones who, in the prophecies of *Isaiah,* accept the Messiah.

Theology of Poverty

In Luke's theology of poverty the Messiah is born, lives and dies poor. ". . . the Son of Man has nowhere to lay his head" (9:58). Jesus' association with the poor is, for Luke, a sign that He is the fulfillment of the messianic prophecies: "The spirit of the Lord . . . has sent me to announce good news to the poor" (Is 61:1ff.).

When the legation from John the Baptist asks Jesus whether He is the Messiah, Jesus calls their attention to the messianic sign: "Go and tell John what you have seen and heard; how the *blind* recover their sight, the *lame* walk, the lepers are clean, the deaf hear, the dead are raised to life, the *poor* are hearing the good news. And happy is the man who does not find me a stumbling-block" (7:22–23). Jesus asserts that He is the Messiah when He says that He does all the prophets said the Messiah would do. This explains why Luke so frequently calls his readers' attention to Jesus' association with these people; it is a basis for their confession of faith in Jesus as the true Messiah.

Are the "poor" to whom Luke refers the economically poor? The general lines of Luke's doctrinal context indicate the answer. The poor are basically those who are receptive, who open themselves to the divine charity. The tax-gatherers, the Gentiles and the sinners like Mary Magdalen, who could purchase a costly ointment for Jesus, were not all economically poor. And yet they were poor in the sense that they recognized their poverty before God; they were *receptive* of His Messiah, of His salvation, of the forgiveness of their sins. And for all these divine benefits repayment was impossible.

In another respect, however, economic poverty was included in a special way. Divisions within Jewish society at the time of Jesus were based more on religious than on economic grounds, more on knowledge and exact observance of the Law than on wealth and poverty. The Scribes and Pharisees were highly respected because they were literate. And the special privileges and particular marks of respect which they enjoyed they owed more to their religious instruction than to their wealth. All of this is true. It is likewise true that the economically poor were not despised because of their poverty. Yet it happened that, precisely because of their poverty, they lacked that instruction in the Law and that ability to observe it carefully that were necessary for being highly regarded. Long work-hours precluded exact observance as well as the time for theological speculation. So it happened that the poor, the economically destitute, were the despised ones, the "sinners."

In conclusion, then, we can say that, in Luke's theology, the poor were all those whom the religious leaders of Israel at the time of Christ considered, for one reason or another, as hopelessly excluded from the kingdom of God. They were the marginal men living on the fringes of Jewish society precisely because they deviated from the religious ideals of the Pharisees. Luke shows that social and economic poverty actually fostered the receptivity requisite for the acceptance of the Messiah.

Universal Charity

The great banquet parable teaches, as opposed to the Pharisees' exclusiveness, God's universal love and invitation. God rejects no one. The pericope preceding the parable (14:12–14) teaches the same attitude of universal charity in such a way that the authenticity of charity is gauged by one's attitude towards the poor, the contemned people on the fringes of society who cannot repay us.

The exclusiveness of the Pharisees is wrong because it is diametrically opposed to the spirit of God and that of His Messiah, who expresses God's universal charity in the banquet parable and in His own life. Men receive this spirit from God through the Messiah, but express it towards their neighbor primarily by giving. Once a man has accepted God's invitation through Jesus, he is able to do what God does. His love of the poor, therefore, is a criterion of his communion with God, of his present membership in the eschatological banquet community. Thus, those who love the poor, invite them to their tables, share their lives and goods with them (14:12–14), have already become the blessed "poor" of the parable.

Luke sees the revelation of universal charity in the light of the traditional Old Testament principle that if God acts in a certain way, His sons will, by the fact of their sonship, act accordingly. This is the Lucan doctrinal context necessary for seeing the unity between Jesus' advice in the pericope (14:12–14) and the main point of the parable that follows. Luke had enunciated this principle before: ". . . love your enemies, do good to them, lend to them without any hope of a reward; then your reward will be a rich one, and you will be *sons of the Most High,* because he is generous to the thankless and the unjust. Be merciful as your Father is merciful" (6:35–36). Again: "Forgive us our sins; we *too* forgive all those who trespass against us" (11:24).

Summary

There is a very close interconnection among the Lucan themes of happiness, poverty and banquets. The word for "happiness" is used fifteen times by the evangelist. Always it refers to those who are receptive to the word of God, the poor, the afflicted and the despised; these are they who find happiness. Happiness comes to the man who has accepted community with God and his neighbor. "Happy are you poor . . . you hungry . . . you who weep now. . . ." (6:21–22). "Happy are those who hear the word of God and keep it" (11:28). "Happy are those servants whom the master finds alert when he comes . . . he will seat them at table" (12:37). "When you give a banquet . . . invite the poor . . . and you will find happiness" (14:13). In this final statement all three themes find expression in one thought.

Happiness, banquet and poverty theologies, therefore, overlap. And all are subdivisions of Luke's theology of salvation through the community. Jesus, the Messiah, re-establishes the community of friendship between God and man. No one is excluded. Jesus' cure of the man at the banquet of the leading Pharisee is a messianic sign of the Holy One sent to the "poor, the cripples, the blind and the lame." The physical cure enabled man to re-enter human community. For Luke this symbolized the re-entrance into community with God, and this is the scope of the Messiah's mission of reuniting men divided among themselves and separated from God by sin. Jesus the Messiah belongs to the community of the poor, because they alone receive Him and because He is sent to them (4:18, 7:22). To enter into communion with the Messiah is to enter into His community of the poor and thus find the happiness promised at the resurrection.

The banquet is now prepared. Jesus the Messiah is present among the dinner guests. Only those who have nothing to impede their acceptance of His invitation have responded. These are the poor, those who are receptive to the "giving" of God. The attitude of giving that man is required to have towards his fellow man is counterbalanced by the attitude of receiving that he must have towards God. The banquet community, therefore, is made up of such "poor." They share now, and will share perfectly "at the resurrection of the just," the messianic happiness of those who sit at the table with Jesus the Messiah. "I have longed to share this paschal meal with you . . . I shall not eat it again till it finds its fulfillment in the kingdom of God. . . . I shall not drink of the fruit of the vine again till the kingdom of God has come" (22:15–16).

8
Leading Ideas
in St. John's Gospel

Clement of Alexandria called the fourth Gospel a "spiritual Gospel." It is evidently not a simple account of our Lord's miracles and popular teaching, but a deeply meditated representation of his person and doctrine by a contemplative inspired by the Holy Spirit.

In the second part of his profound work, *The Interpretation of the Fourth Gospel,* C. H. Dodd presents a study of what he calls the leading ideas of the Gospel. It is our purpose here to take these headings as proposed by Dodd and comment briefly on them; it will be obvious that there is no attempt here at an exhaustive treatment. It is hoped, however, that the remarks will be suggestive of the deep insights provided by this Gospel and a spur to further study.

Symbolism

The explicit use of such symbols as the true vine, the good shepherd, living water, and bread of life characterizes St. John's

89

Gospel. The Synoptic parables, on the other hand, offer a real life situation which the hearers will recognize and judge. There is no need, therefore, for an elaborate interpretation of the details; these have, for the most part, no bearing on the single point intended by the parable.

The story of the Good Shepherd illustrates the difference between the Johannine allegory (10:1–18) and the Synoptic parables in *Matthew* (18:12–14) and *Luke* (15:4–7). In the latter accounts the details clearly have no independent significance; they are merely part of a narrative which aims at evoking the judgment that a fit shepherd must have a specific attitude. Jesus has this attitude in his concern for the "lost sheep of the house of Israel."

When John tells the same story, Jesus becomes the real subject of all the statements made. Here the details have meaning. The pastoral imagery is a series of symbols for the diverse aspects of Christ's work. The shepherd is Jesus himself who enters by the door, knows his sheep, leads them to pasture, promotes their well-being, and risks his life to save them from danger. A Jewish audience would be familiar with the Old Testament symbolism: the people of God are the flock of Yahweh, and Yahweh himself or his representatives are the shepherds; the evil rulers of Israel are unworthy shepherds.

Again, in the allegory of the vine (15:1–8), the metaphorical use of language is clear: Christ is the vine, his Father the vine-tender, his disciples the branches. This same symbolism had appeared in *Isaiah* (5:1–7), where the vine, or vineyard, symbolized the people of God, planted or constituted as a nation by Yahweh. In *Jeremiah* (2:21), Yahweh complains that although he had planted a vine of high quality, it has degenerated.

The images of bread and water were also symbols for religious conceptions. Furthermore, there exists an intrinsic unity of symbol and thing symbolized: the healing of the blind by Christ *is* the cleansing of the soul from error. Christ's act is a significant act which corresponds with something divinely ordained that takes place in the real world.

These acts of Christ are called "signs" by John, and a sign, in Johannine theology, is already the first manifestation of the reality signified. The feeding of the multitude, for example, is a sign of the life that Christ will give to man in all fullness through his death and resurrection; it anticipates that life in an initial manner. The events of the fourth Gospel, therefore, are significant events inasmuch as they point forward to and anticipate the great reality of God's climactic intervention. Phenomena image the eternal in a world where the Word is made flesh.

Eternal Life

The term "life" occurs fifty-five times in John's Gospel in either noun or verb form. "Life" is a dominant theme, and expresses the purpose of the book: "that believing you may have life in his name" (20:31). For this reason Christ became man: "I came that they may have life, and have it more abundantly" (10:10).

Before the raising of Lazarus, Jesus states: "He who believes in me will never die," implying a further notion: the believer is already living in a sense which excludes the possibility of ceasing to live. In this way, the resurrection of which Jesus has spoken may take place before bodily death, with the result that the believer possesses eternal life here and now. John, therefore, envisions a realized eschatology, a climactic intervention of God that is already realized in this life. In a real sense the reality of divine life is already possessed by man here below.

Life, which is perfect and absolute, timeless in quality and therefore exempt from death, consists in the knowledge of God: "Now this is everlasting life, that they may know thee, the only true God" (17:3). John regards this life as possible for men here and now, but to be realized in its perfection beyond the grave.

Knowledge of God

The Greeks considered knowing as analogous to seeing, that is, contemplating an object from a distance and attempting to grasp or master its reality. The thing in itself, the permanent essence to be grasped, was conceived as something static. For the Hebrews, on the other hand, knowing involved an experiencing of the object on the part of the knower. To know something was to be aware of it as immediately affecting oneself. The Hebrew knew things in their activity and in their effects rather than in themselves.

The knowledge of God for the Greeks meant the contemplation of ultimate reality in its changeless essence, the most highly abstract form of contemplation. For the Hebrews, to know God was to acknowledge him in his works and to respond to his claims, to experience God's dealings with men in time, and to hear and obey his commands.

In the fourth Gospel there is an interweaving of both conceptions. When John says that the world does not "know" God (17:25; 1:10), he does not refer to the God who is essentially unknowable; for it is implied that God is in the world to be known through the presence of the Logos. But the world has not accepted the offer of knowledge of God. As St. Paul states, the will and not only the intelligence is at fault in the failure to *choose* to know God: ". . . and they refused to recognize God any longer" (Rom 1:28). The willing acknowledgement of God is Hebraic.

For John the knowledge of God is the knowledge of Jesus, who as the Logos or Son is the divine object of man's knowledge, and simultaneously the subject of God's knowledge of man; but Jesus, as man, is also both the object of God's knowledge of man and the subject of man's knowledge of God. Only between the Father and the Son is there full mutual knowledge (10:14–15). In his relation to the Father, as knower and known, Jesus is the eternal mediating Logos who alone can reconstitute that divine-human relationship for men by himself standing in the place of God, as knower and known.

The Greek identification of knowing with seeing is observed in passages where the knowledge of God is associated with vision of God: "If you had known me, you would also have known my Father. And henceforth you do know him, and you have seen him" (14:7). Jewish piety, on the other hand, lays little stress on the vision of God as a form of religious experience; this was a blessing reserved for the "age to come." John can assert that men know and see God without contradicting the fundamental assumptions of Judaism because the "age to come" has come and eternal life is here. It is true that John also says, "No one at any time has seen God" (1:18). This is because Jesus alone has the direct vision of the Father (6:46) which the Greeks desired and which the Jewish thinkers reserved for the "age to come." This knowledge which is vision he mediates to men in the sense that "he who sees me sees also the Father" (14:9); "he who sees me sees him who sent me" (12:45).

When John states that "we saw his glory" (1:14), the meaning is that those who, whether in actual physical presence or in retrospect through the witness of the Church, contemplate the historic life of Jesus and recognize the divine quality of it—his "glory"—have attained a knowledge of him which is the real "vision of God." John's concept of the knowledge of God is without parallel: it consists in vision, not mediated in abstractions, but embodied in a living person.

Truth

Truth is the object of that knowledge which "will make you free" (8:32). Christ promises his disciples liberty through knowledge of divine reality. This knowledge liberates men from subjection to the world, the flesh and the devil. Eternal reality as revealed to men through Christ emancipates man from sin: ". . . everyone who commits sin is a slave of sin" (8:34). Christ declares *the* truth, the revelation of eternal reality which stands above the world of transient phenomena; the devil, on the other hand, utters *the* lie, the final denial of divine reality. There is nothing in the devil which corresponds with the eternal reality.

Jesus is the manifestation, the incarnation, of ultimate reality. He is the truth (14:10) and the revealer of the truth. Ultimate reality has become identified with a concrete person known to history. Through Jesus men know the truth, not only by hearing his words, but also by being united with him who is the Truth. True knowledge of God is impossible without a personal union with Christ, through whose mediation men possess truth, knowledge and life.

Faith

Faith, in John's Gospel, is a form of vision. Opposed to faith is that purely physical vision whereby Jesus' contemporaries saw him without any saving effects. But simple vision with faith leads to a deeper vision. Although no one has a direct vision of God, the man of faith has eternal life. He has the equivalent of the life-giving vision, or knowledge of God. Jesus told Martha, "If you have faith, you will see the glory of God" (11:40). With faith men apprehend and acknowledge Christ's deity through the veil of his humanity. Faith remains the capacity for seeing the glory of God, even now when Jesus is no longer visibly present. The believer attains eternal life through the vision and knowledge of God. He who has seen Christ has seen the Father. To see the Father in Christ is to see his glory. This is as possible and necessary for men today as for those who saw him in the flesh. Faith is thus a form of knowledge or vision peculiar to those who find God in the person of Jesus, the object of saving knowledge, the truth and the life.

Union with God

For the fourth evangelist union with God is based on *agape,* the love which gives itself. *Agape* originates in God, who, loving his creatures, raises them to himself. Only in so far as the love of God acts upon him and in him can man have *agape*: "We love because he loved us first" (1 Jn 4:19). There is, ultimately, no *agape* but the love of God. Wherever his love becomes effective, the glory of God is manifested: supremely in the self-offering of Christ, but also in those who through Christ live by the love of God.

Through faith in Christ man enters into a personal community of life with God which has the character of *agape,* which is essentially supernatural and yet operates in this world, not only because real *agape* expresses itself in practical conduct, but also because the pre-eminent act of *agape* took place on Calvary. This concrete, actual and divine love enables man to enter into the relation of *agape*: we may dwell in God and he in us, in the sharing of divine life.

John presents parallelisms regarding the mutual indwelling and mutual knowledge of God (Christ) and men: the Father knows the Son (10:15); the Son is in the Father (14:10–11, 20; 17:21). The Son knows the Father (10:15); the Father is in the Son (14:10–11; 17:21, 23). The Son knows men (10:14); men are in the Son (14:20; 17:21). Men know the Son (10:14); the Son is in men (14:20; 17:23, 26). Men know the Father and Son (14:7–8); men are in the Father and Son (17:21). All of these expressions reveal the depth and intimacy of the relationship that John saw in the life of Christian man with God.

Light, Glory, Judgment

John says the archetypal light is in some way interchangeable with life (1:3–4). This light shone in the darkness of non-being, ignorance and error. Jesus is the Light in which we see light, truth and revealed reality. For John, the light coming into the world (3:19; 12:46) is Jesus appearing in history, mediating the knowledge of God which is life. Though we see other things by means of light, light is known by itself alone. When Jesus, for example, tells his adversaries that he knows whence he comes and where he goes (8:14), he means that he has perfect knowledge of himself, necessarily shared by no one else, so that his own testimony is the only testimony available. In other words, his claims are self-evidencing. His claim to be "the light" can only be substantiated by the shining of the light. His work is self-evidencing; his deeds are luminous (5:36; 14:11).

The "glory" of God refers to the manifestation of the divine nature, character and power in time, through the incarnate Logos. This glory is seen only by those who have faith. It is a vision of God under the conditions of life in time and space, and the pledge of the ultimate vision of God beyond this life. For his disciples Christ prays "that they may behold my glory" (17:24): the manifestation of God's presence and power in a vision promised to faith (11:40). Christ brings the radiance of God within human experience and expresses it most perfectly in his loving death for man's salvation. The "glory" of Christ's death consists in the manifestation of the Son's loving obedience to the Father and God's love for mankind. All the deeds of Christ are signs manifesting the glory of God to men of faith.

As for "judgment," Christ says "I judge no one" (8:12). This is true in that those who do not respond to Christ prefer darkness to light and condemn themselves. Christ had come into the world that all men should no longer walk in darkness (12:46–40); his purpose is wholly positive and creative, not destructive or negative. Man pronounces his own "judgment" in his choice between truth and falsehood, good and evil, reality and self-deception.

Spirit

Spirit is related to truth in its Hellenistic sense of reality, reality as apprehended. "Spirit," in the fourth Gospel, is the vehicle whereby knowledge of unseen and eternal reality is given to men. It also stands for ultimate reality itself. John defines deity as spirit. The living, powerful, life-giving spirit is contrasted with powerless flesh. Man can only rise above this lower form of life if he be reborn of the spirit. The Incarnation makes this spiritual birth possible. The gift of the spirit to the Church is the ultimate climax of the personal relations between Jesus and his disciples (20:22). The spirit is the vehicle of life (6:63) and the medium of rebirth (3:5).

Messiah

Nowhere in the New Testament do the messianic titles receive such prominence as in John's Gospel. He catalogues many of these titles in his first chapter to emphasize that his teaching rests directly on the messianic beliefs of the early Church: "Messiah" or "Christ" (1:41, 45); "King of Israel" (1:49); "Son of God" (1:34, 49); "Son of Man" (1:51). The Messiah as king is especially prominent. When Jesus says "My kingdom is not of this world," he admits by implication that he is a king in a non-worldly sense which he explains: "For this was I born, and for this I came into the world, to bear witness to the truth. Everyone who belongs to the truth hears my voice" (18:7). The Messiah's kingship is the sovereignty of the truth which he embodies and reveals, and in virtue of which he demands the obedience of men.

Son of Man

"Son of Man" is another theme which occurs frequently. The Son of Man is more than an individual. He represents the human race in perfect union with God, in a union which others can attain only as they are incorporated in him; the mind whose thought is truth absolute (14:6), which other men think only after him; the true life of man, which other men live by sharing it with him (14:6, 20; 6:57).

Son of God

"Son of God" is a title which expresses the eternal relation of Father and Son, which, with the humanity of Jesus, is projected upon the field of time. The love of God, thus released in history, brings men into the same unity of which the relation of Father and Son is the eternal archetype. The love which the Father bore the Son "before the foundation of the world" and which the Son perpetually returns is dynamically operative throughout the life of Jesus. This love creates and conditions an active ministry of word and deed, in which the words are spirit and life and the deeds are signs of the eternal life and light (8:28–29; 16:32).

Logos

The prologue of this Gospel is an account of the life of Christ under the form of a description of the eternal Logos in its essential relations with the world and with man. The rest of the Gospel is an account of the Logos under the form of a record of the life of Jesus. The proposition "The Word became flesh" binds the two together: that Logos whose varying relationship to man was expressed in the preceding verses is now said to have identified itself with man by becoming man. This man is Jesus, whose life will be a realization of the relationships already expressed. The prologue, therefore, gives in brief outline the whole story of salvation-history realized in Jesus; the Gospel will fill in the details of the story.

9
Signs of
an Authentic Christian Witness

In virtue of Christ, the Christian belongs to the sign-bearing, evidence-giving, witnessing People of God. He individually and corporately communicates Christ through history. This is his vocation mission and privilege.

The Synoptic Gospels often express authentic Christian witness, or discipleship in terms of "following" Jesus:

And Jesus said to them, "Follow me and I will make you become fishers of men." And immediately they left their nets and followed him (Mk 1:17).

And as he passed on, he saw Levi the son of Alphaeus sitting at the tax office, and he said to him "Follow me." And he rose and followed him (Mk 2:14).

And he called to him the multitude with his disciples, and said to them, "If any man would come after me, let him deny himself and take up his cross and follow me" (Mk 8:34).

You lack one thing; go, sell what you have, and give to the poor, and you will have treasure in heaven; and come, follow me (Mk 10:21).

Truly, I say to you, in the new world, when the Son of man shall sit on his glorious throne, you who have followed me will also sit on twelve, judging the twelve tribes of Israel (Mt 19:28).

"Following" clearly means more than physically accompanying Jesus; rather, it implies sharing his life and, therefore, living the way he lives. The true disciple shares his mission, his commitment. The mission of Jesus, according to John, involves a Father-Son relationship which parallels the Jesus-Disciple relationship:

As thou didst send me into the world,	. . . so I have sent them into the world (17:18).
As the Father has sent me, . . .	. . . even so I send you (20:21).
. . . He who receives me receives him who sent me (13:20).	He who receives any one whom I send receives me (13:20).

The calling of the twelve disciples, in Mark's account (3:13–19), indicates that the disciples share Jesus' mission: Jesus gives them the authority to preach and to cast out devils. These activities are signs of Jesus' divine mission, which he extends in history through his disciples. In virtue of his authority, presence and power the disciples preach his word. Elsewhere, Mark (6:6–13) asserts that the mission charge of the Twelve includes summoning men to repent, casting out devils, and anointing and healing the sick. Thus, the Twelve share the life and activities of Jesus; their words and actions are signs for men of faith that the Kingdom of God is at hand: "Heal the sick . . . and say to them, 'The kingdom of God is at hand' " (Lk 10:9). Men are responsible for the way in which they receive the signs proffered by Jesus and his disciples. They were to tell those who rejected the signs of their divine mission that "Even the dust of your town that clings to our feet, we wipe off against you; nevertheless know this, that the kingdom of God has come near" (Lk 10:11).

Luke describes Jesus as "the sign to be spoken against" (2:34); towards the end of Acts (28:22) Luke notes that those who follow Christ are also spoken against. Luke would seem to imply that they offer the same sign as Christ himself; therefore, they provoke the same reaction. Jesus is "approved by signs and wonders" (Acts 2:22); the ministry of his disciples is described in the same way (Lk 4:40; Acts 5:12–15). Their words and works are living signs of the Risen Christ, bearing witness to his promise: "I will give you a mouth and wisdom which none of your adversaries will be able to withstand or contradict (Lk 21:15). What the disciples say and do are signs of the Lord's presence. The lame man healed (Acts 4:14) is a sign which the opponents of Peter and John cannot contradict.

In a very special sense, Stephen is the Church's first "witness" to Christ. His mission, speech, and death recall Jesus. Stephen, full of grace and power, performs great wonders and signs among the people (Acts 6:8). His adversaries cannot withstand the wisdom and the Spirit with which he speaks (Acts 6:10; cf. Lk 21:15). As with Jesus, the evidence against Stephen is taken from false informers (vv.11,13). The charges brought against him are the same as those brought against Christ: "This man never ceases to speak words against this holy place and the law; for we have heard him say that this Jesus of Nazareth will destroy this place, and will change the customs which Moses delivered to us" (vv.13–14). The historical review of Israel's history, constituting Stephen's speech, echoes the discourse of the risen Christ on the road to Emmaus: "And beginning with Moses and all the prophets, he interpreted to them in all the scriptures the things concerning himself" (Lk 24:25–27). His speech expresses the same kind of historical judgment found in Jesus' speech in the synagogue at Nazareth (Lk 4:25–27), or in the woes on the scribes and pharisees (Lk 11:47–51). Stephen dies praying for the forgiveness of those who kill him (Acts 7:60). The Church regards Stephen, its first martyr, as its first witness *par excellence.* His words, actions and death manifested the fulness of his participation in Christ's life; his life, taken as a whole, is a living sign of the love, wisdom and power of the Risen Christ revealing itself through history.

The concept of witnessing has its roots in the Old Testament, where Israel's responsiveness to Yahweh in faith and obedience is a sign pointing to Yahweh himself, "the faithful witness." "Witness" ('edh) and "sign" ('oth) are used synonymously in Isaiah 19:20, where in the Age to Come an altar and a pillar will be "a sign and a witness to the Lord of hosts in the land of Egypt." The Messiah will be given to Israel as a "witness" (55:4). Israel becomes an authentic witness when he responds to Yahweh; for by the recognition of Yahweh's signs, Israel becomes a sign. The mission of Israel is to witness, to be a sign: "You are my witnesses," says the Lord, "and my servant whom I have chosen" (Is 43:10). Thus, the responsiveness of the disciples to Christ in faith and obedience is a sign, a type of evidence, pointing to the effective presence of Christ in their lives, in the Church and in history:

And they went forth and preached everywhere while the Lord worked with them and confirmed the message *by the signs* which attended it (Mk 16:20).

The disciples' lives, words, and actions are living signs pointing beyond themselves for comprehension in faith; they reveal the disciples' whole-hearted acceptance of the summons of Jesus to share in his divine sonship. The signs are specific, because the disciple has committed himself to Christ's specific way of life, which he, in turn, shares with his Father:

> Love your enemies and pray for those who persecute you, so that you may be sons of your Father who is in heaven (Mt 5:44; Lk 6:27).

> You, therefore, must be perfect as your heavenly Father is perfect (Mt 5:48).

> Be merciful, even as your Father is merciful (Lk 6:36).

The basic presupposition is that the son acts like his father, because he receives his life from his father. The Christian also receives his life from his Father, not directly, but through Christ his Son. Christians, therefore, address the Father as "sons in the Son" (Gal 4:6; Rom 8:15). The authentic Christian acts like Christ, because he receives his life from Christ. The signs indicating authentic sonship will be much the same in both Old and New Testaments. The underlying principle is the oneness of God and the oneness of his saving activity. From the beginning he has had one plan for man's salvation and his operation of it is constant, expressing his holiness, mercy, and salvific will. As he has acted towards men, so does he and so will he act. There is a constant pattern in his graces and mercies to prehistoric mankind, to Israel, at the Incarnation, in the life of the Church and at Christ's second coming. All who respond in faith and loving obedience to the divine initiative become "sons in the Son," the Word of God, through whom the Father addresses and expresses himself to mankind.

Sonship is basically established by the reception of one's life from another. Jesus receives his life from his Father; the disciple receives this same life from Jesus. John shows the parallelism of dependence between the Father-Son and Jesus-disciple relationships:

> The Son can do nothing of his own accord but only what he sees the Father doing; for whatever he does, that the Son does likewise (5:19) Apart from me you can do nothing" (15:5).

> "As I live because of the   . . . He who eats me will
> Father . . .   live because of me" (6:57).

> I have given them the words which you gave
> me (17:8); also (12:49; 14:10; 15:15).

The disciples are empowered to witness, to give evidence or "signs" of their Father, because they share his life as "sons in the Son" through whom they are actually receiving the Father's life. This is essentially a relation of sonship and dependence because both the Son and the disciples *receive* the Father's divine life. (The disciples, however, receive it only through and in the Son, who alone—together with the Holy Spirit—is equal to the Father.)

The New Testament writers have specified the signs, the living evidence, of authentic sonship and communion with God in Christ. Loving one's enemies, for example, is only one of the signs. Selflessness, total dedication, and renunciation are other signs:

> If any man would come after me let him deny himself and take up his cross and follow me (Mk 8:34).

Loving obedience and responsiveness are signs:

Why do you call me "Lord, Lord," and not do what I tell you (Lk 6:46).

Whoever does the will of God is my brother, and sister and mother (Mk 3:35).

The service of others, undertaken willingly, is a sign:

You know that those who are supposed to rule over the Gentiles lord it over them and their great men exercise authority over them. But it shall not be so among you; but whoever would be great among you must be your servant [*diakonos*], and whoever would be first among you must be the slave of all [*doulos*]. For the Son of man also came not to be served but to serve, and to give his life as a ransom for many (Mk 10:42ff.).

If anyone would be first, he must be last of all and servant of all (Mk 9:35).

Jesus confirms his instruction by his own example:

Which is the greater, one who sits at table, or one who serves? Is not the one who sits at table? But I am among you as one who serves (Lk 22:27).

However, the sign *par excellence* of genuine sonship, the most convincing evidence that a Christian actually shares the life of Christ and his Father, is the unity of mutual love:

A new commandment I give to you, that you love one another, even as I loved you, that you also love one another.

By this all men will know that you are my disciples, if you have love for one another (Jn 13:34f.; cf. Jn 15:12).

The unity of mutual love draws attention to the social character of bearing witness and of being a living sign of a living God. From the very beginning, the biblical revelation has always demanded that those who profess to be the People of God must verify their claims by the evidence of their words, actions, attitudes and entire lives. The biblical revelation has always obligated the People of God to the mission of witnessing God in history as a living sign bearing evidence of his gracious purpose on behalf of all mankind. If God had made a promise to Abraham, it was ultimately that through him and his people all mankind would be blessed:

I will make of you a great nation, and I will bless you . . .
and through you all the peoples of the earth shall be blessed
(Gen 12:2–3).

The People of God are appointed to be "a kingdom of priests." It is their freely accepted and divinely imposed obligation to represent God to the world as a light for the Gentiles (Is 42:6). The People of God, even before the Incarnation, had recognized its mission and obligation of witnessing, of being the living sign offering evidence challenging all mankind to believe that God has acted, is acting and will continue to act in history through his people on behalf of all mankind. Israel serves Yahweh in witnessing him:

I will give you as a light to the nations, that my salvation may reach to the end of the earth (Is 49:6).

"You are my witnesses," says the Lord "and my servant whom I have chosen" (Is 43:10).

The People of God recognized, at least implicitly, the world context for the command which specified the character of their witness:

> You shall be holy; for I the Lord your God am holy (Lev 19:2).

With the fullness of revelation in Christ, the People of God understands that it must be holy because Christ is holy; and he is the holiness of God incarnate:

> The disciple is not above his master: but everyone when he is perfected shall be as his master (Lk 6:40).

> "It is enough for the disciple that he be like his master" (Mt 10:25).

The entire biblical revelation of both Testaments never ceases to stress the obligation of verifying one's claim to belong to the People of God by giving specific evidence, particular signs and a living personal witness that is accessible to others. The obligation, whether of the individual or of the People of God as a whole, is basically social. The stress placed on authenticating one's adherence to the People of God is not primarily a private matter; it does not primarily concern a personal examination of conscience. The stress is based primarily on God's will for the salvation of all men, which Christ expressed in his command:

> Go therefore and make disciples of all nations, baptizing them in the name of the Father and of the Son and of the Holy Spirit, teaching them to observe all that I have commanded you; and behold, I am with you always, even to the end of time (Mt 28:19–20).

The People of God as a whole and as individuals are charged with a mission to the world; consequently, both as a body and as individuals the People of God must verify its claim of communion with God before the world. If God has so loved the world that he gave his only-begotten Son as a living sign, as his personal witness and challenging evidence of his love; then, those who claim to be his People, to share his life in Christ Jesus, must do what he does. They will love the same world in virtue of the same divine love; they will share Christ's mission, for this is to share his life; they will authenticate their claim to belong to the People of God as living signs bearing witness to God's love for the world in Christ. The quality of their lives will challenge the world to *believe* that God is love and loves it. As authentic witnesses, their lives will have the character of a sign: signs are always meant to be of service to others, and they point elsewhere. The authentic Christian is a living sign for others, directing them to Another. Witness is service.

The frequent stress on service (Mk 10:42; Mk 9:35; Lk 22:27) becomes more understandable in the context of witness; for service is a sign that points to another. The servant belongs to another and works for others. Again, there is a parallelism between the Father-Son relationship and the Jesus-disciple relationship: the Son of Man comes to serve (Mk 10:42), and the authentic disciple is the servant of all (Mk 9:35). As the Father sends Jesus to serve, Jesus sends his disciples to serve (Jn 20:21). Thus, the service of Jesus is a visible sign giving effective witness to his Father; the service of the disciples is a participation in the life-mission of Jesus, and as such it bears witness in history both to Jesus and his Father. Christ serves and is served through his witnesses.

Jesus lives out and fulfills the content of the prophetic passages (Isa. 53) on the Servant of Yahweh. He is *called* in the eternal purpose of God (Is 49:1; 42:1); he is a *sign* to the nations (Is

42:6; 49:6); *humiliation* and *obscurity* characterize his role as *servant* (Is 42:2; 53:7); it is a way of *suffering* (Is 50:5), *intercession* (53:12) and *vindication* (52:13). For men of faith, Jesus' humiliation, obscurity, suffering and life of loving service, were evidential signs which authenticated his claims and verified his witness to his Father. "Son of Man" is a title which the New Testament writers regarded as interchangeable with "Servant." Thus, the Son of Man is *called* to a mission which he accepts in obedience (Mk 14:21; 10:45; Lk 19:10). His life is a *sign* of the times (Lk 11:30; Mk 2:9). It is a life of *humiliation* and *obscurity* (Lk 7:34; 9:58). He *suffers* (Mk 8:31; 9:12) and *intercedes* (Lk 12:8). He is vindicated in *glory* (Mk 8:38; 9:9; 13:26; 14:62; Mt 19:28). Thus, the life of the Son of Man is a life of service, of loving witness as the Servant of Yahweh, which points beyond itself as a living sign of the living God in history.

Paul describes the signs of an authentic Christian witness in terms that closely parallel what both Testaments have revealed about the Servant of Yahweh and the Son of Man:

As servants of God we commend ourselves in every way: through great endurance, in afflictions, hardships, calamities, beatings, imprisonments, tumults, labors, watchings, hunger, by the Holy Spirit, in genuine love, truthful speech, and the power of God; with the weapons of righteousness for the right hand and for the left; in honor and dishonor, in ill repute and good repute.

We are treated as impostors, and yet are true,
  as unknown and yet well known,
  as dying, and behold we live;
  as punished and yet not killed;
  as sorrowful yet always rejoicing;

as poor yet making many rich;
as having nothing, and yet possessing everything (2 Cor
6:4–10).

Thus, the alternating rhythm of the Christian life is a sign of the
Lord's life for those who respond to it in faith. And because it is a
participation in and a manifestation of the Lord's life, it will
also have the character of a *skandalon,* "a stumbling-block," "a
hindrance." The *skandalon* implies moral responsibility, inasmuch
as it does not accidentally trip one up. It bespeaks a situation
which precludes neutrality, because it challenges us to a decision
for which we are accountable. When discerned and accepted,
the sign becomes a blessing; when ignored and falsified, the sign
is a *skandalon:*

Blessed is he who shall not be scandalized in me (Mt 11:6).

Blessed are your eyes for they see (Mt 13:16).

Paul calls attention to other signs of communion with God in
Christ, which offer evidence of and witness to the Risen Lord's
life and activity prolonged in history. Although these signs do
not compel faith from those who do not believe, they are nevertheless conditions for it; for there must be some historical evidence
in terms of personal witnesses which renders the Christian kerygma
and way of life humanly plausible. Christ is not dead; he has really
risen and is actively present in the lives of those who believe in
them. The quality of life, the personal witness of committed
Christians, offers plausible evidence to all men, challenging them
to believe that Christ has risen and is with us now and forever.
Paul specifies the characteristics of the authentic Christian, the
evidence of his personal life, which renders the Christian message
plausible:

Gal 5:22 f		Col 3:12-55	
(The fruits—"evidence"—of the Spirit are:)		(Christians must "put on":)	
love	goodness	compassion	patience
joy	faithfulness	kindness	love
peace	gentleness	humility	peace
patience	self-control	gentleness	
kindness			

These are constants of the Christian life. For men of faith, they are signs of Christ's continuing presence; for non-believers, they are an effective witness rendering the Christian kerygma plausible. In either case, the social character of Christian witnessing is unmistakable; for these are all qualities which others can enjoy and which help others in their quest for happiness. The notion of service underlies them. Communion with Christ, the Servant of Yahweh, is witnessed by the selfless service of others:

> We who are strong ought to bear with the failings of the weak, and not to please ourselves: let each of us please his neighbor for his good, to edify ["help him develop" or "encourage"] him. For Christ did not please himself; but, as it is written, "The reproaches of those who reproached thee fell on me." . . . Welcome one another, therefore, as Christ has welcomed you, for the glory of God (Rom 15:1-3, 7).

Witnessing, bearing evidence, both in one's personal life and corporately as the People of God, to the continuing action of God in history, belongs to the pattern of revelation. The mutual love of the People of God is effective evidence which evokes the wonderment of non-believers. Seeing how much they love one another, non-believers are challenged to believe the Christian explanation for the remarkable phenomenon: that Christ has risen and is living among us.

Matthew, in terms of light, touches upon the Christian's obligation to give witness, to manifest the signs of his communion with God in Christ:

> You are the light of the world. A city set on a hill cannot be hid. Nor do men light a lamp and put it under a bushel, but on a stand, and it gives light to all in the house. Let your light so shine before men, *that they may see* your good works *and give glory to your Father* who is in heaven (Mt 5:14–16).

Matthew clearly sees the connection between the evidential signs of the risen Christ's effective presence in our lives and the transmission of Christ's revelation and life to others. Our good works must be seen because they are simultaneously Christ's works; they are the evidence which Christ gives of himself and of his Father, and which we simultaneously give of Christ. The good works are ours, Christ's and his Father's; they are signs of the one divine life which Christ receives from his Father and which we receive from Christ. Thus, it is equally true to say that God reveals himself through his own works and we reveal him through our own (clearly not in the exclusive sense!) works. Matthew understands the importance of evidence (i.e., good works-witness-signs) as the means for the transmission of the Christian revelation in history. The evidence is not documentary; it is persons. As Christ is the "sign" of his Father, the committed Christian is the sign of Christ and his Father. Matthew implies that just as Christ is the indispensable sign for the revelation of the Father in history, the committed Christian is the indispensable sign for the revelation of Christ and of his Father in history: ". . . that they may see your good works and give glory to your Father" (5:16).

If Matthew speaks of the disciples in their revealing, witnessing capacity as "the light of the world," he also describes Jesus in the same way, implying the revelation of God, when he quotes Isaiah:

The land of Zebulun and the land of Naphtali, toward the
sea, across the Jordan, Galilee of the Gentiles—the people
who sat in darkness have seen a *great light,* and for those
who sat in the region and shadow of death light has dawned
(4:15–16).

When Matthew describes the revealing Jesus as the "great light"
and the disciples as "light," whose good works enable other men
to glorify God, he clearly implies that the disciples are the light
of the world in virtue of the "great light." In both cases, the
context is that of revealing God to the world through persons:
Jesus, in the first instance, the disciples in the second. The revelation of God is contingent upon persons and their way of life:
Christ and his disciples. They are conditions for the transmission
of revelation, for the knowledge of Christ and his Father in history.

10

On Giving Christian Witness in John 13:35

"By this all men will know that you are my disciples, if you have love one for another" (Jn 13:35).

The mutual love of Christ's disciples is a form of Christian witness; it is an efficacious sign which enables men to know that the disciples adhere to Christ. Mutual love enables knowledge: "all men will know." It enables a knowledge of Christ through the attitude and conduct of other men: "that you are *my* disciples."

Mutual love is Christ's new commandment: "A new commandment I give to you, that you love one another; even as I have loved you, that you also love one another" (Jn 13:34). Therefore, the obedience of the disciples to the commandment of Christ enables all men to know that they are genuine disciples of Christ. Responsiveness to the Word of God in Christ is evidence of the disciple, which causes knowledge in others: "By this all men will know."

Mutual love enables all men to know that Christ has loved his disciples, because it is the expression of Christ's command to love, "even as I have loved you." Thus, mutual love is a sign which communicates knowledge to all men of the love of Christ experienced by the disciples.

Because the motive and norm of mutual love is the love of Jesus for his disciples, it constitutes a "new commandment" (Jn 15:12; 1 Jn 2:7–10; 3:11–23; 2 Jn 5). The mutual love of the disciples, like the love between the disciples and Christ, is paralleled with the mutual love of the Father and the Son: "As the Father has loved me, so have I loved you; abide in my love. If you keep my commandments, you will abide in my love, just as I have kept my Father's commandments and abide in his love" (15:9–10). The union of mutual love among the disciples is a sign of the loving union of the Father and Son; therefore, the knowledge which the mutual love of the disciples causes in all men is, by implication, a knowledge of the loving union of the Father and Son, as well as, of the loving union of Christ and his disciples.

Christ prays for the union of mutual love among his disciples: "I do not pray for these only, but also for those who believe in me through their word, that they may all be one; even as thou, Father, art in me, and I in thee, that they may also be in us, so that the world may believe that thou has sent me" (17:20–21). Christ prays for mutual love in order that the world may believe in him as having been sent by the Father. Loving union, according to John's implication, is a means whereby faith in Christ is communicated; it would seem to be something like an efficacious sacramental sign which reproduces the same loving union and faith in others.

The union of mutual love is a gift of God: "The glory which thou hast given me I have given to them, that they may be one even as we are one" (17:22). Christ gives his disciples the gift of "glory" to unite them. John, therefore, implies that the unity of mutual love has been given to the disciples through the gift of "glory" which Christ has received from the Father and, in turn, communicates to the disciples. That the divine glory is the divine excellence proper to God is explained by T. Barrosse in "The Relationship of Love to Faith in St. John," *Theological Studies* 18 (1957) 553. The Son of God made man has it, but, like everything else he has, he has it from the Father; his glory is the glory which the Father also has and which the Father has given him as Son (Jn 1:14; 17:5). By manifesting his proper excellence, Christ manifests his glory; he shows himself to men as he really is: the Son of God made man (Jn 2:11; 11:4). The gift of his glory is the gift of himself which enables the disciples to carry out his salvific mission. The accomplishment of his mission includes leading men to faith or to the recognition of Christ for what he is. The unity of mutual love, therefore, reveals the self-gift of the Father and of the Son which draws all men to the recognition of Christ for what he is among his followers.

Christ prays that his disciples may share the same mutual love that unites him to his Father: ". . . that they may be one as we are one, I in them and thou in me, that they may become perfectly one, so that the world may know that thou hast sent me and hast loved them even as thou hast loved me" (17:23). Unity of mutual love among the disciples is the efficacious sign which causes the world to recognize that unity of mutual love which unites the Father and the Son, as well as the Father and the disciples. One and the same divine love unites the disciples, the Father with his Son, and the Father and Son with the disciples. The mutual love of the Father and Son is essentially a self-giving which creates the unity of mutual love among the disciples, so that the disciples are united by the same love whereby the Father and his Son are united.

Christ's prayer, viewed negatively implies that, to the extent believers are not united by that mutual love which proceeds from the Father and the Son, the world will not know that the Father has sent the Son, and that the Father loves believers. John implies that disunity and discord are signs of the absence of God; they represent the failure to give that efficacious witness whereby the world may come to the knowledge of God's love for it.

The unity of mutual love is the criterion of Christian witness and the efficacious sign of communion with Christ and his Father. Jean-Louis D'Aragon's study of the Johannine concept of unity (cf. "La notion johannique de l'unité," *Sciences Ecclésiastiques* 11 [1959], 111–119) provides a key for comprehending the nature of mutual love as the efficacious sign of Christian witness.* Because the unity of believers is a unity of mutual love, whatever explains the one explains the other. If the nature of unity in Johannine thought is tridimensional, the unity of mutual love is tridimensional. D'Aragon considers three aspects of this unity on three levels: (1) between Father and Son, (2) among believers, (3) between the Father and Son, and the totality of believers absorbed into the unity of the Father and Son.

Thus, D'Aragon understands the unity of the Father and the Son as based on the mutual knowledge of Jesus and his Father: "The Father knows me, and I know the Father" (10:15). D'Aragon points out that the mutual love of the Father and Son receives more attention in John's Gospel than their mutual knowledge. Jesus affirms that his Father loves him (3:35; 17:23–26). D'Aragon asserts that the Father's love is communicated and manifested in his liberality towards his son. The gifts which Jesus receives from his Father are related in two ways to his Father's love for him: "the Father *loves* the Son and he *has given* all things into his hand" (3:35; 5:20); ". . . the glory which you *have given* me, because you *have loved* me" (17:24). D'Aragon notes that the Father has given the son his "name," which the son reveals to men (17:11–12); the entire "work" of his ministry (17:4),

* A grateful acknowledgement must be made to the editors of *Sciences Ecclésiastiques* and Father Jean-Louis D'Aragon for their permission to use and paraphrase so much of Father D'Aragon's splendid article.

which embraces both "works" (5:36) and "words" (17:8); "power over every creature" (17:2); "all power to judge" (5:22); "life in himself" (5:26) whereby "he gives life to whom he will" (5:21); the entire messianic ministry as expressed in the "commandment" of his Father (12:49), which determines the character of his mission, and the "chalice" of the Passion (18:11); his "disciples" are equally gifts from the Father (6:37; 10:29; 17:2; 18:9). The eternal liberality of the Father towards his Son is limitless; he gives himself entirely to his Son so that the Son is equal to his Father: "everything that the Father has is mine" (16:15), and "all thine is mine" (17:10).

D'Aragon observes that in the Fourth Gospel emphasis is placed on the responsiveness and obedience of Christ, on the concrete expressions of the Son's love for his Father, which correspond to the Father's gifts, the expression of his love for the Son; consequently, it is not surprising that the love of Jesus for his Father is expressly mentioned only once (14:31), despite frequent mention of the Father's love for his Son. The close bond between love and the responsiveness of obedience in the life of Jesus is clearly affirmed: "so that the world may know that I love the Father and that I do what the Father has commanded me" (14:31). The attitude of total responsiveness, or obedience, manifests Christ's vital union with his Father: "my food is to do the will of him who sent me" (4:34; 12:50); "I have come down from heaven not to do my own will, but the will of him who sent me" (6:38).

D'Aragon notes that the mutual immanence, the living communion, which unites Father and Son is expressed in the Johannine formulas, "I am in my Father" (14:20) and "you Father in me"; "the Father is in me and I am in the Father" (10:38). Mutual immanence presupposes a certain identity and implies that the knowledge of Jesus is knowledge of the Father (8:19); in other words, "he who has seen me has seen the Father" (14:9). Thus, the presence of the Father in the Son underlies such assertions as: "The word which you hear is not mine, but that of the Father who sent me" (14:24). Mutual immanence appears in parallel sentences on the same subject, where in one sentence an action is attributed to the Father, and in its parallel expression it is assigned to Christ: "if you ask anything in my name, I will do it" (14:14) and "If you ask anything of the Father, he will give it to you in my name" (16:23). It appears in the sending of the Paraclete: "But the Paraclete, the Holy Spirit, whom the Father will send in my name . . ." (14:26), and "But when the Paraclete comes, whom I shall send to you from the Father . . . (15:26); similarly, eternal life is possessed by "he who believes in the Son" (3:36), or by "he who believes in him who sent me" (5:24). Christ's communion with his Father grounds these affirmations. Their unity of mutual love and knowledge is absolute: "The Father and I are one" (10:30); "that they may be one *as we are one*" (17:11, 22; 1:1).

The second aspect of D'Aragon's consideration of unity in Johannine thought is the unity of the disciples, or believers. This unity is rooted in the believers' mutual love which manifests the same life animating them. Christ speaks of the unity which draws and holds his disciples together (ch. 17); he exhorts them to love one another (13:34). John, therefore, insists upon the absolute necessity of mutual love among Christians (1 Jn 2:9–11; 3:11–18; 4:7; 5:1). Mutual love, the only authentic Christian love, can exist only in virtue of Christ's love for his own, the proto-type and cause of mutual love in his disciples: "love one another *as* ("*kathōs*" is comparative and causal) I have loved you" (13:34; 15:12). Love for others includes even the sacrifice of one's life: "he has laid down his life for us; we should also lay down our lives for our brothers" (1 Jn 3:16; 15:13).

The immediate source of mutual love among believers is Christ's love for them; its ultimate source is the Father's love for his Son:

"as the Father has loved me, I also have loved you" (15:9). Love, as life itself, proceeds from the Father; believers acquire love through the mediation of the incarnate Son. Fraternal love is a requisite for and manifestation of a new life in Christ (1 Jn 4:7); through this all who have believed in Christ are regenerated (1:12). Christians, therefore, are really "children" of God (1:12; 11:52), truly "brothers" among themselves (21:23), because they have been engendered by the same Father (1 Jn 3:9; 5:1) and are all brothers of the risen Christ (20:17). They must love their brothers, for they bear within themselves the mark of the same Father who has given them life (1 Jn 5:1).

The mutual love of Christ's disciples assures the cohesion of the Christian community; it distinguishes it from adversaries, whose natural tendency is to hate: "he who loves his brother abides in the light . . . ; but he who hates his brother is in darkness" (1 Jn 2:9–11); "The children of God and the children of the devil are recognized by this" (1 Jn 3:10). Just as love must necessarily flow from the divine life, so too does hatred constitute the normal sentiment of those who are in no way united to Christ in Christian unity. Thus, fraternal love (13:35) and the unity which derives from it (17:21) possesses the value of a sign which indicates to all men the presence of the Father acting in his Son whom he has sent into the world. Jesus presents the unity of his authentic disciples as the sign *par excellence* of the Gospel: "so that the world may know that you have sent me and that you have loved them as you have loved me" (17:23).

Fraternal love is the Christian witness to the love of God in Christ, because the existence of a community unified in this way cannot be explained except by the effective action of God in Christ. Through the mutual love and unity of believers God reveals to the world the very love which characterizes his tri-personal existence (1 Jn 4:7) and which he manifests in sending his Son (3:16) and the Spirit of his Love (14:24; 15:26).

The totality of believers, assimilated into the unity of the Father and the Son, is the third aspect which D'Aragon considers. This unity is the perfection of mutual love. Before the Good Shepherd gathers them into a single flock (10:16) men are scattered and divided (11:52). Dispersion and alienation, the negation of unity, appears as the natural state of men outside the Church. Dispersion, alienation, separation and hatred characterize "the world" which does not adhere to Christ in faith. "The World" for John generally represents all those who refuse to believe; it does not indicate any positive unity.

The transition from separation to unity is not the consequence of a simple agreement based on the friendly feeling which happens to exist among men; it derives from the redemptive death of Jesus (11:52) which enables a new creation when believers are reborn into a new life that makes them brothers of Christ. Christian unity and mutual love derive from the adhesion of all believers to Christ, from the insertion of all the branches into "the true vine" (15:1-8). The ties that bind believers to their Lord establish them in a relationship of faith and knowledge, of love and obedience, and of mutual inhabitation in Christ.

The allegory of the Good Shepherd expresses the mutual knowledge of Christ and his disciples (10:1-18, esp., v. 14). Christ *knows* all the members of his flock (v. 3 "he calls his sheep each by its name"), and they *know* him (vv. 3-4: "The sheep hear his voice . . . they know his voice"). The same relationship appears in Christ's statement, "My sheep hear my voice, and I know them, and they follow me" (v. 27). John places greater emphasis on the necessity of knowing Christ (14:7, 9); this is an indispensable condition for eternal life, so that knowledge of Jesus is practically the equivalent of possessing eternal life (17:3).

The knowledge of Christ is joined with faith: one "believes" and one "knows" that Jesus is the Christ, the Son of God (6:69; 20:31), that he it is whom the Father has sent (8:24; 17:3),

that the Father is in him and that he is in the Father (10:38).
Consequently, the relationship of the Christian to Christ, founded
upon faith, is not clearly distinguished from that which is established by knowledge. This is corroborated by those texts which as-
sociate belief and knowledge (6:69; 10:38; 17:8). D'Aragon
shows how one verb can replace the other with no great change
in meaning. "To know," however, signifies something more profound and perfect than "to believe" (8:30–32), which would seem
to be more concerned with the prolongation of faith. Faith and
knowledge in John's thought represent an absolute commitment
to Christ of the entire person. He who believes "hears" the word
of Jesus (5:24) and "observes" (i.e., "lives by") it (8:51); his
internal acceptance and conformity to it in obedience governs his
conduct, determines his way of life. The believer "comes" to Christ
through the sacrifice of his egoistic self-interest and autonomy
(5:40; 6:35, 45); he "follows" Christ in sharing his destiny
(10:27; 12:26). Faith is necessary for adherence to Christ; it is
associated with the possession of eternal life: "he who believes in
the Son has eternal life" (3:36); he who does not, dies in his sins
(5:38; 8:24).

Mutual love, as well as faith and knowledge, unites Christians
to Christ. The life, death and ministry of Jesus reveal his extreme
love for his own (15:9–10). With respect to the future, Jesus
promises his love to all who observe his commandments (14:21).
Following the pattern of the Father's love for his Son, the love of
Christ for his faithful followers is extended in various gifts: "the
words" or "the word" of the Father (17:8, 14; 1 Jn 5:20); "the
power to become the sons of God" (1:12); "eternal life" (17:2);
"the food which endures to eternal life" (6:26); "another Paraclete" (14:16); "my peace" (14:27); "the glory received from
the Father" (17:22).

The disciples, on their part, must be responsive to Christ's love
(14:15, 21; 21:15–17). As the love of the incarnate Son for his

Father is expressed in his obedience, the love of Christians for their Lord is authentic in the measure that their conduct accords with his commandments (14:15; 15:10), and especially with the "new commandment" of fraternal love (13:34; 15:12; 1 Jn 2:7–8).

The union of Christians with Christ culminates in a mutual indwelling: "you in me and I in you" (14:20). This reciprocal presence of Christ in his and of his disciples in him is especially evident, D'Aragon notes, in his discourse on the bread of life and the allegory of the vine. Jesus affirms that his flesh and blood communicate life and assure the believer's lasting union with him: "He who eats my flesh and drinks my blood has eternal life. . . . He who eats my flesh and drinks my blood remains in me and I in him" (6:54, 56). The theme of mutual indwelling pervades the allegory of the vine in which Jesus insists on the need for his disciples to adhere to him. Only those Christians who share Christ's life are able "to bear fruit," to offer God a genuine service by their total responsiveness, expressed in their obedience to his commandments or word. This holds especially for the commandment of mutual love (15:12–17); it is the basis for the urgency of his exhortation "to abide in" Christ (15:9) and to "abide in my love" (1 Jn 2:27).

D'Aragon notes the striking correspondence between the relationships which unite believers with Christ and those which unite the Son with the Father. In both, John underscores a threefold mutual relationship of knowledge, of love, and of indwelling implying a vital communion. This correspondence becomes explicit in those statements where Jesus compares the relationship of his disciples to himself with the relationship which binds him to his Father: "As I live because of the Father, so he who eats me will also live because of me" (6:57); and, "As the Father has sent me, so I also send you" (20:21). This parallelism is the result of the incarnate Son's mediation, which forms the core of John's thought. Christ is the "gate" through which men are able to enter the fold and become members of the one flock (10:7, 9). There is no other mediator through whom man has access to God (14:6).

The mediation of the incarnate Son, D'Aragon remarks, appears as the result of a twofold union: that of Christians with their Lord and that of the Son with the Father. By uniting in him "all those who have received him", Christ endows those who abide in him with a participation in his sonship as the only-begotten Son; they became sons of God in the Son of God (20:17: "my Father and your Father"). The Son is so united with the Father that he who sees Jesus has also seen the Father (14:9). Thus, in the case of the Christian: he may be so united with Christ that he who knows him has also known Christ, and that he who loves him has also loved Christ. As a result of the union of believers in Christ and of the union of the Son with the Father, the faithful are reunited with the Father, and the reciprocal relationships expressing the unity of Christ and his own, as also that of Christ and his Father, are rediscovered between the Father and Christians. (D'Aragon observes that John gives little attention to the relationship between God and the faithful, lest one think man encounters God directly without the mediation of the Son.)

The Father, D'Aragon continues, has known, selected and given the disciples to his Son (10:29; 17:2, 6, 9, 24). He loves them as his Son: "You have loved them as you have loved me" (17:23). The Father's liberality manifests his expansive love: the gift of the Spirit, the Paraclete (14:16), the gift of "the true bread from heaven" (6:32), the gift of "eternal life . . . in his Son" (1 Jn 5:11), and the gift of whatever the believer will request "in the name of Christ" (15:16). Finally, there is the Father's gift of himself, insofar as he dwells in those who love his Son (14:23).

D'Aragon notes that John expresses God's dwelling in the Christian in terms of the presence of divine attributes in man. God is where he acts. Because he is a living God, the authentic Christian is only he who bears signs of that life: "the truth" (1 Jn 1:8); "his word" (1 Jn 1:10); "unction" (1 Jn 2:27); "the love of God" (1 Jn 2:5). The disciples maintain the same relationships with respect to the Father. They know him (14:7); they love him (1 Jn 4:10) and they reveal their love in their total responsiveness and obedience to his commandments (1 Jn 3:22), and most of all in their fidelity to the commandment to believe in the Son and to love one another (1 Jn 3:23); they remain in him (17:21). "We are in him who is true (God) and in his Son Jesus Christ" (1 Jn 5:20): this, according to D'Aragon, is the perfection of the unity of mutual love by which all men recognize Christ's disciples. The unity of mutual love is the communion of all believers gathered together in and by Christ, who unites them to his Father: "I in them and you in me, so that they may be perfectly one" (17:23).

Thus, D'Aragon has enabled us to understand the effectiveness of Christian witness insofar as it is caused by the tri-dimensional, tri-personal unity of mutual love (of the Trinity) between the Father and the Son, among believers themselves, and ultimately in that between all the believers and the Father and Son, into whose unity of mutual love they are absorbed. The unity of Christians in mutual love reveals the mutual love of the Father and Son as effectively present in the lives of believers whom their love unifies. In the mutual love of Christians men encounter the mutual love of the Father and the Son; theirs is the love whereby Christians love one another and communicate the knowledge and love of God to all men.

This study considers the meaning of Christian witness in John 13:35 from the standpoint of the tri-dimensional union of mutual love; however, the Johannine understanding of Christian witness also includes other aspects, such as the notion of mission. The Father sends his Son who sends his Spirit that all mankind may eventually share in their unity of mutual love. Jesus sends his disciples as apostles (4:38; 13:16; 13:20; 17:18; 20:21) to do the work for which he was sent into the world. Their mission is Christ's mission of communicating the mutual love uniting him to his Father. In the mission of Christ and in the mission of the apostles, the world is confronted by God Himself in the mutual love and unity of the Father and Son. Christ prays that his Father will send the Spirit in his name to complete his work. Thus, the Father, Son, and Holy Spirit are all involved in the mission of unifying mankind in their mutual love. When men receive or reject Christ, they receive or reject God (13:20). Jesus' witness to himself is true because he knows his origin and his destiny; it is not a solitary witness because he is not alone (8:16). The Father who sent him is the witness to Jesus (8:18). Jesus is not alone; what he says and does is initiated and directed by the Father and pleases the Father (5:19) as his Son's witness to their unity in mutual love. This is the mission and life of Jesus in which the disciples and all believers participate. Thus, when men receive or reject the evidence of the mutual love uniting believers, they receive or reject Christ, his Father and his Spirit.

Christian witness in the thought of John may also be considered from the standpoint of glory. The Son's glory is the glory which he has received from his Father (7:18; 14:13; 17:4). The Father is necessarily glorified with his Son: "He who has seen me has seen the Father" (14:9). The incarnate Son is the visible manifestation of the Father's glory; the two cannot be glorified separately, because the manifestation of the excellence or glory of one is the revelation of the excellence or glory of the other. When the Son glorifies his Father, he manifests his own glory (17:1, 7, 11); he manifests the unity of their mutual love, their divine excellence. The same holds for the relations of the disciples and Christ. If the Father has given glory to his Son, his Son has given the very same glory to them (17:22). They share in Christ's glory; their lives manifest the divine reality which they have received from Christ, and this glorifies Christ (17:10) and the Father (15:8). This manifests their participation in the glory of God, in the divine life of mutual love which they have effectively received. The mutual love and union of believers glorifies God because it manifests the divine glory, the Father's and Son's life of union and mutual love into which the believers have been assimilated. Thus, believers, by manifesting God's life and activity, are simultaneously glorifying God and being glorified by God, who is giving them a participation in his life, activity, or glory (5:23; 8:49; 12:26). Thus, men encounter God in his glory, when they encounter believers united in mutual love; it is the effective means of God's self-revelation, the efficacious sign of his presence and activity enabling all men to know him.

11

On Remembering: Divine Gift and Human Obligation

Remembering is essential to the life of the people of God. Christ commands his disciples to commemorate what he has done: " 'This is my body which shall be given up for you; do this in remembrance of me'. In like manner also the cup, after he had supped, saying, 'This is the new covenant in my blood; do this as often as you drink it, in remembrance of me'" (1 Cor 11:24–25). Commemoration is a Christian obligation: "Do this in commemoration of me" (Lk 22:19); Christians are to reenact Christ's sacrifice in the eucharistic celebration. The sacramental liturgy of the Church is the active expression of her memory.

The Eucharistic celebration, as the paschal meal in the Old Testament, is ordered to action, to a way of life. The Christian memory, in this respect, expresses a loving fidelity to the New Covenant of Christ. The fulfillment of Christ's eucharistic command is evidence that the Church abides in his love: "All who keep his commandments abide in him, and he in them" (1 Jn 3:24). To remember is to obey and to love; it is evidence of union with Christ.

Anamnesis is the Greek word for "remembrance" used in the above passages. It refers to the process in which one reflects upon the important historical events that form the basis of one's life. Thus, the particular way in which one remembers the past expresses one's self-understanding. In the Old Testament, for example, the celebration of the Pasch was characterized by the remembering of the Exodus as the decisive and still effective act whereby God saved his people; and this way of recalling to mind the past witnessed Israel's self-understanding as a people whom God had saved and was continuing to save. The Pasch was the annual remembering of Israel's first Passover in Egypt and of God's establishment of his people by liberating them from Egypt.

When Jesus celebrated the Last Supper, he instituted the New Covenant in anticipation of his death, within the framework of the Old Testament Pasch, acting as the father of the household when he distributed his offering of bread and gave the chalice to those who were dining with him. Thus, the Christian celebration of the Eucharist simultaneously commemorates the institution of the Old and the New Covenant. It is a remembering of the entire salvation history, which takes the form of cult. The remembering involved in the Eucharist is the ceremonial re-presentation of a saving, historical event in order that the efficacy of this event may perdure in the present historical situation of the celebrant. The Eucharistic commemoration presupposes that although Christ's saving death has and retains its historical uniqueness, it nevertheless remains vitally present in its effects.

Because the Eucharistic liturgy is not only a commemoration of Christ's passion, but also of his resurrection and ascension, it is characterized by the affection of joy: "breaking bread at home, they did take their food with gladness and singleness of heart, praising God" (Acts 2:46). The affection of joy is rooted in that faith which wills to express itself repeatedly in the actualization of those memories of the historical events which called that faith into being.

Liturgical remembering demands the expression of the whole man in an attitude of joy: "I know, my God, that you scrutinize the heart, and have pleasure in righteousness; in the righteousness of my heart I have freely offered all these things, and now I have seen your people, who are present here, offering freely and joyously to you" (1 Chr 29:17). Isaiah laments the liturgical recollection of God's saving events which is not accompanied by a sincere affection of joy and gratitude: "this people draw near with their mouth and honor me with their lips, while their hearts are far from me, and their reverence of me is a commandment of men learned by rote" (29:13).

To be a Christian, therefore, not only demands the remembering of specific acts of God in history, but it also demands that these interventions be recalled in a certain way. The authentic Christian remembers what God has done for him; secondly, he remembers it in a spirit of loving gratitude and joy.

The role of memory in the attainment of union with God is basic. It is especially manifest in the Eucharistic liturgy of the Church; however, it is also manifested, in various ways, throughout the entire biblical revelation. A consideration of certain aspects of remembering, as found within the biblical revelation, deepens our appreciation of the role of memory in the Eucharistic liturgy and man's personal communion with God.

God's remembering implies his action directed towards someone. The divine movement towards the object of his memory may be positive or negative. Nehemiah asks that God "remember for good" what he has done (5:19). The psalmist requests that God credit to David's account all his suffering (132:1). The Lord remembers in Israel's favor the fidelity of her youth: "I remember the devotion of your youth, your love as a bride, how you followed me in the wilderness, in a land not sown" (Jer 2:2). Jeremiah does not interpret the Lord's remembering as a nostalgic reflection; it is rather a reckoning of this previous fidelity to Israel's account. When God remembers, he acts toward someone because of his earlier commitment.

God also remembers in one's disfavor: "Remember, O Lord, against the Edomites the day of Jerusalem, how they said, 'Raze it, raze it! Down to its foundations'" (Ps 137:7). The Psalmist begs that the sins of his fathers should not be held against him: "Do not remember against us the iniquities of our forefathers" (Ps 79:8). Isaiah implies the unfavorable remembering of God: "I will not remember your sins" (43:25); "Be not exceedingly angry, O Lord, and remember not iniquity forever" (64:8). Jeremiah warns: "he will remember their iniquity and punish their sins" (14:10).

God's remembering is also associated with existence. Whoever the Lord does not remember has no existence: "I am . . . like one foresaken among the dead, like the slain that lie in the grave, like those whom you remember no more" (Ps 88:5). When God forgets sin, he forgives: "I will forgive their iniquity, and I will remember their sin no more" (Jer 31:34). The Psalmist understands the existence of Israel's history as the effect of God's remembering: "He remembers his covenant forever, the word that he commanded, for a thousand generations" (Ps 105:8). Israel exists, because God remembers: "For he remembered his holy promise" (Ps 105:42).

The complaint psalm, whether individual or communal, usually opens with a direct appeal to God to remember. The complaint states the problem of either the individual (Ps 25:6, 7; 119:49) or the community (Ps 74:2; 79:8; 106:4; 137:7; Is 64:8; Jer 14:21; Lam 5:1; Neh 1:8). The Lord is asked either to remember (Ps 74:18) or not to remember (Ps 79:8): "Remember how the enemy scoff"; "Do not remember against us the sins of our forefathers." The plea to be remembered appeals to the Lord's earlier commitment to his people: to his covenant (Jer 14:21); to his loving kindness (Ps 25:6); to his promise (Ps 119:49); to his congregation (Ps 74:2). It is an appeal to his past actions in history, which is hopefully recalled by the individual and the community.

In the Psalms, God always remembers the covenant people and not single individuals. His remembering of individuals occurs only within a few prose narratives (Gen 30:22; 1 S 1:19). Israel praises his faithfulness in remembering his covenant: "He has remembered his covenant forever" (Ps 105:8; Ps 106:45; 1 Chr 16:15). His efficacious memory is seen as constituting Israel's history through his covenant loyalty (Pss 98:3; 106:45; 136:23), through his continuing blessings (Ps 115:12) in the fulfilment of his promise to Abraham (Ps 105:42). Israel praises the divine memory which creates its existence. Israel remembers its past only in virtue of the divine remembering creating its history.

What God remembers is not limited to the past alone. He is remembering Israel in the present because "He is always mindful of his covenant" (Ps 111:5). The psalmist understands a continuity in God's remembering which perdures from the great acts of the exodus (Ps 103:7) to the present memory of Israel's weakness: "As a father pities his children, so the Lord pities those who fear him. For he knows our frame: he remembers that we are dust" (Ps 103:13–14). God's remembering transcends time, inasmuch as his mighty acts, the *magnalia Dei,* are not restricted to the past; they relate also to the present and to the future. God's remembering is not understood as the mere actualization of a past event; rather, historical events derive from the eternal purpose of God. His remembering is not a re-creating of the past, but a continuation of his same purpose. God's memory creates and embraces his entire relationship with his people; therefore, it includes both the *magnalia Dei* of the past as well as his continuing concern for his people in the future. Israel's history is the unfolding of the one eternal act of God's remembering; it is only from Israel's point of view that each remembrance is past.

God remembers those with whom he has made his covenant (Noah, Gen 8:1; Abraham, Gen 19:29), and the covenant itself. Israel's history evolves within a series of covenants which imply the reciprocity of remembering between God and his people. History begins with creation and moves to a covenant with Noah and finally to an eternal covenant with Abraham which is ultimately fulfilled in the new covenant of Christ. Israel's history is the created effect of God's eternal remembering expressed in terms of the covenant relationship. Israel has a history only because God remembers her and his covenant.

God always remembers his covenant; however, Israel can forget it (Dt 4:23). One aspect of Israel's rebellion consists in her failure to remember what God has done for her: "Remember and do not forget how you provoked the Lord your God to wrath in the wilderness; from the day you came out of the land of Egypt, until you came to this place, you have been rebellious against the Lord" (Dt 9:7). The failure to remember is sin: "And the people of Israel did not remember the Lord their God" (Jg 8:34); "and our fathers refused to obey, and forgot the wonders which you performed among them" (Neh 9:17).

Israel's remembering is often associated with doing. This is especially true in the context of the commandments: "remember to do" the commandments (Nm 15:39); "So you shall remember and do all my commandments" (Num 15:40); "You shall remember that you were a slave in Egypt and the Lord your God redeemed you from there; therefore I command you to do this" (Dt 24:18; 15:15; 24:9).

Israel's remembering is also expressed in terms of thanksgiving for the *magnalia Dei:* "Remember the wonderful works that he has done, the wonders he wrought, the judgments he uttered" (I

Chr 15:12). Thanksgiving is expressed for the Lord's remembering which had wrought Israel's liberation (Jon 2:8). Memory of the Lord's great works evokes trust as well as gratitude (Ps 119:52).

Brevard Childs, in his monograph, *Memory and Tradition in Israel* (London: SCM Press, 1962, pp. 50ff.), offers a stimulating analysis of the theological usage of the Hebrew verb "to remember" (*zkr*). His investigation begins with Dt 8:2: "And you shall remember all the way which Yahweh your God has led you." The appeal to remember is set within the hortatory framework of vv. 1 and 6: "Keep the commandments," which sets the purpose of the discourse. Verse 2 places v. 1 within the context of covenant history. The claims of God upon Israel can be understood only in terms of historical memory. The commandments are not abstract laws, but historical events in the life of Israel. Like their ancestors of the Exodus, the present people of Israel are still being tested in a perduring covenant history. Israel's memory links present commandments as events with her covenant history. The purpose of Israel's remembering is not to relive the past, but to find motivation for obedience in the future.

Israel's remembering establishes continuity between the present and her covenant history: "you shall not be afraid of them, but you shall remember what the Lord your God did to Pharaoh and to all Egypt" (Dt 7:18; also 9:7; 24:9; 25:17). Israel becomes aware, through remembering, of the unity of her one redemptive history; she remembers what Yahweh has done to her Egyptian enemies, and concludes that he will continue to act in the same way against her present enemies. Yahweh's commandments continue to confront anew each generation with the choice between life and death; they are the decisive events of her covenant history through which the divine plan for Israel unfolds within her present situation. They repeat their claims on each generation.

If basic to the covenant were the specific promises to Abraham of a land and a people, they occur within a conditional framework. Israel must obey the claims of the Mosaic covenant; otherwise, the promises of a land and a people will not be fulfilled. If God's remembering his covenant to Moses included a renewed promise of the land (Ex 6:8) and the preeminence of the covenant with Abraham as the basis of that hope (Lv 26:42), Israel's remembering makes her constantly aware of her own covenant pledge as well as of God's gracious acts.

Israel's festivals served to arouse her memory: "You shall eat no unleavened bread . . . in order that you may remember the day you came out of Egypt" (Dt 16:3). Israel observes the Sabbath to remember the events of her liberation: "You shall remember that you were a servant in the land of Egypt, and the Lord your God brought you out with a mighty hand; *therefore* the Lord your God commanded you to keep the sabbath day" (Dt 5:15).

The Sabbath and festivals are days set aside for remembering and for relating the present to the past historical interventions of Yahweh: "Remember the days of old, consider the years of many generations; ask your father, and he will show you; your elders, and they will tell you" (Dt 32:7). Memory maintains Israel's traditions. Her observance of the Sabbath is a sign of her continuing relationship with Yahweh, and that she continues to participate in the liberation of the historical Exodus event. It is the time for remembering; it is the faithful response of Israel to the demands of the covenant: "You shall remember that you were a servant in the land of Egypt . . . therefore the Lord your God commanded you to keep the sabbath day" (Dt 5:15). Thus, in Deuteronomy, Israel's remembering becomes an act of loving obedience toward Yahweh (8:18); it is contrasted with "forgetting him" (8:19).

Israel's remembering is essential for her continued existence as Yahweh's covenant people; forgetting his redemptive acts would bring her destruction: "You shall remember the Lord your God

. . . that he may confirm his covenant which he swore to your fathers, as at this day. And if you forget the Lord your God . . . I solemnly warn you that you shall surely perish" (Dt 8:18–19). To remember is to obey; to forget is to rebel. Joshua commands his people to "remember the word which Moses commanded you (Jos 1:13). The people reply (v. 16): "All that you have commanded us we will do. . . . Just as we obeyed Moses . . . so we will obey you." Thus, Israel celebrates her festivals in order to remember. Her remembering links the present to the past, to the tradition of Moses, to her redemptive history and covenant God. Through her remembering, Israel's redemptive history continues in a living tradition where the divine commands perdure as historical events challenging successive generations to decision and that obedience which enables Israel to share in the redemption of her forefathers.

Israel must remember in order to participate in the great acts of redemption: "O my people, remember . . . what happened on the way from Shittim to Gilgal that you may know the saving acts of Yahweh" (Mi 6:5). Israel must remember to know the saving acts of Yahweh. Israel's failure to understand what God has done leads to a rupture in her relationship with Yahweh. It is by remembering that Israel "knows"; that she has that intimate encounter with the great acts of Yahweh. Through memory Israel transcends the time gap which separates her present generation from the *magnalia Dei*. Liturgical worship nourishes the memory of Yahweh's acts (Mi 1:2; Is 1:2; Jos 24; Ps 105:5), in which Yahweh has revealed his righteousness. Through a righteous response Israel actually participates in Yahweh's redemptive acts. Her remembering actualizes Yahweh's original purpose for his people.

Isaiah's concept of memory and history is characterized by an eschatological hope. He urges his exiled people to recall all God's historical interventions on behalf of Israel in order that they may understand his absolute control over history: "remember the former things of old for I am God . . . declaring the end from the beginning" (46:9). God is accomplishing his redemptive purpose from the beginning to the end of history. Israel's remembering relates herself to her former covenant history, which becomes her future, because both past and future are united in the divine purpose. The unity of historical memory coincides with the oneness of God, who calls forth Israel's response of faith from beginning to the end of history. Because God's purpose embraces all history, he can proclaim his will in the past and accomplish it in the future: "I am the first and I am the last" (Is 44:6); "Who has announced from of old the things to come? Let them tell us what is yet to be. Fear not, nor be afraid; have I not told you from of old and declared it? And you are my witnesses" (Is 44:7–8); "Remember these things, O Jacob and Israel, for you are my servant . . . you will not be forgotten by me" (Is 44:21).

Israel's history is marked by continuity between the past and the future, which is rooted in the unity of the divine purpose; however, there is also an element of discontinuity which derives from her lack of responsiveness to the divine purpose manifested in the great acts of God. Israel's failures require a new quality within history that will enable a recapitulation. In this context the prophet urges: "Do not remember the former things, nor consider the things of old" (43:18) and "Behold I am doing a new thing; now it springs forth, do you not perceive it" (43:19)? Continuity with God's redemptive action in history is reestablished when Israel looks to his future actions (65:17), and does not remember her sinful days (Ez 23:19, 27).

Remembering in Ezechiel is consistently linked with the formula: "they (or you) shall know that I am Yahweh" (6:10; 16:62; 20:44; 36:23). Yahweh's nature is revealed in the prophet's proclamation of the divine intervention; he is known in remembering these historical revelation-events. Israel's remembering

is a response to the divine initiative. Each generation's remembering is a new actualization of the faith response to the original
Exodus events; it is no less authentic than the original response
to the same events. It is an acknowledgment of the same significance affirmed by the original witnesses to the *magnalia Dei* in
the continuation of the same historical witness throughout history.
It is in no way inferior to the original acknowledgment. In both
cases, the same divine reality enters the historical present in the
revelation-faith response event; both share the same redemptive
history, despite the separation of space and time. Memory enables
the same faith response; it spans the gulf separating generations,
as a condition for the continuation of redemptive history.

Remembering approximates an act of repentance when it refers
to a discernment or recognition which turns one toward God. The
psalmist, cut off from access to the temple, stretches out toward
God; he seeks to reestablish contact with God and to overcome
his isolation by remembering himself as a part of the community
in Jerusalem: "These things I remember, as I pour out my soul:
how I went with the throng, and led them in procession to the
house of God, with glad shouts and songs of thanksgiving, a
multitude keeping festival" (Ps. 42:4); "I consider the days of
old, I remember the years long ago. I commune with my heart
in the night; I meditate and search my spirit: 'Will the Lord spurn
forever, and never again be favorable?'" (Ps 77:5–7). Remembering is a type of reflecting, meditating and prayer. In psalm 77,
remembering begins with an intense sense of alienation and rejection (2–11) and suddenly turns to hope (12) when the psalmist
encounters God through memory: "I will meditate on all thy
work, and muse on thy mighty deeds. Thy way, O God, is holy.
What god is great like our God?"

In psalm 137 Israel recalls the day of Jerusalem's destruction
and curses herself if she should ever forget her commitment to and
unity with Jerusalem (137:6). Israel feels cut off from the

presence of God in Babylon; she feels separated in time and space from the sphere of his revelation and seeks to find him (Ps 42: 137). Through her remembering Israel encounters anew the Lord of her history and shares in his redemptive purpose. Israel's remembering is her prayer and communion with God; despite the absence of her temple, the established means of access to God, Israel seeks and finds him in the remembering that is prayer and communion. In remembering, Israel reexperiences the presence of God in the land of exile.

If Israel's complaint psalms implore God to remember, the psalms of praise proclaim that God has remembered. Common to both was the belief that God's remembering, rooted in his prior commitment to Israel, results in his gracious aid. Israel's liturgical memorials bring Israel to God's attention and assure his continuing intervention on Israel's behalf. They assume that he is always present, transcending time and space. The question at issue is whether God would withdraw his gracious assistance because of Israel's disobedience or continue to take care of Israel as he had in the past. In other words, would he continue to remember a people who had forgotten him in their disobedience?

Israel's memory contemporized the past tradition and enabled participation in the great redemptive acts of the past, and in their perduring power. Remembering made relevant the great redemptive acts which she recited in her tradition; it achieved solidarity with her fathers. Von Rad writes: "We have in Deuteronomy the most comprehensive example of a theological restatement of old tradition in which later Israel contemporized the message of Yahweh" ("Das formgeschichtliche Problem des Hexateuch," in *Gesammelte Studien zum Alten Testament,* pp. 33ff.). God's redemptive interventions in history are not confined to the past. The Deuteronomist sense of history understands the continuity of these great acts throughout history. The theology of memory reveals the condition for the continuity of God's one purpose in history.

God's redemptive action continues in the present when the son asks the meaning of the commandments and is told the historical tradition of Israel's redemption, and is admonished to obedience (6:20). Every new generation is called upon to respond in obedience to God's commands, expressed in terms of Israel's tradition. The restatement of God's claims to each new generation manifests the continuation of his redemptive action in history.

Israel's obedience is a condition for maintaining the continuity of God's redemptive intervention in history. Israel must obey the commandments in order to remember the redemptive history. Israel must observe the Sabbath in order to remember and to participate in the redemptive power of God's great acts. Israel's liturgical acts share the quality of the great historical acts of the Exodus; they are genuinely historical, non-repeatable and once-and-for-all in character. The liturgical recital is a particularization of the divine intervention of the past which has entered the world of time and space at a given moment, yet causes a continuous reverberation beyond its original entry. Israel's remembering, therefore, is not a return to the original event, but a continuation of the original event. The Word of God creates history; God's redemptive historical interventions continue to confront and are contemporary with every new generation.

The Old Testament events have a once-and-for-all quality: there is only one Exodus, one desert wandering and conquest of the land. Although they do not repeat themselves, they do not remain static. The redemptive events are a beginning. Redemptive history continues when every new generation is confronted anew by these same challenging events which continue to establish the people of God through time and space. Although the date of the Exodus event is fixed in time, it continues as a redeeming event to reverberate in the life of Israel. It is much more than the continuation of an idea or a meaning; rather, what God has done at the Exodus continues as an event which redeems and transforms successive generations, living within their concrete historical situation. The historical redemption-event of the past has initiated a genuine redemptive encounter in the present, in which God continues to challenge Israel to an obedient response through the medium of her tradition. Remembering is a *conditio sine qua non* for its continuing efficacy.

In every generation there are witnesses to these saving events. Some are closer in chronological time to the original historical happening than others; nevertheless, all share in the same witness to the same event. The saving events have always been witnessed events, interpreted events and never "bare facts." The remembered event is no less a valid witness to Israel's encounter with God than the first witness. Israel's redemptive history is the story of remembering; it can be expressed in terms of God's remembering Israel which, in turn, enables Israel to remember God: it is the outcome of God's action and Israel's response.

Every generation reinterpreted the same saving events in terms of its new encounter. The historical biblical revelation consists of layer upon layer of Israel's reinterpretation of the same great acts of her Exodus liberation and constitution as a people; every generation reinterpreted the same past in the light of its own experience with the covenant God who encounters his people through a living tradition. God's continuing call throughout history and Israel's response to his initiative form a unity, a witnessed, interpreted event. The perduring witness of all the different generations in their response to the divine initiative yields an understanding of Israel's redemptive history, in which the *magnalia Dei* are continually interpreted in terms of her on-going experience with her covenant God.

There is need for a developed theology of remembering which will enable a deeper understanding of the historical evolution of the biblical revelation and its impact on the contemporary world. The Christian liturgy and ascetical life would also be illuminated by such a theological investigation. Remembering is a fundamental obligation of the people of God, who are constituted as a people precisely insofar as they share the same memories. To forget the *magnalia Dei* would be to abandon the people who remember them and the Lord who wrought them.

The Christian Church's self-comprehension and understanding of her past is a divine gift which implies her remembering. It is the fulfillment of Christ's promise to send the Holy Spirit who would *remind* the Church of everything that Christ had revealed: "The Holy Spirit, whom the Father will send in my name, he will teach you all things, and remind you of all that I have said to you" (Jn 14:26). Through the Holy Spirit, the Father and the Son communicate the power of remembering to the people of God. It is the power to carry out the command to remember: "Do this in remembrance of me" (1 Cor 11:24). It is the power to obey, to accept lovingly the Word of God requiring this remembrance, whether in terms of the Eucharistic liturgy or of embracing the word of God. The capacity to remember, to commemorate, is the gift of the Father, Son, and Holy Spirit; and, as all the gifts of God, Christ's eucharistic commandment proclaims that it must be used. Thus, in the New as in the Old Testament, God's remembering enables man's; through his Spirit, God has given his people the capacity to remember, so that our remembering is the correlative of the divine remembering, the human response is itself a gift of the divine initiative, of the covenant God who remembers his people and thereby maintains them in existence.

In Luke's Gospel, for example, the good thief expresses the Christian's utter dependence on his Lord's remembering, with his prayer, "*Remember* me, Lord, when you enter into your kingdom" (23:42). In the Resurrection narrative, the angel commands the women coming to Christ's tomb to "*Remember* how he told you when he was still in Galilee that the Son of man must be delivered into the hands of sinful men and be crucified, and on the third day rise" (24:6). The women obey the angel's instruction, "And *they remembered* his words, and returning from the tomb they told all this to the eleven and to all the rest" (24:8–9). Thus, Luke clearly recognizes the Lord's remembering as the grace enabling the sinner's entrance into the Kingdom of God, as well as the Christian's obligation to remember the words of his Lord, as a necessary means for communicating the mystery of the resurrection.

12
On Returning:
The Process of Conversion

Conversion is both a state and a process. Once a man has turned to God, he is in the *state* of grace and communion with God; however, he has entered into a dynamic relationship. His initial conversion represents the establishment of a personal relationship with God; in this respect he has returned to God, he has been converted, he is in the state of grace. However, conversion also represents the initiation of a process of returning to God, of "putting on Christ" (Gal 3:27); thus, the converted sinner is in the process of completing his conversion. It is only at the resurrection of the just that the process terminates; only then has he returned, is in perfect communion with Christ; only then has the work of his salvation been finally accomplished.

Comprehension of conversion as a process helps one to understand why the Church's officially canonized saints so often expressed a keen sense of their distance from God, of their "sinfulness" or sense of alienation. Their basic psychological attitude is no different from that of a recently converted sinner. Both are converted, yet both are in the often agonizing process of completing their conversion. Thus, a man may be converted and yet fail in many ways to respond to the divine interventions in his life that would contribute to the completion of his conversion. Such was the case of the Rich Young Man. The Church's liturgy for Advent and Lent implies her profound realization that every Christian is in the process of returning, of repenting and of completing his conversion. Both the Old and New Testaments express her understanding of conversion as a continuing, life-long process of returning to God in the responsive spirit of faith, hope, and love.

The Hebrew word *shubh* is the most common expression for conversion or repentance in the Old Testament; it means "turn back" or "return" (Jer 8:4; Ez 33:19). The Septuagint translates this verb by *epistrepho*, "turn about," and *apostrepho*, "turn back." The New Testament employs the verb *metanoeo* to express repentance and changing one's attitude; it uses the verb *epistrepho* in the sense of turning back, or of being converted.

The basic presupposition of conversion, or repentance, in both Old and New Testaments is that man lives in a state of alienation from his Creator; something has gone wrong with man. The universality of human guilt is evidence that man cannot return (*shubh*) to his Creator, if left to his own resources. There is the understanding of the fatal human tendency to resist God, to oppose his will, to reject his guidance and to grasp shortsightedly at the nearest human expedients. Paradoxically, man is capable of committing sin, however he cannot remove or undo it. God alone, in his mercy, can do that.

The Israelite realized that God alone could restore him and overcome the frustration of his innate longing to be at peace with God. He recognized that God was not the cause of this alienation, because he is good and such an evil can in no way be attributed to him. The alienation of man's sinful condition was actually against

God's will; therefore, he prayed that God would "return" him, convert him, bring him back to himself: "Thou hast chastened me, and I was chastened, like an untrained calf; bring me back that I may be restored, for thou art the Lord, my God" (Jer 31:18). In Psalm 80 the following refrain is repeated three times: "Make us return, O God; let thy face shine, that we may be saved" (vv. 3, 7, 19). Israel prays that God cause a return, because Israel believes that it is only God who can initiate and effect a return which utterly transcends human resources.

The concept of conversion, or repentance, is expressed by certain formulas: it is "seeking God" (Dt 4:29; 2 K 12:16; Amos 5:4; Os 10:12); "seeking his face" (Os 5:15; Ps 24:6); "to humble oneself before him" (1 K 21:29; 2 K 22:19); "to set one's heart on him" (1 S 7:3). It is to desire God with the whole heart and soul (Dt 4:29, 30:2; 1 K 7:3); it is directing the heart to God (1 K 7:3). The Old Testament conceives sin as a turning away from Yahweh, so conversion is understood as a turning back to him, a return.

Conversion consists essentially in the complete return of the entire person to God: "And when thou shalt seek there the Lord thy God, thou shalt find him; yet so, if thou seek him with all thy heart, and all the affliction of thy soul" (Dt 4:29). Conversion, therefore, implies that man surrenders himself completely to a new purpose, a new cause, in the loving response to God. It implies that he reinterprets the meaning of his existence, which he now understands as completely reorientated, restructured and renewed.

Conversion always presupposes human freedom and decision. The Word of God confronts man with a crucial choice: "And when all these things come upon you, the blessing and the curse, which I have set before you, and you call them to mind among all the nations where the Lord has driven you, and return to the Lord your God, you and your children, and obey his voice in all that I command you this day, with all your heart and with all your soul" (Dt 30:1–3, also 4:25–31). The prophet expresses the Word of God challenging man to decision: "Return, faithless Israel, says the Lord. I will not look on you in anger, for I am merciful, says the Lord; I will not be angry forever" (Jer 3:12; also 3:1, 7, 9, 14, 22 and 4:1).

Conversion is decisive; it is a complete and resolute return to God. Consequently, repentance is described as the breaking of new ground: "Break up anew your fallow ground, and sow not upon thorns" (Jer 4:3); "Sow for yourselves righteousness, reap the fruit of steadfast love; break up your fallow ground, for it is the time to seek the Lord, that he may come and rain salvation upon you" (Os 10:12). Conversion is a radical change of heart and mind which hinges on a firm decision to seek the Lord.

Conversion is man's appropriate response to God's call. God calls man to return; he is not indifferent to man's alienation. God takes the initiative: "The Lord God called Adam, and said to him: Adam, where are you" (Gen. 3:9)? He refuses to abandon man; he calls out for him even after man has turned away from him: "When Israel was a child, I loved him, and out of Egypt I called my son. The more I called them, the more they went from me; they kept sacrificing to the Baals, and burning incense to idols" (Os 11:1–2). He calls Israel to return in a continuing present: "O that *today* you would listen to his voice!" (Ps 95:7). The call to return, to conversion and repentance is a call to salvation through union with God. His saving call is gratuitous. He calls Abraham from Ur to found a new people. He calls Joseph into Egypt and captivity to save his people. He draws his people to the rivers of Babylon in exile to create a new spirit in them. He calls his mother out of her native land of Galilee to found a new people with the birth of the New Man. The calling of important people away from their homelands, out of their familiar human setting and way of life, for great missions seems to be a standard pattern of Providence in effecting man's return. It is almost a symbol of what happens interiorly: a man is drawn out of and beyond the confines of his narrow ego for the accomplishment of a great purpose. Great men seem to die outside their hometowns. God's call to return is incompatible with human egoism.

Conversion is a response to the Word of God. Through the Word of God, man is summoned to conversion, to return and enter into a personal, covenant relationship with his Creator. God enters history through his Word, spoken by the prophets and incarnate in his Son, calling man to return. If man and the universe were created by the Word of God, they are also restored, "returned," converted by the same Word. Sin can be understood as a human failure to respond and pay attention to the Word of God; it is a turning away from the Word of God, uttered throughout history. Conversion, therefore, implies a return to the Word of God, which is creating the order of the universe from which man has deviated. If sin is the culpable deviation from this order, conversion is the return to it. Conversion, in this sense, is a return to the Word of God spoken within the human conscience. The Word of God expresses God's activity in creation, providence, revelation and redemption. To heed the Word of God, therefore, is to return to him through the means that he is actively creating, providing, revealing and also redeeming mankind. Ultimately, it is to return to God through and in Christ Jesus, the Word of God. *Whenever man encounters the Word of God, he hears the call to return.* And whenever God calls man, it is to himself and to his Son that he calls him.

Conversion means a return to the covenant commitment of the People of God. It involves a return to a regularized and official relationship with the divinity which is central to the entire Judeo-Christian tradition. The Old and New Testaments express the old and new covenants in which the Word of God has revealed the way of man's return to God. God entered into a covenant relationship with the tribes of Israel which was characterized by definite stipulations which he imposed upon them. The tribes of Israel solemnly swore to observe these conditions (i.e., the Ten Commandments), which constituted a code of religious and social law, later to be developed into the various other law codes of Israel. By infidelity to the covenant, the People of God would forfeit all claim on God's protection and salvation; they would be turning away from his loving kindness by failing to measure up to the terms of his covenant love. Osee complains of Israel's alienation from God, which derives from her failure to keep the covenant: "Hear the word of God, O children of Israel, for the Lord has a quarrel with the inhabitants of this land. There is no truth, nor kindness, nor knowledge of God in the land. Swearing and lying, and killing and stealing, and committing adultery—they break all bounds" (Os 4:1–2). Fatal results follow upon Israel's flouting of the creative Word of God, expressed in the covenant conditions: "Since you have forgotten the law of your God, I likewise will forget your children" (Os 4:6). Rejection of the Word of God, which created the world and keeps it in existence, is to choose self-destruction. Conversion is a return to the creative order of God which he has expressed in his covenant stipulations; it is a return to him through a way of life his wisdom has revealed through his Word, spoken by the prophets and apostles, incarnate in his Word encountered in the Christian community, the Church, which is brought into existence and kept in existence by the Word of God made flesh and proclaimed throughout history.

Revelation specifies the way of return and conversion. In the Old Testament, God reveals the way of return through the law, the prophets, and wisdom. Covenant love motivates the observance of those conditions which enable its fulfillment. Law expressed the will of God, the obligations of covenant love, the way of return, and communion with God. The prophetic interpretation of history revealed the way of return, so that history with all that it involves is understood as grace. The prophet speaks the Word of God, revealing the meaning of God's activity in the present situation; he instructs men on how they must accomplish God's will in this situation, because the accomplishment of the divine will in history is the way of return. John L. McKenzie (*Dictionary of the Bible* [Milwaukee: Bruce Publishing Co., 1965], p. 737) describes wisdom as follows:

> Wisdom, however, is also a charisma and it is the gift of Yahweh. It does not deal with cosmic and historical events, but with the will of Yahweh as it governs the ordinary events of the life of the individual person. This revelation is more strongly the preservation of a tradition than even the law. Thus in all three of these sources of revelation (i.e., law, prophets, wisdom), the self-manifestation of Yahweh as lord of history, creator and lord of nature, and source of law and wise conduct, is seen to be the governing factor of Israelite life and belief to the point where there is no other factor. Human intelligence and prudence best fulfill themselves by learning what Yahweh is. The result of revelation in the OT is knowledge which is not the philosophical knowledge of understanding but the knowledge of the living and active personal reality of Yahweh, experience of Yahweh as He is and as He acts.

Thus wisdom structures the ordinary events of the believer's daily way of life which constitute a way of turning to God. In the New Testament Christ is revealed as the Law, the Prophet, and the Wisdom of God, the way of return.

Creation and nature also point beyond themselves for an explanation, and offer grounds for turning to God. The mother of the seven martyred Maccabees understands creation's witness to

God: "My child, look up at the heavens and the earth, and see all that is in them, and perceive that God did not make them out of the things that existed, and in that way the human race came into existence" (2 Mac 7:28). God reveals himself as lord of creation through his continuing creative activity and presence. Man's failure to respond to the Creator, to return to him through creation, is reprehensible: "For men are foolish by nature, and had no perception of God, and from the good things that were visible they had not the power to know him who is, nor through paying attention to his works did they recognize the workman" (Wis 13:1 ff.). The failure to find God through creation is inexcusable: "They are not to be excused; for if they had the power to know so much that they could speculate about the world, why did they not more quickly find its Lord" (Wis 13:8–9)?

Paul also finds that the Gentiles have been indifferent to the Lord of creation: "For what can be known about God is clear to them, because God has shown it to them. Ever since the creation of the world, his invisible nature—his eternal power and divinity —have been clearly perceptible in what has been made. So they have no excuse, for, though they knew God, they have not honored him as God or given thanks to him, but they have indulged in speculations, until their stupid minds have become dark" (Rom 1:19–21). For Paul, God manifests himself in his creation in such an unmistakable way that the failure of men to return to him in adoration and thanksgiving indicates their perversity. The Creator calls man to return through his creation; he is understood as continually creating the way for man's return in a universe which expresses his divine wisdom. Parenthetically, both human speech and creation have spiritual significance as instruments for spirit's expression; the created universe is just as apt an instrument for God as the human tongue is for man. Creation, in this sense, is God's cosmic word inviting man to return to him in the recognition of his divinity and the acceptance of his creation.

Man returns to God through history. Through the remembrance
of the great acts of God in history, Israel repents and returns to
God. Israel turns to God through memory: ". . . you must not be
afraid of them (i.e., nations greater than Israel), remembering
rather what Yahweh did to Pharaoh and all Egypt" (Dt 7:18);
"Remember, never forget, how you provoked Yahweh to anger
in the desert" (Dt 9:7). He remembers the creation, the beginning
of history (Sir 42:15–43:33); the historical covenants God made
with Noah, Abraham, Moses and David (Gen 8:1; 9:15; Ex
2:24; 2 S 7). History remembered reveals the way to return to
God: ". . . and you shall remember all the way which Yahweh
your God has led you" (Dt 8:2). Thus, the way to return to God
is the same way she has lived under God in history. Israel believes
that the Lord of History is accomplishing his one great saving purpose in history which embraces past, present and future; therefore, Israel returns to, is converted to, God in the present when
she recalls what he has done for her in history. It is a way of
seeking God in her present situation. She focusses her mind and
heart on God by remembering the meaning of what he has done
for her in history and by giving thanks for this.

If Israel returns to God by remembering what he has done for
her in history, she becomes alienated from God when she forgets
his great acts on her behalf: "I fed you in the wilderness, in the
land of drought; but when they had fed themselves full, their
heart became arrogant, and so they forgot me" (Os 13:6); "Because you did not remember your youthful days, but roused me
to wrath with all these things, I will requite your doings upon
your head" (Ez 16:43). If it is the Lord of history who gives
meaning to history, then Israel can repent and return to him by
recalling the meaning of her past. This is the way she turns her
heart and mind to God and reenters the sphere of his saving purpose. To forget her history is to forget God; to remember it is to
remember God, her beneficent Creator and life-giver, who con-

tinues to communicate his goodness to her in the present. The Israelite turns to God when he recalls that in the entire unfolding of history the Lord of History is creating the way for his return and final conversion. History, past, present and future is understood as the Lord's loving invitation to return.

Conversion, in its positive aspect, implies a return to God who calls man through his word in the cosmos, history, law, the prophets, traditional wisdom, and ultimately in Christ. Although conversion assumes action on man's part, this action always has the nature of a response to the divine initiative. Man cannot return on his own resources alone: "Convert us, O Lord, to thee, and we shall be converted!" (Lam 5:21); "bring me back that I may be restored, for you are my God" (Jer 31:18). Although the free response of the human will is an indispensable condition for conversion, nevertheless, man's coming back is always the correlative of God's bringing him back. Man's returning is the free and appropriate response to the divine call simultaneously empowering it. Conversion is man's participation in God's creative initiative; in this respect, conversion represents the characteristic state of the true Israelite or Christian, constantly growing in the knowledge and love of God through his continuing faith-interpretation of his historical experience.

Paradoxically, God's lordship of history is always creative, despite its occasionally negative or apparently disruptive aspects. The faith of Israel interprets historical misfortune as a grace which is intended to turn Israel to her God: "Whereupon I have given you want of bread in all your cities, yet you have not returned to me. . . . I have also withheld the rain from you, when there were yet three months to the harvest . . . yet you did not return to me" (Amos 4:6–8). The Lord of History intends that whatever happens in history should progressively turn Israel toward him; consequently, every historical event is interpreted by faith as a grace mediating Israel's salvation. National calamities represent Israel's painful education by Yahweh, whereby Israel "will know that I am Yahweh" (Ez 25:7). The psalmist understands his personal history as the means whereby God has revealed himself: "O God, you have taught me from my youth, and till the present I proclaim you wonderous deeds" (Ps 70:17).

Conversion, in its negative aspect, is characterized by sorrow, or contrition, over the estrangement and alienation from God, experienced by the man reaching out for God. He confesses his estrangement and expresses it liturgically: "My sacrifice, O God, is a contrite spirit: a contrite and humbled heart, O God, you will not despise" (Ps 50:19); "I have given it (i.e., blood of sacrificed animal) for you upon the altar to make atonement for your souls; for it is the blood that makes atonement" (Lv 17:11). If such liturgical expression could not take place, the "contrite heart" would appear sufficient (Is 66:2; Ps 50:19). Psalm 50, the *Miserere,* exemplifies the sentiments of genuine repentance and conversion. The entire prayer expresses the resolution to please the Lord, and to seek him with a renewed spirit. He rejects those evils, which he understands as an offence against God. What matters is that the disillusioned sinner shall be freed by the grace of God from the tyranny of a good that is only limited and particular but without which life seemed unbearable and for the sake of which he had defied God's will. Conversion can also be seen as a process of liberation whereby God's love is empowering a man to love him more freely. In this respect, the pious Israelite and Christian alike experience sentiments of contrition in proportion to their progressive liberation of heart from creatures. The degree of contrition is relative to the extent of liberation; for, once liberated, the Israelite or Christian recognize their former ingratitude to their God. Recognition of his offended loving kindness, based on the total or partial rejection of his gracious call to return to him, grounds personal sorrow for sins, failures or indifference. Paradoxically, the unliberated man has no spirit of contrition or sorrow;

he has already found and is preoccupied with his creature-gods. Secondly, the relatively unliberated man experiences far less contrition, because this is a sentiment based on the recognition of what *had*, and no longer, separated man from God: "The Lord is saving the contrite of heart" (Ps 34:18).

Conversion in both the Old and New Testaments involves the community of the People of God. In the communitarian perspective of the historical biblical revelation, man returns to God through the mediation of other men within the community. Thus, Moses attempted to make expiation for the sin of his people (Ex 32:30–34). Jeremiah interceded vainly for the pardon of Israel (Jer 18:20; 7:16; 14:11). Ezechiel symbolically took upon himself the sins of Israel (4:4). To take upon oneself the sins of the community (*nasa' avon*) describes the work of the Servant of Yahweh (Is 53:4), whose intercession takes the form of martyrdom (Is 53:12). He is the innocent lamb of the Pasch (Is 53:5), whom God leads along the path of suffering, the mark of sin, to a sacrificial death (Is 53:10).

Solidarity in sin presupposes solidarity in salvation. God calls men to return through his word, spoken by the prophets. The prophets' vocation joined them to the people. The prophets were responsible for them (Ez 4:5; 33:1, 9), and interceded for them (Amos 7:1–6; Jer 18:20). Man's alienation, estrangement or "sin" becomes incarnate in social structures, in value systems, in ideologies, in traditions, habits, collective behavior and the dominant climate of opinion. The individual is born into this society and swept along by his surroundings through education, through a spontaneous mimicry, the spirit of gregariousness, his personal interests, to perpetuate this state of estrangement, this unjust social order of oppression, racism and collective indifference to God and neighbor (C. Tresmontant, *La doctrine morale des prophètes d'Israel* [Paris, 1958], p. 146). Consequently, the prophets addressed themselves to society in virulent criticism of its evils. Isaiah calls Jerusalem by the name of Sodom (1:10). The condemnation of cities reveals the communitarian dimension of sin and salvation. Man returns to God through society, with the help or hindrance of his contemporary social order, which may reflect the carnality of Sodom and Gomorrah (Gn 19) or the arrogance of Babel (Gn 11; Is 47). The Word of God calls for man's return through society, which must be reformed through the power and wisdom of God, creating the way of return within it.

Conversion implies a return to the creative, dynamic order of God. The dynamism of this order is expressed in God's laws: "The law of the Lord is perfect *converting* the soul" (Ps 19:7). It is expressed by God's word, structuring a man's life in a creative process that progressively turns him to God: "the testimony of the Lord is true, *making wise* the simple; the precepts of the Lord are right, *rejoicing* the heart; the commandment of the Lord is pure, *enlightening* the eyes" (Ps 19:7–8). The order of law and wisdom through which man turns to God, is not understood as a set of abstract rules. A return to God through the covenant laws and traditional wisdom of Israel represents a reentry into the sphere of God's ordered creation-activity; it is a responsiveness to and a participation in the life-giving wisdom-activity of God, giving meaning to the universe, history and Israel; it represents *the way man lives with God.* It is the way of living which the Lord of History is creating and returning man to himself, progressively liberating him from whatever does not leave man free to love him. Ultimately, God reveals that his Son is the law of Christians who turns—or "returns"—man to God.

From the beginning of his public ministry, Jesus, the Word of God, calls out for man's return: ". . . be converted" (Mt 4:17). Jesus is the incarnation of God's efficacious will for man's conversion and of his initiative in the process of returning. His miracles are signs of his efficacious lordship which empowers those who believe to return. Healings, exorcisms, resurrections, and miracles over the forces of nature, bear witness to Christ as the Way of man's return to God: "I am the way, and the truth, and the life; no one comes to the Father, but by me" (Jn 14:6). Christ's miracles are the testimony of God enabling man to recognize him as the Way of return. When he enables the paralytic to walk as a sign of his divine authority to forgive sins, men of faith exclaim: "We have seen marvellous things today" (Lk 5:26). The Jews believed that sickness and death are the wages of sin and the symbol of man's alienation from God; consequently, Christ's miracles of healing and resurrections are convincing evidence in the context of Israel's revelation that God is restoring and returning man to himself through Christ. They are meant to convert men to Christ. The restoration of sight to the blind enables man to see the way of return in Christ; the restoration of hearing to the deaf enables man to hear the Word of God calling for his return in Christ. In the context of Jewish anthropology, the salvation of the body was always, in a sense, the salvation of the whole man.

"The people who sat in darkness" (Mt 4:16) return to God through the saving compassion of Christ. The loving kindness of Christ is the characteristic of the divine power which overcomes man's alienation and draws him back to God; this is the greatest gift of God to man. The self-giving compassion of Christ empowers man to respond to the Word of God calling for his return. Jesus loved people: "Now Jesus loved Martha and her sister and Lazarus" (Jn 11:5). John records that at the death of Lazarus, "Jesus wept. So the Jews said, 'See how he loved him'" (11:35–36). Jesus reveals that loving kindness is God's basic attitude toward man. The awareness of this love, incarnated in Christ, conquers man's self-centeredness and alienation. It evokes a progressive response of self-giving which constitutes repentance, conversion, or return. Baptism efficaciously symbolizes the beginning of man's returning, which continues throughout his life. Man's conversion is ultimately accomplished only at the resurrection of the just and the beatific vision; it is only then that man has finally returned. In the humanity of the Risen Christ, God's loving kindness has achieved the perfect conversion or return of man to God.

The process of conversion faces many threats and obstacles which may either retard it or bring it to a halt. The parable of the sower reveals that the Word of God calling for man's return, even after the enthusiastic response of the believer, can be obstructed by human inconstancy and the attachment to temporal goods and cares (Mt 13:1–9, 18–23). This parable (found also in Mk 4:1–9 and Lk 8:4–9) describes three types of people in whose lives the return to God is fatally interrupted. Matthew describes them as the man who does not understand, the man who does not persevere in persecution, and the worldly man whose temporal interests turn his mind and heart away from God. The shallow mind, the hard heart, and the distracted life fail to return.

Christ's words on the narrow gate and the difficulty of justice reveal that the return is a process which involves sacrifice: "Enter by the narrow gate; for the gate is wide and the way is easy that leads to destruction, and those who enter by it are many. For the gate is narrow and the way is hard that leads to life, and those who find it are few" (Mt 7:13–14). Jesus teaches that the return to God demands that man must struggle against his more easily satisfied instincts and the distractions of the world. In this perspective, conversion involves a constant turning away from anything or anyone, either preventing or diminishing one's free response of love for God; this is the correlative of the total adherence of the disciple to the person of Jesus and his cause. The Rich Young Man was pleasing to Jesus; however, he was not fully converted: "You lack one thing; go, sell what you have, and give to the poor, and you will have treasure in heaven; and come follow me" (Mk 10:21).

The parables of the pearl and of the treasure (Mt 13:44–46)

imply that the return to God merits any sacrifice; and that the final expectation, motivating man's life-long process of conversion, should suffice to inspire even the most difficult renouncement. The power of man's faith, of his hope and of his love, is the divine grace which enables him to persevere in the life-long process of turning to God; viewed negatively, it is the same power which enables him to transcend whatever would turn him away from the Lord who is calling him back.

The parable of the prodigal son (Lk 15:11–32) is the classic story of repentance and conversion. It begins with the relationship of sonship. The relationship is ruptured by the son's assertion of independence and his departure. The relationship is remembered as having been a happy one. The relationship is reestablished when the son changes his mind, decides to return and is welcomed back by his father. Although the father respects the freedom of the son in allowing him to depart; nevertheless, the son is dependent from beginning to end. His departure is an assertion of independence; however, even this depends on his receiving his share of his father's property. Only when he squanders everything, and is left with nothing but the memory of his former relationship of dependence, does he decide to return. However, he returns with trepidation because he realizes that the reestablishment of his former relationship ultimately depends on the willingness of his father to receive him.

Conversion is a relationship (a state and a process) to which God calls all men. To those who were shocked at seeing him eat with "publicans and sinners," Jesus responds, "I have not come to call the just, but sinners" (Mt 9:9–13; Mk 2:14–17; Lk 5:27–32). Jesus ironically refers to the Pharisees and those who reject his call to conversion as "the just." Although they, too, stand in need of conversion and are also called, nevertheless, they refuse to admit their alienation and confess their sins. The publican attains righteousness through the confession of his sins (Lk 18:13); and there is joy in heaven at a repentant sinner more than there is for the righteous who do not need conversion, for these are the "righteous" who fail to admit their need for righteousness, conversion and repentance. Their "righteousness" is, in fact, merely a self-righteousness which counts for nothing. True righteousness derives from Christ alone; therefore, only he who confesses his sins and turns to Christ for salvation attains forgiveness (Acts 5:31). Man returns to the Father through Christ, and anyone who refuses to repent and be converted to him is in danger of perdition (Lk 13:3–5).

All men are called to return. God has made conversion and repentance possible for the Gentiles as well as Jews (Acts 11:18). Luke concludes his Gospel with the affirmation that repentance and forgiveness of sins should be preached in Christ's name to *all* nations (24:47). Conversion is not to be regarded as the privilege of race, but rather as the gift of God, the call of God, to all men. It is the work of Christ's lordship and service on behalf of all mankind: "The Son of Man has not come to be served but to serve, and to give his life as a ransom for many" (Mt 20:28; Mk 10:45).

A basic assumption of the New Testament teaching on return, conversion, or repentance is that God's invitation and call to return in Christ is inseparable from his work in the past. Only God the Creator can be God the Renewer or Restorer. The Pharisees acknowledged this implicitly when Christ cured the paralytic and forgave his sins. They protested, "This man is blaspheming" (Mt 9:3), because they understood that the forgiveness of sins is a form of restoration which only God the Creator can effect. Conversion expresses the re-establishment of God's creative order which is his efficacious will to save (Is 63:7–14). The Creator reintegrates man through his saving will expressed in Christ Jesus (Tit 3:5). He turns man to himself through his loving kindness in Christ (Eph 2:4–10); the result is the good order of peace which comes through union with Christ (Phil 4:7). Christ himself is the incarnate communion of God and man, the living and efficacious symbol of the return of man to God which he achieves: "For he is our peace, who has made us both one, and has broken down the dividing wall of hostility, by abolishing in his flesh the law of commandments and ordinances, that he might create in himself one new man in place of the two, so making peace, and might reconcile us both to God in one body through the cross, and thereby bring the hostility to an end" (Eph 2:14–16). Conversion to Christ is an entry into the new order of peace which God has created; it is to have communion with God in Christ, who is himself the incarnation of this communion, and the first man to have returned. The peace of Christ represents the dynamic order and process of man's life-long return to God which achieves its ultimate fulfilment in the resurrection of the just.

Jesus describes the process of conversion as becoming like a child (Mt 18:3): "Unless you are converted and become like children, you will never enter the kingdom of heaven." Conversion is not here understood as something completed; it clearly involves a process of change and development in which one progressively humbles himself before God as a child (18:4). Becoming like a child suggests the development of an attitude of complete dependence and reliance upon God, which would be opposed to one of self-reliance. It suggests a parallel in the final attitude of the prodigal son, who returns to his father, helpless and humbled after the folly of a disastrous self-assertion. Conversion involves the constant recognition that everything a man is and possesses is a gift of God.

In the apostolic preaching the summons to conversion is primary: "Repent and be baptized every one of you in the name of Jesus Christ for the forgiveness of your sins. . . . For the promise is to you and to your children and to all that are far off, every one whom the Lord our God *calls to him*" (Acts 2:38). The call of God to return through and in Christ Jesus is expressed by the Apostles: "Repent and be converted, that your sins may be blotted out, that times of refreshing may come from the presence of the Lord" (Acts 3:19). To be converted is to turn to God. For pagans, this involves the decisive step to monotheism (Acts 26:20); but there is a sense in which the Jews themselves must be "converted to God" (Acts 20:21). The return is preached with the formula "conversion to God, and faith in Jesus" (Acts 20:21). Baptism was preached as an act of adherence to Christ and as a washing from sin (Acts 22:16). Thus, Baptism is an efficacious symbol of adherence and repudiation, the positive and negative aspects of conversion. Baptism symbolizes not only the beginning of a new life in Christ, but also the end of the old life of sin (I Cor 6:11; Eph 5:28).

God's will is accomplished in all men who are actually returning to him; it is not fulfilled in those who resist and reject the grace of his call. Thus, God's will is man's salvation-return; sin is precisely the failure to respond to his Word, calling for and empowering the sinner's return. Paul speaks of the Word of God as the "gospel of your salvation", affirming that "it is the power of God for salvation for everyone who has faith" (Eph 1:13). The man of faith lives by the Word of God which endows his way of life with the quality of a return; he is being returned progressively by the wisdom and power of loving kindness of the divine Word, which is transforming and structuring his existence into a more perfect communion with God. Thus, Paul describes the man of faith as the work of God being created in Christ Jesus (Eph 2:10); he is God's new creation (Gal 6:15), growing progressively in the image of his creator (Col 3:10). Paul's concept of the Christian's development and "putting on" Christ (Gal 3:27) implies transformation: something is left behind and something else is acquired. He implies that two aspects characterize the Christian's life-long conversion process. The negative aspect is what the maturing Christian leaves behind, old views and values, former preoccupations and habits; the positive aspect consists in the new views and values which take their place. The former things are repudiated because they are now understood to be incompatible with a more serious and loving commitment to Christ; he turns away from them to the extent that he is progressively turning toward ("returning"), Christ. He is assuming a higher viewpoint in "putting on" Christ which involves continual renewal; he willingly accepts the liberating action of God who is removing every impediment to his free response. The "turning-away" process enables him to love more freely through the acceptance of new commitments or the implications of former ones to which the love of God directs his heart (2 Th 3:5).

Paul repeatedly reminds Christians of their commitment to conversion, to growth in Christ: "You have put off your old man with his habits, and you have put on that new man, constantly being renewed in view of perfect knowledge in the image of his Creator" (Col 3:9–10). It is "in the image," in the likeness of Christ who is God's perfect image that the Christian "grows" or "returns" to God (2 Cor 3:18).

In Christ's humanity, God has wrought a new creation, "the Last Adam" (1 Cor 15:45), "the first-born from among the dead" (Col 1:15), the "first-born before all creatures" (Col 1:15), the "image of the unseen God" (Col 1:15). He is the prototype of conversion as the first man perfectly united to God, the first converted man, the first man to have returned to God, absolutely and finally transcending mankind's alienation from God. By being baptized into Christ and putting on Christ, the Christian enters into the attitudes and affections of *the* converted man, of the first man to have returned to a state of perfect union with God. Baptism incorporates the Christian into the Body of the Converted Man, the Church; it effectively symbolizes a "new creation" which will attain its full perfection—perfect union or return—in the resurrection of the just. The Risen Christ is Man Returned, Man Converted, man at one with God, "the redemption in Christ Jesus" (Rom 3:24), which might be expressed as "the return" or as "the restoration" in Christ Jesus. Thus, the Christian is one who dynamically participates in the life of "The Returned," in virtue of which he is returning. He is in the process of assimilating the attitudes and values of "The Returned," through and in whom he is returning, being "led by the Spirit" (Gal 5:18) to the ultimate return that is constituted in the resurrection of the just and the beatific vision.

Notes

The following definitions of conversion and *metanoia* are relevant. They are taken from Karl Rahner, Herbert Vorgrimler, *Theological Dictionary,* trans. Richard Strachan (New York: Herder and Herder, 1965), pp. 102, 287.

Conversion: The biblical *metanoia;* primarily any sort of religious or moral transformation, especially the radical venture of entrusting oneself to God and his gracious guidance by a radical and fundamental religious act. It is always a matter of religious experience and of the subjective certainty bound up with this latter, though the personal question whether God has effected a particular conversion by an intervention that can be directly ascertained must often be left in abeyance. Conversion of this kind can and must often occur where faith has already been received and within the Church.

Metanoia: A religious term of OT origin, meaning conversion to God and already used in the OT of man in all his dimensions, that is *metanoia* (Gr. Μετάνοια, change of mind) is not only based on a change of attitude (Jer 8:4 ff.; 31:18 f. and *passim;* Ez 18) but must also be shown externally (Confession of guilt, fasting, etc.). Similarly John the Baptist preached a *metanoia* which is above all the absolute demand, sanctioned by the threat of God's judgment, that all men without exception must comply with (Mt 3:7 ff.; Lk 3:7 f.). Instead of repeating traditional exhortations to *metanoia* he preaches and administers a "baptism of penance" (Mk 1:4 f.). Jesus adopts this notion of *metanoia* and makes it the heart of his gospel, with less stress on the threat of judgment and more on the role of faith in true *metanoia* (Mk 1:15). The idea of a repeated *metanoia*, already to be found in later Judaism, becomes a great problem in the later writings of the NT (Heb) in view of the slackening enthusiasm of the Christian communities; it is even said (Heb 6:6) that there can be no repetition of *metanoia* (psychologically, not theologically speaking) in the case of a Christian who falls away. The sense of *metanoia* is conveyed today by the genuinely theological notion of faith and contrition rather than "penance" (with its strong suggestion of external works).

13

On Showing Mercy:
The Good Samaritan

Exegetes have given the parable of the Good Samaritan different interpretations. One of these interpretations is christological, and the other is moralistic. The christological interpretation was universal during the patristic period and seems to have remained the only interpretation until the end of the medieval period, or the beginning of the Renaissance. As early as the sixteenth century, Maldonatus (*Commentarii in quattuor evangelistas* [Mainz, 1578], *ad loc.*) pointed out the unanimity of the Fathers on the parable. Calvin (*Comm. sur le N.T., ad loc.*) and Maldonatus (in the above work) were among the first proponents of the moralistic interpretation; whereas, Luther maintained the traditional christological interpretation (*Evangelienauslegung* III, p. 138). The christological interpretation was definitely rejected in Jülicher's classical work on parables (*Die Gleichnisreden Jesu*) which appeared in 1899, and greatly influenced Protestant writers. Today, the moralistic interpretation is dominant. In the present context, the observation of J. Jeremias in the summary of his important work on the parables is most significant: "All the parables of Jesus compel the hearer to react to his person and his mission. For they are filled with the 'mystery of the Kingdom of God'" (*Die Gleichnisse Jesu,* 4th ed. [Zürich, 1956], p. 194), they are all "veiled christological self-evidence"; (M. Hêrmaniuk, *La Parabole Evangélique* [Univ. Cath. Lov., Ser. II, Tome 38], Paris-Louvain, 1947, p. 281 ff.): "the parables of Jesus appear as symbolic revelations of mysteries." The work done on parables by recent generations shows us that they must be divested of their moralistic significance in order to reveal their eschatological, original meaning" (Jeremias, *op. cit.,* pp. 23, 32). Hoskyns, Daniélou and Gehardsson are among those who support the christological interpretation of this parable. Their interpretation does not exclude the moralistic interpretation; however, it would definitely subordinate it. David M. Stanley, S.J., who is among Catholicism's outstanding New Testament scholars, in a letter to this writer (March 29, 1966) stated: "I am quite persuaded that the Christological interpretation is a valid one, and also one which makes much better sense theologically than the usual 'good-doer' interpretation of the Good Samaritan parable. Certainly Gehardsson's opinion is one that is not lightly to be discarded." The following essay suggests a consideration of those elements which would seem to support the christological interpretation.

Five parallel pericopes in the Gospel of Luke corroborate the hypothesis that Jesus is the Good Samaritan. In these five pericopes there are three common elements which also occur in the Good Samaritan story: (1) Jesus travels. (2) He encounters evils, moral or physical. (3) He shows mercy, expressing his saving purpose.

I. Jesus is journeying to Jerusalem (9:51–56). The village of Samaritans will not receive him. When his disciples urge that he should destroy it, Jesus rebukes them: "The Son of Man did not come to destroy men's lives, but to save them" (9:56).

II. Jesus is journeying to Jerusalem (13:22). He is told to de-

part because Herod wants to kill him (13:31). However, Jesus
casts out devils and cures people (13:32).

III. Jesus continues his Jerusalem journey (17:11–19). Ten
lepers cry out for mercy. Jesus cures them. (Only the Samaritan
thanks him.)

IV. Continuing his Jerusalem journey, Jesus approaches Jericho
(18:31–43). A blind man asks him for mercy. Jesus restores the
beggar's sight.

V. Jesus enters Jericho, en route to Jerusalem (19:1–11). He
encounters Zacchaeus, a publican and sinner. Jesus enters his home
and declares that "Today salvation has come to this house. . . .
For the Son of Man came to seek and to save what was lost"
(19:9–10).

In the Good Samaritan story, the journey takes place between
Jerusalem and Jericho. In the last two accounts, Luke mentions
both Jerusalem and Jericho. In the Good Samaritan story the
Samaritan encounters a man who has been robbed, beaten, stripped,
and left half-dead. The Good Samaritan, who is also on a journey,
comes, sees the victim, has compassion on him, and takes care of
him. An interesting contrast: all the evils befall the man who is
going away from Jerusalem, in the Good Samaritan story; whereas,
in the five above pericopes, Jesus is journeying to Jerusalem to
accomplish the salvation of mankind. This contrast would tend
to rule out the hypothesis that Jesus is the victim. During his
journey to Jerusalem, Jesus affirms that the Son of Man "must be
rejected by this generation" (17:25). This rejection by the official
leaders of Judaism would suggest a reasonable basis for his being
a "Samaritan."

The cure of the ten lepers offers another parallel with the Good
Samaritan contrast between the actions of the priest and Levite
and the Samaritan. Jesus sends the ten lepers to the official leaders
of Judaism, to the priests; however, it is implied that they do not
recognize the significance of the evidence Jesus sends them. Con-

sequently, they reject him and the claims which he bases on this evidence. It is only the Samaritan, one outside the sphere of official Judaism, who is capable of recognizing the significance of God's action in Christ.

The hostility of the Samaritans who will not receive Jesus is not directed against his claims and mission; rather, their hostility is directed against him because of his journey to Jerusalem, which implies his association with official Judaism.

Jesus is always the subject of Luke's basic threefold pattern. The frequency with which Luke repeats this pattern as well as its correspondence with the Good Samaritan pattern strongly suggests that Jesus is also the subject of the Good Samaritan story.

Noteworthy subordinate elements also support this interpretation. The Samaritan's reaction on seeing the wounded man is described with the word *"splagknidzesthai,"* which is a technical term for the action of divine love. This word has a particular usage in the New Testament literature and in the Apostolic Fathers; it always has God or Christ for its subject. Only two seeming exceptions are found. One is in the *Shepherd of Hermas* (*Sim.* VI), where the word is used of an angel, the other is in our parable, used of the Samaritan. It would appear, therefore, that the Samaritan is no ordinary man, but Christ.

The messianic symbols oil and wine ought also to be noticed. Although they were common medicines in the Near East, one should not lose sight of the traditional connection with the Shepherd and King of Israel, God himself or his Anointed One. The symbols oil and wine belong to the complex of sayings about the Messiah.

Furthermore, two accounts mention Samaritans (17:11–19; 9:51–56) and imply their conflict with official Judaism; two different accounts, among the five considered, specifically cite Jericho within the context of Jesus' Jerusalem journey (18:31–43; 19:1–11). A third element of comparison is the concept and word for mercy. The Samaritan is identified as, *"the one who showed mercy"* (10:37). Just as the Good Samaritan is "the one who showed mercy" (*eleos*), it is Jesus who shows mercy to the ten lepers (17:13) and to the blind beggar (18:38–9) when he cries out "Have mercy!" (*eleison*). The Greek noun appears in the Samaritan story; whereas the verb form for mercy appears in the Jerusalem journey accounts. The literary correspondence would seem to imply a doctrinal correspondence: the mercy which God shows, precedes and enables the mercy which Jesus requires of men in his command, "Go and do likewise." In terms of the Good Samaritan story's eternal life theme, the obvious implication is that *he who possesses eternal life shows mercy.* This is the answer to the lawyer's initial question: "Master, what shall I do to inherit eternal life?" (Lk 10:25). Just as God, who is Eternal Life, shows mercy, those who possess eternal life also show mercy. In other words, showing mercy is what a man does when God, Eternal Life, possesses his whole heart, mind and soul. Thus, the Good Samaritan story spells out the meaning of the Great Commandment.

Samaritans appear three times in the Gospel of Luke. Christ is forebearing with the inhospitable Samaritans who would not receive him en route to Jerusalem (19:51–56). Christ is implicitly identified as the Good Samaritan (10:29–37). Christ extols the faith and gratitude of the Samaritan leper whom he has healed (17:11–19).

"Samaritan" was a term of contempt among the Jews. Enraged Jews attacked Jesus with the words "You are a Samaritan and have a demon" (Jn 8:48). If orthodox Jews prided themselves on being the Chosen People of God, nothing could be more detestable than false religious pretensions of the Samaritans. The rival temples of Jerusalem and Mount Gerizim symbolized the intransigent hostility between Jews and Samaritans; each claimed to be the one true sanctuary of the Deuteronomic law (Dt 12). Samaritan priests claimed to be descended from Levi. Although the Samaritan temple had been destroyed in 127 B.C., they still retained their altar. At the time of Christ, there was no trace of either polytheism or syncretism. They were more conservative than the Jews. They acknowledged the Pentateuch alone as being properly canonical. They rejected the Prophets, the second part of the Jewish Bible. However, they, too, looked forward to the coming of the Messiah. And the belief is attested in the Talmud that the Messiah would come from the northern tribe of Ephraim, one of the tribes from which the Samaritans were descended.

The Samaritan is the symbol of the man whom official Judaism rejects on religious grounds. The Samaritan is consequently shunned as an outcast because of his false religious claims; he is despised as a sinner.

There are many reasons for believing that Luke's Good Samaritan is Jesus himself. He is a Samaritan because official Judaism has rejected him for his "false" religious claims.

The immediate context of the Good Samaritan story would seem to support this interpretation. The story is told not so much in terms of the Jewish lawyer's second question, "Who is my neighbor?", but in terms of his first question, "What must I do to inherit eternal life?" (10:25). The lawyer is primarily interested in eternal life. Jesus assures him that he will have eternal life, if he observes the Great Commandment of loving God with his whole heart, soul, strength, and mind and his neighbor as himself. Consequently, when the lawyer asks who is his neighbor, he is asking for an explanation of the Great Commandment, the means of attaining eternal life. Christ's answer, the Good Samaritan story, explains the Great Commandment; it explains, therefore, the means for inheriting eternal life. The lawyer's second question must be understood in the context of his first question. The Good Samaritan story answers his first question about what he must do to attain eternal life, precisely because this story is merely an explanation of the answer to the first question. In other words, Jesus replies that he who possesses the spirit of the Good Samaritan possesses eternal life; presupposing that this man not only loves his neighbor as himself, but also loves the Lord with his whole heart, mind and soul.

In the two other places where Luke speaks of life, there is more indirect evidence for interpreting the Good Samaritan as Christ himself. Luke emphatically underscores the relationship between the source of eternal life and the men of Israel: "But you *rejected* the Holy and Righteous One, and asked for a murderer to be granted to you, and killed the *Author of Life,* whom God raised from the dead" (Acts 3:14–15). The angel, releasing Peter from prison, tells him "Go and stand in the temple and speak to the people all the words of *this Life*" (Acts 5:20). The Greek word for "life" in these texts (*Zoē*) is the same as that in the lawyer's question. Although not conclusive proof, it is noteworthy, inasmuch as three Greek words for "life" appear in Luke. The other two are *psychē* (12:20) and *bios* (8:14). Consequently, the Good Samaritan would seem to be the same *"Author of life,"* rejected and despised by official Judaism because of his "false" religious claims. The implication is that eternal life is possessed through communion with the Author of life whom official Judaism has rejected.

Luke's presentation also contrasts the Great Commandment, the means of acquiring eternal life, understood as a written law with the Great Commandment understood as embodied as a way of life. It is the contrast between "What is written in the law? How do you read?" (10:26–27) and the living spirit and life of that law incarnated in the Good Samaritan. It is the contrast which Luke implies between the written law of Judaism and the living expression of that law in Christ, the law of Christians. The Good Samaritan expresses what eternal life means: Christ, and his living spirit. The Good Samaritan answers the question "What must I do to inherit eternal life?"

The story of the Good Samaritan contains two elements which support the hypothesis that Christ is the Good Samaritan. The first is the contrast between the actions of the official representatives of Judaism—the priest and the Levite—and that of one whom Judaism has officially rejected on religious grounds, the Samaritan. The antithesis between the leaders of Judaism and the rejected Samaritan is superfluous if the purpose of the story is merely that of promoting the ethics of universal brotherhood. If this were the case, the point could be equally well made by making the Samaritan the half-dead victim.

Secondly, the universal brotherhood theme would render superfluous the part of the story concerning the following day, when the Samaritan pays the innkeeper two denarii, telling him that he will be repaid for whatever more he must spend. The Samaritan concludes that he will return (10:35). The neighborliness of the Samaritan, or any other character substituted for him, would have been sufficiently well established without protracting the story to the following day and the promise of the Samaritan's return.

The tone of Luke's entire Gospel[2] supports the interpretation that the Good Samaritan is Christ. Luke is not proclaiming the ethics of neighborliness, but rather the divine message of universal salvation through Jesus Christ. In his Gospel, Christ is preeminently the savior of all men; in fact, the terms "savior" and "salvation" (*sotēr* and *sotēria*) do not occur in the other Synoptics. The general context of Luke's Gospel reveals that salvation consists in the first place in the physical healing of persons to whom Jesus addresses himself (8:48); elsewhere, salvation is explicitly the forgiveness of sins (7:50; 17:19). However, in both cases, salvation comes only to the man of faith: "Thy faith has healed thee" (7:50; 8:48; 17:19; 18:42). Jesus can act as Savior, he can heal and forgive, only when man reacts in faith. The Good Samaritan would seem to be the Jesus who acts on behalf of an afflicted mankind; it is the Jesus who saves, who heals and forgives. Salvation is eternal life through and in Christ.

In terms of eternal life and salvation, the Good Samaritan story implies a twofold alienation on the part of the leaders of Judaism. The priest and the Levite are alienated from the half-dead victim, because they do not bring him salvation. They are also alienated from the Good Samaritan, who actually brings salvation, on religious grounds. The Samaritan is rejected for what he is in the eyes of official Judaism: an imposter with false claims to the truth about God. The twofold alienation of the Jewish leaders is reprehensible, because the priest and the Levite could and should have done something for the salvation of the half-dead victim; and because *the* Samaritan is the "Good" Samaritan, the priest and Levite have no justification for their alienation from him. Judaism has failed to bring salvation to an afflicted mankind; rather, it is Christ, the Good Samaritan, rejected by the leaders of Judaism, who brings salvation. Eternal life comes from a "Samaritan," from one whom the leaders of Judaism have rejected and despised. Luke implies that it should have come from Judaism. He implies that the alienation of official Judaism from an afflicted mankind derives from its alienation from the "Samaritan," from the Righteous One through whom salvation actually comes. Official Judaism's rejection of the *Author of life,* the Good Samaritan, explains its reprehensible failure to bring eternal life to mankind. The Old Israel had failed in its role of service to an afflicted mankind in need of salvation; nevertheless, in spite of official Judaism's rejection, salvation comes to mankind through the "Good Samaritan." The tragedy which Luke implies is that salvation could have and should have continued to come through Judaism. Had Judaism accepted Christ, the story would have to relate how the priest and the Levite had served the half-dead victim, how they had bound up his wounds and brought him to an inn and took care of him.

The final part of the story strongly supports the interpretation that the Samaritan is Christ. Several elements clearly support an eschatological interpretation. If salvation is in one respect an immediate reality which Christ has inaugurated, it is also to some extent future; only after the last judgment will mankind be definitely and completely saved. Luke uses verbs in the future tense, with regard to salvation, which imply that salvation is ultimately accomplished through the redeeming work of Christ after the judgment (8:50; Acts 16:30ff.). In a strict sense, believers are in the process of being saved.

The process of salvation is indicated by that part of the story in which the Good Samaritan entrusts the victim to the innkeeper, saying "Take care of him; whatever more you spend, I will repay you when I come back" (10:35). The Good Samaritan has inaugurated the process of salvation; however, it would not seem to be complete until he returns.

Luke uses the same verb for "return" in only one other case (*epanerxomai*), which is remarkably similar to this one. Luke tells of the man who goes to a distant country to receive the royal title of King. He tells his servants to trade while he is away. His fellow-citizens hated him and sent messengers after him to say that they would not have him for their king. The verb appears in the phrase, "When *he returned,* having received his kingly power, he commanded these servants . . . to be called before him, that he might know what they had gained in trading" (19:15). There is an echo of the same rejection implied by the word "Samaritan" in hatred of the "fellow-citizens" who will not have him as king. There is a parallel of sorts between the service of the innkeeper, promised repayment for whatever he spends, and the servants of the parable, rewarded for their faithful work during his absence. The Good Samaritan and the nobleman who becomes king are both men of means who have entrusted men with a task; both will return to judge or to repay the service done on their behalf. By analogy, the Good Samaritan would seem to be Christ, returning in glory at the final judgment.

Luke uses the same verb in its simple root form (*erxomai*) to describe the coming of Jesus to men to save that which is lost (9:56; 19:10); to call sinners to repentance (5:32); to kindle a fire on earth. It describes the eschatological coming of the kingdom of God in the Our Father (11:2). This coming is identical with the eternal life given those who leave everything to follow Jesus (18:30). The coming of the kingdom is linked with the *parousia* of Christ (23:42). It refers to the eschatological coming of Christ to judgment in the parable of the fig-tree. When the Lord finds that his tree has produced no fruit, he orders its destruction (13:6).

The word for repaying (*apodidomai*)—"I will repay you"— also suggests the final judgment. God and man are not equal partners in their mutual relationship. God is never the recipient in relation to man. It would be self-deception to regard the status of a creature as one of autonomy; rather, it is a personal relationship of man, the recipient, to God, the Giver, to whom man is bound for his very existence. Thus, repayment belongs to God, whose love is creation and forgiveness. The Greek word used for expressing repayment is sometimes rendered in our translations as "reward," "recompense." It is the recompense due to a workman for his work (10:7), or for a service rendered (Acts 1:18). It is also divine retribution, repayment or punishment for evil (Acts 22:12). In any case, retribution, repayment or recompense belongs to God alone. In the context of the Good Samaritan, the word suggests that the Samaritan is he who alone can repay man for his services.

Repayment, in this case, reward, is for a service. The Good Samaritan's order, "Take care of him," expresses the character of this service. This is the very service which the Good Samaritan himself had rendered; in other words, the Good Samaritan rewards those who do his work of taking care of the half-dead man. Luke uses the Greek verb for taking care only twice in his Gospel. The verb (*epimeleomai*) first describes what the Samaritan does: ". . . he brought him to an inn, and *took care of* him" (10:34). Secondly, it defines what the Good Samaritan requires of the innkeeper: "*Take care of* him" (10:35). This parallelism is a typical literary device whereby Luke manifests his didactic method. In his balanced literary structure he presents one truth which complements and explains another; he thereby creates a didactic unity. This unity in the Good Samaritan story is composed of three elements: (1) Christ is the Good Samaritan who possesses eternal life and brings salvation; (2) however, to possess eternal life and to bring salvation means that Christ is a servant, acting as one who takes care of everyone who needs his help; (3) therefore, to possess eternal life means that the Christian does what Christ does, because Christ lives in him. He collaborates with Christ in bringing salvation, in "taking care of" everyone who needs help, in a life of service.

Eternal life or salvation is Christ. The Good Samaritan story explains the meaning of eternal life and salvation in Christ and his Church. It implies that Christ is where he acts; that eternal life is where it is lived. Luke explains how Christ acts—as the Good Samaritan—because this is the evidence of eternal life. Christ acts in the Church because the Church does what the Good Samaritan does, fulfilling his command, "Take care of him." The Church is the *locus* of eternal life, because Christ who is eternal life possesses it and has given it the means of salvation to be used in his service of restoring mankind to health, to peace with God: He took two denarii, and gave them to the innkeeper, saying, "Take care of him."

The Good Samaritan story is part of a Gospel which proclaims salvation to all mankind in Jesus Christ. The half-dead victim of the robbers underscores the salvation motif, because the concept of salvation in the New Testament is primarily connected with salvation in the sense of health. It means to restore health to one who has lost it, to restore safety to one who is threatened by danger, to snatch from death someone who is about to perish (Mt 8:25; 14:30; 27:40; Mk 3:4; Lk 6:9; Jn 12:27; Acts 27:20; 4:9; 14:9; Heb 5:7). The Good Samaritan is primarily *a man who saves;* and he orders the innkeeper to help him in saving, in restoring the victim. The priest and Levite do not save; but the innkeeper has the means which the Good Samaritan has given him for the salvation of the victim. The half-dead victim symbolizes the life-and-death aspect of salvation. The arrival and role of the Good Samaritan saves him from death; the innkeeper must also help to save and restore him. Luke implies that the man would have died, if the Good Samaritan had not come. What the Good Samaritan has done, enables the innkeeper to do the same: because the Samaritan has taken care of the victim, the innkeeper is able to take care of him. Because Christ has saved mankind, the Church is able to make his salvation a present reality in its preaching of the Gospel (i.e., proclaiming his salvation), in its celebrating and Eucharist, and in its ministry of the sacraments. Salvation is the new relation with God made effective by the ministry of the Church obeying her Lord's command, "Take care of him."

That the Good Samaritan is Christ would also seem to be supported by its resonance with the earliest forms of the kerygma which Luke records. The kerygma may be summarized thus: (1) There is a new age in Jesus Christ. (2) The ministry, death, and resurrection of Jesus inaugurate this new age. (3) Jesus has been exalted in his resurrection and constituted Lord of all. (4) He pours forth his Holy Spirit upon all who obey him. (5) He will return. (6) An appeal by the preacher for repentance, faith and baptism. (Acts 2:14–39; 4:8–12; 5:29–32; 10:34–43).

In terms of the Good Samaritan story, the kerygma may be summarized thus: (1) There is a new age in the Good Samaritan. (2) The rejected and despised Samaritan's ministry inaugurates this new age. (3) The Good Samaritan is Lord of all with the power to save. (4) He pours forth his Holy Spirit upon all who obey his command, "Take care of him." (5) The Good Samaritan will return and will repay those who obey. (6) "And Jesus said to him (i.e., lawyer), 'Go and do likewise'" (10:37). The Good Samaritan story would implicitly seem to capsulize the kerygma, concluding with an appeal for faith in the saving ministry of Christ and his Church. Thus, the people of God is created by the saving action and word of the Good Samaritan; the people of God represents man as restored by the Good Samaritan's care and as responding in faith to his word, "Take care of him." The people of God is restored by the living Good Samaritan and can restore in virtue of his restoration and life. It is the people for whom the Samaritan cares and through whom the Samaritan cares for all mankind, precisely inasmuch as it is his active caring which actually constitutes the people as such. The people can care for others, precisely because it is being cared for; its efficacy in saving and restoring derives from that life by which it is simultaneously being saved and restored as a people. Because the Church is the recipient of eternal life, it can share this life; furthermore, its very identity is constituted by this reception and sharing, by the care which the Good Samaritan takes of it and by the care which it takes of all those who are "half-dead" and in need of restoration and salvation.

When Luke concludes the story with Jesus' words, "Go and do likewise" (10:37), he is in fact addressing Christians. He is telling them that they must do for others what Christ, the Good Samaritan, is doing for them. He implies that they can "Take care of him" in virtue of the care which Christ has for them. And the care of the Good Samaritan for them transcends time and space only in the sense that it perpetually embraces every time and every place; the Good Samaritan *is* always and everywhere the same Good Samaritan with his eternal response to the human tragedy. He is eternally coming to where the tragedy is; he is eternally seeing it; he is eternally having compassion; he is eternally going to the victim, eternally binding up his wounds and eternally taking care of him: ". . . and when he saw him, he had compassion, and went to him and bound up his wounds, pouring on oil and wine; then he set him on his own beast and brought him to an inn, and took care of him" (10:34). This is the eternal life which the Good Samaritan is eternally giving them; it is his life, as life of loving service, eternally restoring, healing and creating. It is the eternal God revealing himself in the historical Christ.

If the spirit of the Good Samaritan is the spirit of the authentic Christian, it is the spirit which he has received and is receiving from the Good Samaritan himself. It is the gratuitous gift of the Good Samaritan's saving life which heals, restores, and progressively creates the recipient in the image and likeness of the Good Samaritan himself. The nominal Christian reveals that this gift can be lost; the penitent manifests its restoration. In either case, the Samaritan remains unchanging in his eternal presence and readiness to heal, restore and recreate an afflicted mankind. However, his actual efficacy in history, with individual persons, hinges upon the response of the human will to his words, "Go and do likewise." The man who goes and does likewise has in his very response accepted the life of the Good Samaritan. He hears the word of God and does it. He now has communion with Christ the Good Samaritan: "My mother and my brothers are those who hear the word of God and do it" (8:21). He has received the blessing of Christ: "Blessed are they that hear the word of God and keep it" (11:28). His wholehearted response in life and action to the words of the Good Samaritan, "Go and do likewise," is evidence of the Good Samaritan's simultaneous, efficacious, saving care, enabling his response to eternal life in the Word of God. By the very fact of his going and doing likewise, he is being saved by the Good Samaritan; he is receiving life; he is being healed, restored and re-created; he is becoming what the Good Samaritan is, in virtue of the saving life he is receiving from him; and, therefore, he is beginning to do what the Good Samaritan does.

"Go and do likewise," for the authentic Christian, does not express an external, abstract order; it is rather the word of God, expressing the life of God which the Christian lives. It expresses the abiding, spontaneous, internal impulse to do what the Good Samaritan does, precisely because it derives from the saving life of the Good Samaritan which he has received and is receiving. Consequently, the authentic Christian, to the extent of his response within his human limitations, *reveals* the Good Samaritan and his saving life in history; and he also *communicates* the Good Samaritan and his salvation within history. His impact on history will be that of *a man who saves.* It will be that of a man who heals, restores and creates reconciliation among men and between men and God; for no one is reconciled with God, who is not reconciled with his neighbor. The need for salvation derives from the wickedness and hatred of men, from the "robbers, who stripped him and beat him, and departed, *leaving him half-dead*" (10:30). The need for salvation derives from the hardness of heart, irresponsibility, indifference and egoism of men like the Levite, who "came to the place and saw him" and "passed by on the other side" (10:31). It is only the Good Samaritan who saves, and if his goodness is the goodness of God in Christ, it is also the goodness of Christ in man.

Notes

[1] Birger Gerhardsson has published a study, "The Good Samaritan— The Good Shepherd?", in *Coniectanea Neotestamentica* (Uppsala, 1958), xvi, in which he interprets the story of the Good Samaritan as an allegoric parable which contains a christological *didache* valid for all time.

Gerhardsson notes that in the Patristic Age all the church fathers interpreted this parable christologically. The Good Samaritan represented Christ himself who came down to a wounded humanity with healing and deliverance. As early as the sixteenth century, Maldonatus (*Commentarii in quattuor evangelistas* [Mainz, 1578], *ad loc.*) pointed out the unanimity of the fathers on this parable. H. de Lubac lists the relevant texts from patristic literature in *The Catholic and His Church* (New York, Sheed and Ward, 1960, and *Catholicism* (New York, Mentor Press, 1964. Other texts are accessible in Fr. Quievreux, *Evangile et Tradition*, I, *Les Paraboles* (Paris, 1946), p. 82. R. C. Trench presents a synthesis of the "mystical interpretation" in *Notes on the Parables of our Lord* (London, 1902), p. 311. J. Daniélou has also published a study, *Le Bon Samaritain*, in *Melanges Bibliques rédigés en l'honneur de André Robert* (Paris, 1957), p. 457. Daniélou finds the dominant contemporary interpretation unsatisfactory. He stresses the antiquity of the patristic view which was not even new in Irenaeus, and maintains that the New Testament interpretation of the parable is christological. Daniélou agrees with E. C. Hoskyns that the parable is related to the teaching of the Good Shepherd. Hoskyns asserts that the whole background of the parable of the Good Shepherd is not unlike the background of the parable of the Good Samaritan, where the love of God towards the man who has fallen a victim to the brigands is displayed not by the leaders of Judaism (the priest and the Levite), but by the Good Samaritan. Because of the passage which immediately precedes this parable, Hoskyns rejects the interpretation that the Good Samaritan story is merely an exhortation to human kindness (*The Fourth Gospel* [London, 1947], p. 377). The christological interpretation was definitely rejected in Jülicher's classical work on parables (*Die Gleichnisreden Jesu*, I–II [Freiburg im B., 1888–1899], II, p. 585 ff.). This work, appearing in 1899, greatly influenced Protestant writers. Since Jülicher, the parable is generally considered as a story illustrating the meaning of love of one's neighbor as going out to help whoever needs it; therefore, the Samaritan is just a Samaritan. Calvin favored the moralistic interpretation (*Comm. sur le N.T., ad loc.*); whereas Luther accepted the christological interpretation (*Evangeliensauslegung* III, p. 138).

Among the most recent scholars to support the christological interpretation of the Good Samaritan parable is Pierre van den Eynde, in his article "*Le Bon Samaritain*," *Bible et vie chrétienne* (Bruges, 1966), 70, pp. 22–35.

[2] The Lucan account has been called the gospel of mercy. The gift of salvation is itself the loving mercy of God. His two works, Acts and his gospel, continually proclaim: "Such is the merciful kindness of our God"

(Lk 1:78); "He has mercy upon those who fear him, from generation to generation" (Lk 1:50). Christ is the mercy of God, our salvation, and he demands that men be merciful: "Be merciful, then, as your heavenly Father is merciful" (Lk 6.36). Luke alone records the two sayings from the cross, in which Christ to the very end continues to express the divine mercy: "Father, forgive them; they do not know what it is they are doing" (23:34); "I promise you, this day you shall be with me in Paradise" (23:43).

The mercy of Jesus is the mercy of his Father, just as the life of Jesus is the life of his Father: "As your Father is merciful," "Father, forgive them." The divine mercy originates in the Father and is expressed in the life of the Son, for "My Father has entrusted everything into my hands" (10:22). Luke alone records the parable of the prodigal son (15.11–32), which reveals the merciful heart of the Father. Because of the merciful kindness of the Father, the Son has been sent to die for us and the Spirit has been sent for the forgiveness of sins. Jesus Christ is the Father's loving mercy and salvation. Just as the Good Samaritan is identified as *"the one who showed mercy"* (10:37), it is Christ who shows his Father's mercy, man's salvation. Through the gift of his life, Christ mercifully brings a sinful mankind into communion with himself in his Body, the Church; and thus the Church, as the Body of Christ, is the expression of the Father's mercy and salvation in history.

14

On Creation and History

Because divine revelation was and is mediated through history and inspired meditation thereon, the investigations of psychiatry and psychology on how man organizes his past have a theological relevance. The book, *Existence: A New Dimension in Psychiatry and Psychology* (New York, 1958), by May, Angel, and Ellenberger is especially suggestive. This work stresses the capacity to organize the past in the direction of the present and future as a condition for sanity. The inability to have a history, to organize the past, characterizes one type of mental deterioration and psychic trauma. Although a patient may be aware of what actually happened and capable of giving a thoroughly "objective" account of his life, he cannot interrelate the events of his past into a coherent whole; he cannot distinguish between the important and the trivial; he can only record with monotonous accuracy. Because he is not motivated by any reason for living, because he has no direction or future, his past is a meaningless chaos.

According to C. A. Simpson ("An Inquiry into the Biblical Theology of History," *The Journal of Theological Studies* 12,

[1961], 2-3), an examination of the chaos myth in the light of depth psychology should contribute to a deeper understanding of the psychological constant which conditioned the pattern of the human response to what was apprehended as the activity of God in history.

Common to the peoples of the Fertile Crescent was the myth that in the beginning of time there was a Monster of Chaos. In Babylonia he was named Tiamat, in Indic he was known as Vrta, while for the Greeks he was Typhon. In the mythology of the Fertile Crescent it was difficult to differentiate between Tiamat, the chaotic watery ocean itself, and Tiamat the monster that dwelt in the sea. A fusion of ideas was the outcome. In these creation myths of the Near East the various parts of the world, sea, sky, and earth were represented as so many divinities engaged in a life and death struggle, out of which emerges the created world. There are reasons for saying that when the Israelites wished to establish the sole activity of Yahweh in cosmogony and anthropogony, they related his work in familiar terms of the battle and victory over the power of chaos. In combat, Yahweh overthrew the dragon who in the creation stories represents the great ocean and is called Rahab, Leviathan or the dragon (Ps 74:12-17; 89:9-12; Job 26:12-14; Is 27:1; 51:9), before he created the world. Elsewhere it is the ocean itself which Yahweh brings under his dominion (Job 38:8; Prov 8:29; Jer 5:22; Hab 3:9; Ps 18:15, 33:7, 65:7).

In Genesis 1:2-2:3 the world at the time of creation is depicted as an ocean without a shore, wrapped in darkness, a chaos in which water, earth and night were commingled. The Israelites divested the elements of the personalities which they possessed in the other myths; they are not gods, but things.

Genesis reveals that God brought order out of chaos, and light out of darkness. The verb *bara* (create) itself (Gen 1:1) always has God as subject; it represents an act proper to divinity alone.

God, therefore, controls both chaos and darkness. His spirit, his creative purpose in action, *brooded* over the surface of the primordial chaotic mass. This verb is used in only one other instance, when it describes an eagle hovering over her young (Dt 32:11). In both cases there is the intimation of a loving purpose fostering new life by its action. Before God's action, the world is depicted as a chaotic mass in which no life is possible. God's creative action makes life in the world possible.

The theological implication of God's creative act is that history begins with meaning; there is no history until existence becomes comprehensible. The intelligibility of history is the effect of God's creative activity. History begins when God creates meaning. In terms of the Genesis imagery, history begins when God structures the incomprehensible incoherence of chaos according to his gracious purpose. The quality of God's activity is that it creates coherence, meaning, identity, significance, intelligibility; therefore, it creates what is lovable. In this sense, the divine activity makes life in the world possible for man. Thus, history can begin only when it is possible for man to live in time.

Tannin is the monster of chaos common to the various mythologies of the Fertile Crescent. It also means "serpent" in Hebrew and appears in the Exodus account: "And the Lord spoke to Moses and to Aaron saying, When Pharaoh shall speak unto you saying, Show a miracle for yourselves: then you shall say to Aaron, Take your rod and cast it before Pharaoh, and it shall become a serpent" (Ex 7:9). In Job 7:12 and Ps 74:13, *yam*, the sea, is paralleled with *tannin*. The monster of chaos was also called Leviathan: "You break the bands of leviathan in pieces" (Ps 74:14). He was called *behemah* in Ps 73:22. The monster of chaos is visualized as a serpent in Isaiah 27:1: "In that day the Lord with his hard and great and strong sword will punish Leviathan the fleeing serpent, Leviathan the twisting serpent, and he will slay the dragon that is in the sea."

Consequently, Moses would give Pharaoh a sign that Yahweh was in control of all things, even of the incomprehensible, chaotic unknown, whether visualized as the serpent Leviathan or as the sea. Because Pharaoh resists the demonstrated Word of God, Egypt becomes a land of chaos and darkness. The Pharaoh and Egypt are later described in terms of the monster which God must overcome (i.e., "Rahab"): "For Egypt's help is worthless and empty, therefore I have called her 'Rahab who sits still'" (Is 30:7). From the standpoint of history, the term is most appropriate for the menacing forces which would have put an end to Israel's history. Yahweh preserves Israel from oblivion, from the monster of chaos, when he destroys the Egyptian army: "Awake, awake, put on strength, O arm of the Lord; awake, as in days of old, the generations of long ago. Was it not you who cut Rahab in pieces, that pierced the dragon, *tannin?* Was it not you who dried up the sea, the waters of the deep, *tehom;* that made the depths of the sea a way for the redeemed to pass over?" (Is 51:9–10).

The crossing of the Red Sea and the defeat of Pharaoh were divine interventions in history analogous to the primary act of creation with which history begins. In both Yahweh manifests his dominion over the chaotic sea. Out of the waters of the Red Sea come forth a people whom Yahweh has created: "O Lord God of hosts, who is mighty like you, O Yahweh, you rule the raging sea: when its waves rise, you still them. You have broken Rahab in pieces . . . you scattered your enemies with your strong arm" (Ps 89:8–10). The same theme appears in Ex 15 and Is 63.

The Deutero-Isaiah perceives that the disobedient nation could be reborn only by a new divine act of creation-redemption, as at the deliverance at the Red Sea. He declares that he who in the original creation of Israel had cut Rahab-Egypt in pieces and who had smote the dragon of the deep, was he who even now is bringing back his people with singing to Zion; so that Israel might know that this same Yahweh, the "Creator of Israel" (Is 43:15), was the Lord of all the earth (54:5), besides whom there was no other (54:18), and that it was he who had stretched out the heavens and laid the foundations of the earth. The Deutero-Isaiah reinterprets the historical kerygma of Israel, in the light of Israel's Exile experience. It achieves a new understanding of the creative activity of God in history.

Israel's historical existence, constantly threatened by powerful enemies, was viewed as a continuing miracle wrought by the creative power of Yahweh (Is 17:12–13). The prophets appreciated the continuing control which Yahweh exerted over the elemental disorder beneath the surface of life. The entire ordered world could possibly return to chaos (Jer 4:23–29; Is 34:11); however, Yahweh's effective sovereignty governs the whole earth (Is 14:26). He combines the destinies of all nations in one great unity, guiding history in accordance with his mysterious plan, as the master-builder who lays on Zion his precious corner-stone (Is 28:16), thus bringing the Kingdom of God to completion, even when everything seems to be shattered in pieces.

Israel believes the Lord of history will attain his goal, despite disobedience and hostile powers. He is the Lord of history; consequently, he can incorporate hostile powers into his own scheme for history so that they become the instruments of his decrees. Assyria and Babylon are compelled to serve him by the very impulse for conquest which seems to augur the frustration of his redemptive plan in Israel. Their rebellious independence only illuminates more sharply the transcendent power and wisdom of Yahweh, who apportions them their time, and then hurls them back into nothingness (Is 10:5 ff., 14:5 ff., 30:27 ff., 37:22 ff., 44:24–45:13, 46:9 ff.; Jer 25:8–16, 27:5, 51:59 ff.; Hag 2:6 ff.; Zech 2:1 ff.).

Israel believes in the immediate dependence of history, of mankind and the whole of creation, on the controlling wisdom and power of Yahweh, who works purposefully toward the accomplishment of his plan, and brooks no contradiction of his authority. Yahweh's lordship of history is seen not so much as a blessing expected in the future, but as a reality of the present moment. His creative activity did not come to an end with the creation of the world; it is a perduring, present reality which effectively orders the world here and now, structuring history according to his wisdom, creating meaning, and thereby enabling Israel to have a history, to make sense of, to discover a coherent past.

Creation is understood as the work of Yahweh's loving kindness (*hesed*); history, therefore, begins and continues as an act of divine *hesed*. Because Yahweh is Lord of history it is possible to speak of the entire earth's being full of his loving kindness (Pss 33:5; 119:64), and to proclaim that his *hesed* is above all his works. (Pss 36:7; 89:14; 145:9). Yahweh's lordship over history means that he gives man's temporal existence coherence, significance and value, rescuing him from oblivion. Thus Yahweh is effectively creating history and ordering the world; it is to this that man must willingly conform in order to have an authentic meaning and history. Man's conformity, therefore, is an acceptance of and *rapport* with Yahweh's loving kindness unfolding itself in history.

The order which the Lord of history has imposed on creation is a dynamic gift of his loving kindness; it is not the yoke of a tyrant. The coherence which his dynamic order has given human existence and the whole of creation constitutes the vehicle of revelation; it is the meaningful structure of history in which Israel encounters its loving Yahweh and thereby achieves self-understanding and identification as his people (Dt 4:5–8, 32–37). Israel acknowledges Yahweh's dynamic ordering of creation as the saving grace of his love which constitutes her history, and assures her salvation. Yahweh's love is the power which upholds the present order of the universe, creating history for his people, Israel. Obedience to Yahweh's laws, expressing his saving order, is a necessary condition for participating in his redemptive action in history. Obedience is an entering into the structuring salvation activity of Yahweh's love which constitutes that history, endowing the human past, present, and future with coherence and the intelligibility of redemption.

The certainty of Yahweh's love, however, was constantly being endangered by an ever-deepening sense of sin which made men incapable of seeing in Yahweh's lordship over history anything but the threat of retributive justice. Historical misfortunes were interpreted as divine punishment for outrage done to Yahweh or to others (Mi 5:14; Dt 32:35, 41, 43; Jer 11:20; 20:12; Ez 25:12). The only rational attitude to incomprehensible misfortune was to bow to the divine displeasure (2 S 15:26). Elements of chaos disrupting the order of history, such as an extraordinary public calamity, are ascribed to God (Ex 21:13; 8:15; 1 S 6:5). Despite unintelligible, chaos-bringing events, such as the Exile, the coherence of Israel's self-understanding in history perdures. Yahweh is still lord of history, even though Israel's sins may temporarily obscure his lordship. Historical calamities, apparently destroying Israel, are manifestations of the displeasure of Yahweh's unsearchable greatness, and as such transcend human understanding.

Yahweh's lordship of history means that his creative action endowing the universe with meaning never ceases; even if Israel cannot immediately comprehend the significance of a particular historical calamity, she believes that it is not without meaning. There can never be any question of blind rage or despotic caprice in Yahweh's lordship of history. There is no historical event which does not have an explanation in terms of Yahweh's creative wisdom; the lord of history incorporates every historical event into his redemptive action. The sea of chaos and darkness is under his control; and just as history began when Yahweh gave it meaning, he continues to embrace the chaos-bringing events of history into his creative redemptive plan. His wisdom and power controls even that which seems to be beyond his lordship, even that which is beyond Israel's immediate understanding.

The Lord of history proclaims his universal sovereignty through Israel, the nation constituted by its recognition and response to Yahweh's lordship in history. The divine order is represented in Israel as opposed to the chaos of heathenism. The Lord of history establishes a dynamic world-order which saves all who come within its compass, inasmuch as it assures a direct relation to Yahweh. Through Israel, the incarnation of and witness to the divine order, the Lord of history's blessing would work outwards to all the families of the earth (Gen 12:3; 28:14). Israel is the priestly nation mediating to the Gentiles access to the Lord of history (Is 61:5, 6, 9), who has imposed his order on the cosmos as the perfect expression of his power in creation. Israel proclaims the order which Yahweh has manifested in her history as evidence that he is the Lord of history, holding all things in his hands, guiding toward a unity of all life, in which the meaning and goal of human existence is to find fulfilment. Israel's claims were not merely arbitrary or contingent; they were based on a cosmic order fitting both the individual and the nation into an intelligible, universal system in which the meaning of history is revealed.

The prophets adopt the mythological concepts of the Chaos-monster and its slaying at the hands of the Creator of the universe, transferring them to the subjugation of tyrant nations and their rulers by Yahweh (Is 17:12 ff.; 14:12; Na 1 f.; Ez 38 f.). The prophets sketch the evil in man in terms of a demonic cosmic power, embracing in itself all that rejects the Lord of history, and strives against Yahweh's world-order for the domination of the earth. (Is 5:26 ff.; 8:9 f.; 14:26 ff.; 28:14 ff.; Jer 4–6; Zeph 1:2 ff.; Jl 2:1 ff.). Israel's sins, from this point of view, are interpreted as taking sides in a cosmic conflict against Yahweh. Any nation which rejected the exclusive sovereignty of the Lord of history had forfeited the right to exist (Jer 11:9). Isaiah identifies

Israel's incomprehension of the prophetic proclamation of what Yahweh was doing in history with Israel's hardness of heart which results when a people has severed relations with their God. Sin renders Israel incapable of interpreting Yahweh's action in history, precisely because it is an alienation from Yahweh from whom Israel's historical understanding proceeds. (Is 7:9; 28:16; 28:11; 29:9 ff.; Jer 2:25; 2:3; 6:7–15; 8:4 ff.; 13:23.) Because of Israel's sin and moral blindness, history appears as an incoherent, incomprehensible chaos of events.

According to the prophetic interpretation of history, Yahweh's lordship of history is resisted by the anti-God powers. It is in history that Yahweh's struggle to implement his lordship is to reach its consummation. All the events of the past are understood as a connected series, reaching out toward an ultimate decision and final reckoning. The prophets appreciated the real significance of the contemporary situation, which they regarded as a separate phase of Yahweh's struggle to implement his lordship in history. Nothing in the unfolding of history is a matter of indifference; everything leads to the dénouement of the cosmic drama. At every moment, human conduct acquires its own eternal importance and is subjected to the binding obligation of decision. History is taken seriously as the once-for-all reality ordained by Yahweh and pressing for decision. Men must take sides in the cosmic struggle; their choice will be of final and absolute importance.

At the same time, human decisions are not the determining elements of history. Yahweh, the transcendent Lord of history, is omnipotent; he will accomplish his purpose in history despite hostile powers and the disobedience of his people. Yahweh's lordship means that history is always coherent and meaningful, even if Israel's sinfulness occasionally obscures her vision of his wonderful purpose. Proof of his effective lordship of history is that he is able, in the midst of the break-up of the old world, to inaugurate new developments, a new world-order, a second creation. Yahweh, the creator, transforms the world through history; his work of transformation is witnessed by the prophets' radical criticism of the contemporary situation and reaching out toward that enduring order of existence guaranteed by Yahweh's promises.

A genuine comprehension of history, grasping the purpose of its creator, is only possible through participation in the miraculous reality of the divine world. In so far as the People of God are plunged into the sphere of the marvellous, of the spirit of Yahweh, can they grasp the significance of their polyhedral historical experience. All human striving to comprehend the chaos of historical experience is mere foolishness, unless Yahweh himself reveals his transcendent purpose through his prophets who interpret his action in history. Israel's understanding of her historical experience gives coherence to what would otherwise be a chaotic flux of unrelated incidents. Yahweh's communication of an understanding of what he is accomplishing in history, creates history. The prophet, speaking the word of God, is Yahweh's agent; he communicates a new understanding of the divine-human relationship and of history as intermediary of their communication. Both human speech and history have spiritual significance as instruments for spirit's expression; history is just as apt an instrument for God as the human tongue is for man. Because Yahweh transcends history, and is not limited to an understanding of a particular segment of the past, present or future, he alone comprehends the totality and coherence of the entire historical procss from creation to the Last Day; therefore, he alone can communicate the meaning of the entire process and thereby enable Israel to interpret historical events within the framework of a determined, coherent historical structure, in which Yahweh stands at the beginning and end, guiding all according to his saving purpose.

The concepts of creation and history, of the Creator and the Lord of history, are correlative. Yahweh has created the universe according to an order that is dynamic and saving. Yahweh is constantly achieving his cosmic order in a victory over the forces of chaos that is daily renewed. Israel looks to the ultimate lordship of the creator over the forces of chaos, and a restoration of the primordial cosmic order. Chaos and all it represents are not primal; creation is the continuing process whereby the Lord of history gives meaning and coherence to the existing universe. The powers of chaos are mythological personifications of the natural forces governed by the Lord of history (Ps 74:12-17). The prophets applied the creation theme to eschatology, where it became a type of future salvation (Is 17:12-14; 51:9-16; 65:17; 66:22, Hb 3; Apoc 21:1,5). Because creation is effected by God's successive utterances, St. John refers to Gen 1 in his theology of the Word of God found in the prologue to his Gospel. History begins, meaning emerges with the Word of God, which for Israel is the key to the interpretation of history.

The imagery of the creation story is especially suggestive for interpreting Yahweh's creative action in history, for these subsequent actions will always be analogous to the original creation. The chaos imagery is important because it is the foil against which creation takes place; it enables some understanding of creation by antithesis. It is what creative action dispels. Whenever Yahweh acts in history, he acts creatively. He will always be intervening in a situation where there are elements of the original chaos state, of the formless, the unorganized, the meaningless, the empty, the incoherent. Some historical counterpart of that primeval ocean, surrounding the universe as the fearful, menacing, disruptive power beyond human comprehension, will always be the context of divine action in history. Elements of the primeval Deep (*tehom*), of the empty chaos (*tohu wabhohu*), the formless darkness—expressions which are as close as Hebrew could come to describing absolute nothingness—will always characterize divine action in subsequent creation analogies interpreting God's action in history. They will represent, analogously, the state of affairs prior to divine intervention; it is a situation to which God brings meaning, coherence, the grace of a new creation, a new beginning, a restructuring of a new existence, against which the prior state of affairs was in some aspect a *tohu wabbohu.*

Psalm 136 is a commentary on the divine creation of history. The psalm expresses gratitude to Yahweh for his threefold creation: the creation of the world, the rescue from Egypt, and the conquest of Canaan. With each of these three creative acts, the Lord of history wrests meaning from the meaningless: the existing world emerges from empty chaos, Israel from the Sheol of Egypt, and the promised land from the desert. Yahweh's three acts are understood as works of creation extending the realm of meaning. Beginning with the act of creation, the meaning of history develops as God continues his work of creation throughout the stages of history. Because Yahweh is the Lord of creation he is the Lord of history. Psalm 136 surveys the Lord of history's creation-activity from the beginning of time to the establishment of his people in the land of promise. Meaning grows simultaneously with the Lord of history's continuing act of creation.

Meaning ramifies from an experiential nucleus: "A wandering Aramean was my father; and he went down into Egypt, and sojourned there" (Dt 26:4). The Exodus expands into the patriarchal history. To be brought out of Egypt, Israel first had to come into it. Meaning radiates from the Exodus center of Israel's historical experience. Israel understands its history as the creation of the will and wisdom of God. This understanding of her own historical experience becomes the key to comprehending world-history as meaningful in so far as it reveals the ordering will and wisdom of Yahweh in every stage of the process, including the creation of the world itself. Beyond the history of the cosmos, therefore, appears the Lord of history who by his word called Israel and history into existence. Through history he reveals himself as Creator, Lord of history and Savior, a God who creates, controls, and saves when he

acts in history. For Israel, Yahweh is the transcendent answer to
the coherence of the cosmos, historical events and her own continuing existence. Without Yahweh as Creator, Lord of history,
and Savior, these three aspects of Israel's experience would be meaningless. He is the explanation for the meaning Israel finds in the
order of the cosmos, history and her own existence. He is a continuing explanation for this threefold, continuing order which is
daily renewed; and without his constant, miraculous intervention
the cosmos, history, and Israel would disintegrate and lapse into
the primordial meaninglessness symbolized by the dark waters of
the primeval Deep (*tehom*) and empty chaos (*tohu wabhohu*).
Ultimately, it is Yahweh who pours into existence whatever meaning Israel finds.

The emergence and recession of meaning characterize the dramatic pattern of Genesis. The emergence of order and meaning
embodied in the creation account is followed by a recession of
meaningful order in the story of the Fall and the Tower of Babel.
The Lord of history gives new meaning to human existence when
he calls Abraham from Ur to Canaan. A second recession from the
meaningful order of Israel's historical fulfilment occurs when repeated famines drive first Abraham to a temporary settlement in
Egypt and later the Jacob clans to a more permanent one. The
second recession concludes with the oath of the sons of Israel to
takes the bones of Joseph with them, when they return to the
promised land. Creation and Exodus are successive phases in the
unfolding order that gives meaning to existence and history.
Genesis is also the prelude to the second Exodus, the wandering
in the desert and the conquest of Canaan. Psalm 136 reveals the
fulfilment of Yahweh's creative ordering of history in the constitution of Israel as a people and its occupation of the promised land.
Thus, the fulfilment and meaning of Genesis is seen from the
historical present in which the post-exilic redactors still live; it is
seen from the historical present in which Israel is a nation and

possesses its land. All historical interpretation involves the understanding of the significance of the beginning from the end; for, it is in the present that the past achieves its temporary fulfilment and historical meaning emerges. Israel's beginnings are interpreted in the light of subsequent developments.

The present is evidence of the past; it is the outcome of the past which provides the basis for reinterpreting history. Consequently, Israel's understanding of her present existence constitutes her history, her interpretation of the evidence of history. Because the past is actively terminating in each moment of the present, it is continually offering evidence of its meaning. The continuing order of the cosmos is evidence that Yahweh is continually ordering the cosmos in a perduring act of creation. Yahweh *is* creator because he is here and now creating. Similarly, Yahweh is Lord of history because he is here and now structuring Israel's temporal existence so that all events have meaning in terms of his covenant relationship with Israel. Israel's structured present existence is precisely what it is, because it is the continuing terminal point of her structured past. Israel's present, structured according to the covenant, is perduring evidence of the coherence and meaning of her past. Israel is capable of having a history, of interpreting her past, only because she comprehends the significance of her present existence in history.

Israel's history is not static. Israel is always capable of understanding her past more profoundly, because she is capable of penetrating the meaning of her present existence more thoroughly. The complex structure of historical events and causes that are causing Israel to be what it is, are always contemporary; therefore, a growth of self-knowledge in the present implies a better comprehension of her past. It implies that the meaning of Israel's history grows in the present. Israelite history, for example, does not end with the conquest of Canaan. The prophets conceived a community under God that no longer had to reside in Canaan at

all cost. The prophets did not accept the *status quo* as the goal of
Israel's God-directed history. Had the goal of Israel's history been
considered achieved with the conquest of Canaan or the establishment of the Davidic monarchy, the whole succeeding period would
have been regarded as a conservation of something already accomplished; it would have lost the forward thrust that characterizes
a movement striving to attain its goal. The prophets recognized
that communion with God, the goal of Israel's history, had by no
means been realized in contemporary Israel. The ideal divine-
human relationship left much to be desired. The prophetic recognition of the need for a new and more complete union with God
saved Israel from turning in on itself; it preserved her from
stagnation and provided her with a new sense of purpose.

The prophets were charged with a new sense of the reality of
God which would ground a reinterpretation of Israel's past, in
which the nation's history was regarded as a history of failures, sins
and resistance to the claims of Yahweh. Because the prophets could
not accept with complacency the *status quo,* they radically criticized
Israel for her historical ungraciousness and disloyalty to Yahweh.
They frankly confessed and bitterly castigated the infidelity, idolatry and immorality of the people (Is 63–64). Contemporary life
offered ample historical evidence of disastrous effects of Israel's
historical sins. The present testified to Israel's historical failures to
abide by her covenant with Yahweh. Israel's history of resistance
to God's graciousness was the one real obstacle to her receiving
the fullness of his salvation. The only way that present evils could
be put right would be by a complete commitment to Yahweh.
Mere human resources were inadequate for achieving communion
with God. Only an existence that is truly in accord with the spirit
of Yahweh, one which manifests the effects of his divine life,
transcends the limitations and inevitable failures of the merely
human.

If the prophets understood the past in terms of the present, they also recognized that the present was not fully meaningful or intelligible. They recognized that the present pointed beyond itself; that the meaning of the present becomes more fully comprehensible in the future. The prophets looked to the future for the emergence of the fuller meaning for what they grasped of the present. They implicitly recognized that the comprehension of what God is doing in history grows with time and meditation; on the other hand, they believed that God does not do everything at once. He reveals his meaning in history according to the special character and conditions of man's receptive capacity. Because the prophets recognized in their contemporary situation the deeper meaning and further significance of the past, they were able to understand that the meaning of the present would emerge more fully, it would be fulfilled, in the future.

The political subjection of Israel offered a grave challenge to the traditional idea of the supremacy of Yahweh: did it not imply that he was inferior in power to the gods of the Gentiles? This was the challenge confronting the prophets. They proclaimed Yahweh as the Controller of the destinies of all nations; furthermore, he directed them with reference to his people Israel. Consequently, the prophets believed that the full significance of contemporary events would emerge at a later date. They could never have deduced the concept of Yahweh's lordship of world-history from their historical situation; rather, it preceded it, constituting a *datum* of faith in the light of which the prophets interpreted the meaning of the situation.

The apocalyptic second half of the Book of Daniel expresses a view of world-history in which meaning would fully emerge with Yahweh's ultimate triumph over the forces of evil. The Book was written in the context of the conflict between traditionalists and the would-be Hellenizers, backed by the Gentile ruler Antiochus IV. Israel understood the historical political struggle in terms of the cosmic warfare between the forces of good and evil. Israel has an absolute trust in Yahweh's power to save; there is no need to substitute a reliance on human resources, which would be a practical negation of the Covenant. Despite political weakness and complete subjection, Israel believes that the full significance of her contemporary situation will emerge when Yahweh's eternally ordained redemptive plan has been achieved at the end of history. Israel believes that the meaning of Yahweh's plan *is emerging;* in fact, history shall have come to a close when it has fully emerged.

The Lord of history communicates the meaning of history through men interpreting history. The patriarchs were a series of men who claimed attention because they spoke in the name of the Lord; the word of the Lord had come to them, enabling them to comprehend the fact and meaning of his action in history. The prophets were intimately related to the emergence of God's word in history: they were his spokesmen, called and elected by his word, through which they communicated the meaning of history. When they spelled out the significance of history, they proclaimed that history had an ultimate meaning, and that God had elected Israel to play a role in the historical events that contribute to the ultimate realization of this meaning. They shared the common belief in God's lordship over history; they communicated to Israel the meaning of her historical experience. They believed Yahweh is the Creator, the Lord of history, who reveals himself, speaks his word, in acts. The word of God is his deed. Historical events are meaningful because of their place in the redemptive plan.

Israel had historical meaning in terms of her election by his word. God's election gave Israel's historical experience a meaning in his plan. Election pointed to the future, so that the message of the prophets interpreting history, became inevitably eschatological; it implied a keen sense of historical development, evolution and the growth and fulfilment of meaning in history. Israel's eschatological hopes recapitulate the creation theme; they look forward to the creation of a new covenant (Lk 22:20), a new Israel (1 Pet 2:9–10) and their proclamation throughout time. God's word, interpreting history, continues the work of creation in a process where he gives meaning to man's historical experience. John L. McKenzie remarks that the Israelite conception of history is a process governed by Yahweh and moves to a term intended by Him; that history is also "the work of Yahweh," a reality which fulfills the utterance of Yahweh. The word of history is dynamic and dianoetic: dynamic in that it accomplishes what it signifies, dianoetic in that it makes the historical process intelligible. History, McKenzie continues, is the revelation of the purpose of Yahweh, and even more; as the word is a release of the psychic energy of the personality so history is a revelation of the character and personality of Him whose Word it is. The word affirms not only the thing signified but also the person who utters it (John L. McKenzie, S.J., develops this concept in his article, "The Word of God in the Old Testament," *Theological Studies*, 21 [1960], 199–200).

The word of God which the prophet speaks is addressed to the life and problems of his community. It may involve an extrapolation from the present scene, whereby divine commitment to the future is proclaimed in divine judgment or in redemption, or in both; or it may sweep backward in time to bring past events forcefully into the present through reinterpretation of their relevance. But any reference to the past or the future is directly related to, or contingent upon, the present and it is intended primarily for the contemporary community.

At the same time, the prophets understand that meaning is emerging to an ultimate fulfilment because Yahweh is still creating; his power and wisdom are constantly operative (Is 40:21). Creation is regarded as something which vitally regards man's present existence. When speaking of the creative power of God, Isaiah uses the present participle, which stresses the permanent, contemporary aspect of creation: "I am Yahweh who *am making* all things, who alone stretch out the heavens, who spread out the earth—who is with me?" (Is 44:24). In the present, past and future, Yahweh is and remains creator, giving the temporal universe its stability, coherence and meaning. It is the prophets who interpret the meaning of his on-going creation; they proclaim the significance of the past around the direction of the future. Israel's past makes sense in the light of its present under Yahweh pointing toward a future in which the full meaning of history would ultimately emerge.

The progressive emergence of God's word creates a progressive understanding of the meaning of Israel's historical experience. God is where he acts and he acts where he is; his word is his act, as in the creation of his people in the first Exodus event. His constant word recreates and holds his community in existence; it reveals the meaning of history. Israel represents the community of those who interpret history according to the word of God; to interpret history in any other way would represent a divorce from the community united by the word of God. Belonging to the community of Israel meant belonging to those who share in the meaning of what God is doing in history, as specifically proclaimed by the prophets; it implies a conscious sharing in the same interpretation of history.

Israel, thus, is unique among the nations in that its view of history is determined by a person, and not by a theory or philosophy about the nature of man and the world. A personal God controls history. Yahweh creates history, and Israel identifies itself as the people who acknowledge him as Lord of history. For Israel the ultimate meaning of man, the universe and history is found in a Person.

The Christian community, under the same Lord of history, views the past as a series of experiences which have their meaning "according to the definite plan and foreknowledge of God" (Acts

2:23). It affirms its continuity with Israel: "In many and various ways God spoke of old to our father by the prophets; but in these last days he has spoken to us by his Son, whom he appointed the heir of all things" (Heb 1:1–2). The history of Israel is re-interpreted; its ultimate significance emerges in Christ, the Word of God, the Lord of history, who alone comprehends the full significance of history as its beginning and end. Through Christ, the Christian conceives history with an openness toward the future rather than in nostalgic reminiscence of the past. The atheist understands time as passing from the future into the past, carrying him inevitably toward oblivion; whereas, the Christian conceives history as that which leads him with the living Christ into the future. Through Christ, who passed through the jaws of death, who overcame the pastness of the past, the Christian is enabled to live toward the future in hope of the fulfillment of promise given to faith. Time does not carry the Christian to oblivion, nor is history the Great Destroyer; rather, history is the *locus* of man's redemptive encounter with God and bears witness to the unfolding of God's gracious promises.

15

On Being Lord and Servant: "I Never Knew You"

"Not everyone who says to me, 'Lord, Lord,' shall enter the kingdom of heaven, but he who does the will of my Father who is in heaven. On that day many will say to me, 'Lord, Lord, did we not prophesy in your name, and cast out demons in your name, and do many mighty works in your name?' And then I will declare to them, 'I never knew you; depart from me, you evildoers!'" (Mt 7:21–23).

Thus Matthew presents what is perhaps the most terrifying human situation in Scripture: the mistaken assumption of friendship with Christ at the judgment. The situation appears paradoxical. How can Christ fail to recognize those who know him and have received his special charisms? The charisms of prophecy, exorcism and miracles are reasons why the unrecognized protest that Christ should know them. Matthew teaches, however, that the recognition of Christ as Lord and the reception of his gifts are no guarantee that men are Christ's friends.

An appreciation of this pericope demands an investigation of its theological context in Matthew's eschatology of the judgment.

The expression "on that day" indicates that the pericope is eschatological and refers to the final judgment when history shall be consummated and its purpose realized. Matthew's eschatological judgment pericopes focus on the final division of men into those who enter the kingdom and those who are rejected. Matthew's twenty-fifth chapter contains three eschatological pericopes: the foolish and wise bridesmaids (1–13), the parable of the talents (14–30), the final judgment (31–46). This chapter is, therefore, especially helpful for an understanding of Matthew's theology of the judgment, which constitutes the doctrinal context of the "I never knew you" pericope.

Matthew underscores his eschatological doctrine in the last public words of John the Baptist and the last public words of Jesus, in which both speak of the judgment. The Baptist describes the Judge: "His winnowing fork is in his hand, and he will clear his threshing floor and gather his wheat into the granary, but the chaff he will burn with unquenchable fire" (3:11). Christ's final words are: "And they (i.e., the wicked) will go away into eternal punishment, but the righteous into eternal life" (25:46).

It is in the prospect of the judgment that the Baptist warns the Pharisees and demands that they "Bear fruit that befits repentance" (3:8), because "every tree that does not bear good fruit is cut down and thrown into the fire" (3:10). The criterion of genuine repentance is that renewal of life, that change of mind and heart, manifest in a man's words and actions. Matthew recalls the Baptist's words in his criterion for distinguishing true from false teachers: "Every tree that does not bear good fruit is cut down and thrown into the fire. Thus you will know them by their fruits" (7:19–20). He does not teach Christ who does not live Christ. Christ is where he acts; and he is truly known where he is truly operative.

The call of the Baptist (3:2) and Jesus (4:17) for repentance is in terms of the approaching judgment, for which a merciful God has allotted time for decision. The time for renewal and preparation had been prophesied by Malachi: "Behold, I will send you Elijah the prophet before the great and terrible day of the Lord comes. And he will turn the hearts of the fathers to their children and the hearts of children to their fathers, lest I come and smite the land with a curse" (Mal 4:5–6).

Both the Baptist and Jesus, after announcing the kingdom, call disciples whose function it shall be to prepare the world for the day of the Lord (4:18–22). "The day of the Lord" and the expression *"Then* will the kingdom of heaven" (25:1) both refer to the judgment and indicate Matthew's eschatological doctrine.

Matthew's eschatology contrasts present appearances with future reality. God's standards are not those of men. He reverses the positions and judgments that men have made for themselves: "The last will be first, and the first last" (20:16). It is the poor in spirit, the man who mourns, is meek, thirsts for justice, is merciful, pure of heart, a peacemaker and persecuted for righteousness' sake, that finds favor with God. The man of the Beatitudes is first in the kingdom of God, even though his way of life, measured by a purely worldly standard, makes him appear as the least of men.

The Beatitudes (5:3–10) indicate "the fruit that befits repentance" (3:8), the basic attitudes which define a man's life and prepare him for a favorable judgment on the day of the Lord. Matthew implies that the man of the Beatitudes is he whom the Judge recognizes as his friend: "Blessed are the poor in spirit, for theirs is the kingdom of heaven" (5:3). It is this man who shall be comforted, shall inherit the earth, shall be satisfied, shall obtain mercy, see God and be called the son of God.

The theological logic of Matthew implies that, if the kingdom of heaven is promised to the poor of spirit, it is closed to those who claim admission on the basis of their possessions. Those who cried "Lord, Lord" claim the kingdom of heaven in virtue of their charisms, their possessions (7:22). Although the charisms are ex-traordinary gifts, it would seem they had been possessed with the wrong spirit. Had their recipients been poor in spirit, the Lord would have made good his promise to give them the kingdom of heaven; instead, they are told "I never knew you." The judgment is according to what a man has become, what he is; it is not ac-cording to what he possesses. A man cannot buy his way into the kingdom of heaven, even with charisms. The poor in spirit do not regard their gifts as a claim against Christ, as a way of "forcing his hand."

Matthew's eschatological pericope corrects the false assumption that the mere recognition that Christ is Lord and the possession of extraordinary gifts within the Church suffice as a criterion of com-munion with Christ. Contrary to a superficial human standard of judging, Matthew teaches that the esteem a man may enjoy in the Church because of his charisms may be concomitant with his absolute alienation from Christ. This is typical of that contrast between present appearances and future reality which characterizes Matthew's eschatology.

There is a remarkable harmony of doctrine between Matthew and Paul on the relation of charisms and charity. Paul also teaches that charisms are an insufficient criterion of union with Christ: "And if I have prophetic powers, and understand all mysteries and all knowledge, and if I have all faith, so as to remove moun-tains, but have not love, I am nothing" (1 Cor 13:2). Paul's description of love—the ultimate criterion of communion with Christ—squares in many respects with the attitudes of mind and heart praised in the Beatitudes: "Love is patient and kind; love is not jealous or boastful; it is not arrogant or rude. Love does not insist on its own way; it is not irritable or resentful; it does not rejoice at wrong, but rejoices in the right. Love bears all things, believes all things, hopes all things, endures all things" (1 Cor 13:4–7).

Matthew's "Lord, Lord" pericope becomes more intelligible in terms of his theology of the Beatitudes and lordship of Christ. It is the poor of spirit who possess the kingdom of heaven; it is not those who claim the kingdom of heaven in virtue of their possessions. The former are they whom the Lord possesses; the latter are they who believe they possess the Lord, merely because of their faith and charisms which enable them to recognize who he is and to work wonders in his name. Although some call Christ "Lord," their attitudes and way of life imply that they are "Lord." They represent the pride of man arrogating the lordship of the kingdom to himself; whereas the poor of spirit belong to the kingdom because the Lord possesses them as good and faithful servants: "Well done, good and faithful servant; you have been faithful over a little, I will set you over much; enter into the joy of your Lord" (19:21).

When Christ as Judge declares, "I never knew you," he is responding to those who are falsely calling him their "Lord." Christ never knew them as their Lord. In their lives, he was never what they say he was. If they had been poor of spirit, if they had been good and faithful servants, he would have actually been their Lord. They are talking about a relationship which never really existed; for, the word, "Lord," bespeaks a relationship between persons. On the contrary, they were never servants; they were autonomous; they were their own lords, leading their own egocentric, independent lives, *as if* there were no real Lord of the universe before whom they would ultimately recognize themselves as men who had never been servants, and who had never had a Lord.

The final words of the judgment pericope contribute to a further understanding: "Depart from me, you evildoers" (7:23). Matthew clearly implies that if Christ had been their Lord, they would not have been evildoers. Matthew is implicitly explaining what the lordship of Christ means; namely, that Christ possesses a man's inner core, his whole heart, mind, and soul, so that a man's entire way of life is a response to the Lord, who guides, protects, and lovingly cares for him. Consequently, this man's response is one of loving "service," not servility; and it is incompatible with evildoing. His entire way of life is essentially a response to and a communion with a Lord who serves: "the Son of men came not to be served but to serve" (20:28). In this sense, he is following and serving a Lord who is a Servant because he loves him. The lordship of Christ is, therefore, incompatible with evildoing.

Matthew expresses the active lordship of Christ in three ways in the verses immediately preceding and following the judgment pericope. Christ is actually a man's Lord when the man follows the narrow way (7:13–14), produces "good fruit" (7:15–20) and builds on the solid foundation of his word (7:24–27); in other words, a man bases his entire life on Christ. If the gift of faith, therefore, enables a man to recognize that Christ is Lord, it also demands that Christ must *be* Lord. Matthew conceives the life of the Christian as a vital evolution in which Christ is ever more becoming Lord; for the narrow way is to be *followed,* good fruit is to be *produced* and a solid foundation is for a *construction.* The Christian is committed to a Lord who is ever intensifying his personal relationship with him, so that the Christian is, properly speaking, constantly becoming more Christian. He is a Lord who *leads, produces, constructs;* he continues his work of creation in those who have accepted him as their Lord, because he is a living Lord, one who acts where he is. But he is also a Lord whose action has the special quality of love; he is a Lord who serves wherever and in whomever he acts. This means his action is always that of creating. And where his action is personally welcomed, the lordship of Christ begins the work of a new creation in the service of a new man who is becoming a son of God: "Blessed are the peacemakers, for they shall be called the sons of God" (5:9).

The eschatological pericope of the foolish and wise bridesmaids has the same implications as the above three sayings with respect to the lordship of Christ. The foolish bridesmaids, like those who possessed the charisms, also recognized Christ as "Lord, Lord" (25:11). The parallel continues with the Lord's reply, "Truly, I do not know you" (25:12). The foolish bridesmaids were unprepared for the Lord; they are alienated from him. Even though they recognize him, they never personally knew him as their Lord, as one who had creatively structured their lives so that they might be called the sons of God. Consequently, it is false on their part to call Christ their Lord; they had never known him as their "Lord."

There is a difference, however, in these two remarkably similar pericopes. Those who possess the charisms are specifically condemned as evil doers; whereas, unpreparedness is the failure of the foolish bridesmaids. The latter would seem to have been guilty of indifference and spiritual sloth.

The contrast between the wise and foolish bridesmaids echoes the contrast which Matthew has made between the wise man (*phronimos*) who builds on rock and the foolish man (*moros*) who builds on sand. In this contrast (7:24–27), the wise man is he who lives according to Christ's teaching; the foolish man is he who disobeys. The parallelism implies that the wise and foolish bridesmaids are distinguished from one another on the same basis. Secondly, the parallelism of the parable of the bridesmaids with the pericope concerning those who possessed the charisms, would imply that both were unrecognized for the same basic reason. Both had heard the word of God; both knew that Christ was Lord. However, both had remained outside the effective lordship of Christ. If Christ's words express and communicate Christ, then a life of communion with the Lord postulates a life incarnating his word.

Matthew does not see good works as something extrinsic to the Christian, as if Christ demanded a stockpile of good deeds and were indifferent to the individual himself. Matthew is concerned about the quality of the fruit, precisely because it is evidence of the quality of the tree. What the Christian says and does, or fails to say and do, is evidence indicating whether or not Christ is actually his Lord. Because the Lord is a living Person who actively serves, he will always give evidence of his creative presence in the lives of those who love him. And the quality of this evidence has been expressed in his word, in the Beatitudes, the great commandment and entire way of life.

It is good to acknowledge Christ as Lord. No one is condemned for saying "Lord, Lord"; however, men are condemned for lying. Those who say "Lord, Lord" are reprehensible because this affirmation does not correspond to any interior reality; it does not correspond to the existential truth of their lives. A man's words, in this respect, derive their truth and value from the reality of the relationship with the Lord which he affirms. Those saying "Lord, Lord" affirm a personal relationship which is non-existent, and incompatible with their condemnation as evildoers. From a lying mouth, the false claim to Christ as "Lord" merits only condemnation.

Matthew's "Lord, Lord" pericope (7:21–23) reveals an insistence on religious sincerity and genuine interior union with God found throughout his Gospel. Matthew's condemnation of false, nominal Christians is matched by his denunciation of scribes and Pharisees for the same reasons: "they preach, but do not practice" (23:4). The ostensibly pious words and deeds of the Pharisees do not correspond to any genuine internal love of God or neighbor: "They do all their deeds to be seen by men" (23:5). Consequently, their words and deeds are lies, false evidence for an internal communion with God that does not exist: "Woe to you, scribes and Pharisees, hypocrites! for you cleanse the outside of the cup and of the plate, but inside they are full of extortion and rapacity. You blind Pharisees! *first cleanse the inside* of the cup and of the plate, that the outside also may also be clean!" (23:25–26).

Because Matthew's Gospel is written for Christians, it may be safely assumed that his repeated condemnation of scribes and Pharisees for religious hypocrisy is not so much a denunciation of this vice in the Jewish community as in the Christian community. It is Christians who are condemned for saying "Lord, Lord," when in reality they are evildoers. Matthew undoubtedly relates Christ's condemnation of religious insincerity among the Pharisees because of its relevance to the "Pharisees" of the Christian community.

Christ's declaration, "I never knew you," affirms the non-existence of any personal relationship between Lord and servant, even though this relationship is implied by those with charisms and the foolish bridesmaids. In this statement of non-recognition, Matthew presents Christ as a judge who does not cause the alienation of others, but rather as a judge who merely affirms an existing state of alienation. Christ drives no one away from himself and the kingdom. When he asserts that he does not know those crying "Lord, Lord," he implies that there is a continuity between a man's habitual frame of mind and his final state, between a way of life which the Lord had never personally influenced and the final declaration of the truth about a man's way of life.

Because the alienated recognize Christ as Lord, they are guilty. They know what "Lord" means, and, therefore, they know the role Christ should have had in their lives. Matthew's eschatological parable of the talents is the key for understanding the mystery of alienation and why Christ becomes Lord for some and not for others.

This is basically a parable about responsiveness. It explains the meaning of love as responsiveness; it explains why some men respond to the Lord and others fail. It is the story of a Lord who acts and of the reaction he expects. The faithful servants are totally responsive. The Lord's action evokes their total reaction.

The Lord's love and generosity evokes theirs. The Lord's gift of five talents evokes the total, perfect response of five talents; his gift of two talents evokes the same personal, total response. This is Matthew's way of explaining the love of Christ. The Lord's gift makes his servants' response possible; his loving initiative enables man's loving response. And the Lord expects the loving responsiveness of his servants, precisely because he is lovable, and has taken the initiative in loving and providing the means for his servants' reciprocity. His servants have nothing which he has not generously given them. He expects a total responsiveness in terms of everything that he has given them; for *everything* they possess manifests his love for them, therefore, *everything* they possess is a reason for loving him, a reason for responsivness.

This parable (25:14–30) expresses concretely what the Great Commandment states abstractly: "You shall love the Lord your God with your whole heart, your whole soul, and your whole mind" (22:37). The "good and faithful" servant is the incarnation of the Commandment. He is perfectly responsive; everything he has received from his Lord—his whole heart, mind, and soul—have become reasons for his loving him.

The unloving servant considered his Lord as hard and unlovable: "Master, I knew you to be a hard man, reaping where you did not sow, and gathering where you did not winnow; so I was afraid, and I went and hid your talent in the ground" (25:24). His failure to respond to the graciousness and generosity of his Lord is symbolized by his failure to produce one talent. Because he had received one talent, he was capable of responding with one talent; that would have been his total and perfect response. He rationalizes his ingratitude and hardness of heart with the lie that his Lord is "a hard man." Because he fears his Lord, he will not reciprocate according to his capacity; therefore, his life is sterile. He is unloving and therefore unproductive. He has not responded to the creative power of the Lord's love, which leads, produces and constructs (7:13-27) in the service of those whom he is creating in his image and likeness as sons.

The parable of the talents explicitates what is implicit in the "Lord, Lord" pericope. In both cases, the Lord had given gifts, whether the charisms or the talent. Despite the Lord's love and generosity, implied by his gifts, both are condemned as evil: "Depart from me, you evildoers" (7:23), and "You wicked and slothful servant . . . cast the worthless servant into the outer darkness" (25:26, 30). Their wickedness is their ingratitude, unresponsiveness, unloving indifference and hardness of heart. Neither had possessed the Lord's gifts in such a way as to win his approval as "good and faithful" servants in an authentic Lord-servant relationship, based on mutual love. Neither served him because neither loved him. Both are culpable because everything they had was a gift, a reason for loving the Lord whose loving initiative had created the possibility and responsibility for their love.

Matthew's account of the final judgment (25:31-46) also helps to explain the "Lord, Lord" pericope. Both the blessed and the cursed ask, "Lord, when did we see you hungry?" (25:37, 44). Both are equally unaware of having had any contact with the Son of Man beforehand. Both shared a common ignorance of the eschatological significance of their actions; nevertheless, both had acted quite differently. The blessed ask, "Lord, when did we see you hungry *and feed you*" (25:37); whereas the cursed ask merely, "Lord, when did we see you hungry or thirsty or a stranger . . . and did not minister to you?" (25:44).

A comparative study of the final judgment and "Lord, Lord" accounts indicates that it is not man's recognition of the Lord that determines his belonging to the kingdom of heaven; it is the Lord's recognition that is decisive. His recognition hinges upon a man's way of life. Consequently, men who are unaware of his presence may be in communion with him; whereas, many who explicitly recognize him as "Lord, Lord" may be completely alienated from him. Therefore, if the Lord recognizes those who helped men in need, Matthew's theology of the judgment implies that those who cry "Lord, Lord" are not recognized because of their failure to serve their neighbor.

Christ is Lord of those who keep his commandments. These are his authentic disciples because they love him with their whole being and their neighbor as themselves. Their lives are the embodiment of all that the Lord has commanded them. Their lives are the fulfilment of his promise, "I am with you always, even to the end of time" (28:19–20). If the Lord recognizes those whose lives have effectively taught others the meaning of his commandments, Matthew would imply that he does not recognize those who do not live according to his word. If he declares, "I never knew you," he simultaneously denies that "I am with you always," because he does not know those who do not keep his commandments. He knows only those in whom he abides as Lord.

The Lord knows those who follow him. This was Matthew's first experience of Christ's lordship: "As Jesus passed by . . . he saw a man called Matthew sitting at the tax office; and he said to him, 'Follow me.' And he rose and followed him" (9:9). The Lord's call is a free gift: "You received without pay, give without pay" (10:8). Matthew, a publican and sinner outside the bounds of the worshipping community, follows the Lord; whereas, those possessing charisms, juridically within the worshipping community, apparently did not follow him. It is only sinners who are called, and therefore it is only sinners who are really capable of following the Lord: "I came not to call the righteous, but sinners" (9:13). If it is the sinner who becomes the Lord's disciple, it is the sinner whom the Lord knows; it is not the man who claims righteousness in virtue of his charismatic gifts within the Church: "Lord, Lord, did we not prophesy in your name, and cast out demons in your name, and do mighty works in your name?" (7:22). The self-righteous are incapable of becoming disciples because they are incapable of being called. It is only the sinners who will follow a Lord promising salvation because they recognize the absolute insufficiency of their own resources.

The lordship of Christ is absolute, demanding the whole heart, mind and soul, a total response of five talents for five, a precedence over all human ties: "Follow me, and let the dead bury their dead" (8:22); "He who loves father or mother more than me is not worthy of me. . . . He who finds his life will lose it, and he who loses his life for my sake will find it" (10:37–39). If this is the authentic Lord-servant relationship, Matthew implies that those crying "Lord, Lord" had never really followed Christ; they had never relinquished their autonomy and self-centeredness, the necessary condition for finding that life which the Lord promises those who follow him. The Lord recognizes the man who loses his life in order to follow him.

Christ is Lord where he acts; and he gives evidence of his lordship where he acts. The Lord is a servant, and the quality of his action is that of creative service. Therefore, discipleship—following the Lord—means to be where the Lord acts; and, because the Lord is a servant, it means to be where the Lord serves. However, the Lord acts in his servant, and serves in his servant. It is in virtue of the Lord's action and service that the disciple acts and serves; because the disciple is where the Lord acts. The Lord-disciple relationship is a dynamic one in which the Lord gives evidence of himself in his disciple. The Lord's evidence is correlative to the disciple's witness: "So everyone who acknowledges me before men, I also will acknowledge before my Father who is in heaven" (10:32–33). Everyone in whom the Lord is giving evidence of himself before men is giving witness to the Lord before men and is being simultaneously acknowledged by the Lord before his Father in heaven. This is the man whom the Lord knows and is recognizing. He is not the evildoer with charisms, who says "Lord, Lord," of whom the Lord can only say "I never knew you." The Lord is not giving evidence of himself in this man; and this man is not giving witness to the Lord. The failure to give witness to the Lord is the failure to bear evidence of his existence. This is the actual denial of the Lord, of his existence and activity, before men of which the Lord speaks when he says, "Whoever denies me before men, I also will deny before my Father who is in heaven" (10:33). "I never knew you," the divine correlative of the human reality, is the Lord's response to man's denial.

Giving witness to Christ before men, therefore, implies more than affirming that he is Lord; it implies more than prophesying, casting out devils and working miracles in his name. One can do all this and still effectively deny the Lord's existence and activity before men.

The Church invokes the Lord when it administers the charisms in his name (7:22), and when it places the baptized under his lordship (28:19). The Church does not believe in a Lord who is waiting inactively in heaven; rather, it believes in a Lord who vitalizes and serves the Church which obeys him. His lordship is his service to the Church; it is that which creates the faith, hope, and love of the Church. The Lord serves his Church in giving it his life, light and salvation. At the same time, Matthew implies that he is not effectively Lord of all the members of the visible Church (7:23); whereas, he is effectively Lord of many outside the visible Church (25:34–40). Christ is effectively Lord of all who accept the service of his creative influence and who, in virtue of his service, are united with him in serving others. In accepting the service of Christ they accept the Servant Christ and his life of serving others.

Christ's lordship is not something external to man. Matthew understands it as the Lord's activity within a man's dynamic, affective core. The Lord is not a remote juridical authority apart from a man's existence and welfare; rather, the Lord is actively present within the mind and heart of a man, personally structuring this man's life according to the spirit of his own life as expressed in the Beatitudes (5:3–10), the Great Commandment (22:36–40), and in all that pleases the Son of Man at the judgment in those "blessed of my Father" who cared for him when he was in need (25:31–46). The entire Gospel of Matthew expresses the life-spirit of the Lord, according to which he is re-creating his "good and faithful" servants into his own image and likeness of a servant.

The Lord-servant relationship is an intimate personal communion: "If any man serve me, let him follow; and *where I am there shall also my servant be,* if any man serve me, him will the Father honor" (Mk 8:34; Mt 10:38). The Lord is where he acts as Lord, and this is in his servant: ". . . where I am there shall also my servant be." The world encounters the Lord in his "good and faithful" servants. Their lives personally express the lordship of Christ, his existence, and activity.

The Lord-servant relationship is a communion with a trinitarian dimension. The Father expresses himself in Christ the Lord, who alone knows and reveals him: "All things have been delivered to me by my Father; and no one knows the Son except the Father; nor does anyone know the Father except the Son, and him to whom the Son chooses to reveal him" (11:27). The Lord, in turn, expresses himself in his "good and faithful" servants who have received his Holy Spirit: ". . . it is not you who speak, but the Spirit of your Father speaking through you" (10:19). The Spirit of God the Father gives evidence of the truth of Christ's lordship in the lives of the "good and faithful" servants through whom the three Persons speak to the world. Therefore, it is only the "good and faithful" servant that is a credible witness to the reality of the Lord; it is not the evildoer who protests his righteousness with his "Lord, Lord." The Spirit of God the Father speaks to the world of the truth of Christ only in those in whom he acts. The Spirit is where he acts, and this is only in the "good and faithful" servant.

Christ's lordship, in Matthew's Gospel, is not arbitrary; it corresponds to the reality of the universe. Christ is the one and only Lord of the universe (23:10). Men are free to accept him or reject him; however, they are not free from the eternal consequences of their decision, ratified at the final judgment (25:31–46). Refusal to accept the actual lordship of Christ is a vain self-assertion based on an illusory sense of independence and autonomy; it is a refusal to accept the reality of the universe, tantamount to arrogating the lordship to oneself in defiance of the divine lordship.

Matthew's eschatological judgment pericopes (e.g., 7:21–23; ch. 25) teach that human pride achieves nothing but an eternal alienation from the Lord which is eternal unhappiness. Because the lordship of Christ is the happiness of the Christian community, Matthew and the other evangelists understand that separation from the Lord, acknowledged at the final judgment, is eternal unhappiness. The Lord-servant relationship expresses the dynamics of that human happiness which the Lord creates in his "good and faithful" servants. Because it is the relationship of happiness, even now experienced in part by the Christian community, its eternal prolongation is understood as eternal happiness. Matthew's theology of the judgment implies a continuum in the temporal-eternal happiness of the "good and faithful" servant, which derives from his Lord-servant relationship. Its correlative is the temporal-eternal unhappiness of the unwilling, unresponsive servant, which derives from his vain rejection of the Lord-servant relationship.

It is the rejection of reality.

Men are ultimately divided according to their response to the lordship of Christ. And they may respond to it without being aware of it: "When did we see you hungry, and feed you?" (25:37). The Lord is eternally calling "Follow me" (9:9) throughout his universe; he is eternally creating the possibility of a response on the part of all rational creatures. In Christ Jesus the Eternal Word speaks, "Follow me," the eternal invitation, the eternal service, the eternal love creating the possibility of the personal response which is eternal happiness for the "good and faithful" servant who follows. Salvation does not come from the words of men crying "Lord, Lord," but from the Word of God, speaking his eternal "Follow me" which enables man's eternal following. And the eternal Lord knows those who are following him, are responding to the service of his creative love in faith, hope and loving obedience, because he is where he acts. The servant's following is the correlative of the Lord's leading; the servant's reaction is only in virtue of the Lord's action; the servant's love responds to the Lord's word. This is the basic dynamism which establishes the Lord-servant relationship; this is what it means to be Lord and to be servant. They are correlative concepts, representing initiative and response, action and reaction, cause and effect. Thus, Christ is only effectively Lord of the man who responds, the "servant."

The Lord-servant relationship is a dynamic correlation of persons. It means that Christ is effectively savior only in the man he is saving; he is effectively revealing himself only in the man in whom he is revealed; he is effectively speaking only in the man who hears him; he is effectively the happiness only of the man who enjoys him. The Lord-servant relationship is that of a living Lord evoking a loving response, which Matthew expresses in terms of the Great Commandment, the Beatitudes, and the service of those in need which the Son of Man rewards at the Final Judgment. The "servant" is the man who lovingly responds to the Lord's "Follow me," so that his life is a spontaneous following, as opposed to a condition which he regretfully tolerates. He is a servant because he wants to follow and would be unhappy if he did not.

For those who cried "Lord, Lord," the Lord-servant relationship was never actualized; however, it should have been actualized. The Lord's creative initiative, his "Follow me" had enabled the response that would have meant a life of dynamic growth in becoming a son of God: "Blessed are the peacemakers, for they shall be called the sons of God" (5:9). The failure to respond was a reprehensible rejection of life, and an ungrateful refusal to accept the future.

Matthew's concept of the Lord-servant relationship has its roots in the Old Testament, where God is revealed as the Lord who alone exercises power over the universe and all mankind (Ps 135). The Lord is the creator, the disposer of life and death. "Lord" summarizes the faith of the Old Testament, the unique, exclusive relationship of commitment between the Lord and his people, which implied his full control of history, his ability to mold and guide their destiny, and to achieve whatever he desires.

The Old Testament provided Matthew with prototypes of "good and faithful" servants. Abraham, Isaac, Jacob, and Joseph were entirely responsive and loyal to his call, and conformed themselves to his will to the extent that they understood it. They were keenly conscious of their solidarity and union with their Lord. With the Lord's faithful servant Moses, the people of Israel experienced during the Exodus God's mysterious and omnipotent lordship in the achievement of their liberation, which was the Lord's irresistible will.

Israel's covenant acknowledged Yahweh as Lord in the closest possible bond of mutual fidelity and loyalty. The covenant, the prototype of the Lord-servant relationship, obliged both parties, under penalty of destruction and curse, to mutual assistance and support according to capability and need. Mutual fidelity and loyalty were obligatory; love and ready action, on the basis of this bond, were expected from the covenant partner. Thus, the Lord protected and saved his "good and faithful" servants who were true to their covenant obligations.

The Lord's effective lordship was expressed in the love, loyalty and ready action of his servants; in this way, the Lord was protecting and saving them. He is a saving Lord only for those who are united with him; separation implies consequent destruction.

Although the Lord has perfect independence from his creation; he freely chooses to extend his loving care, his *lordship,* to all men. His "good and faithful" servants are not slaves, but his covenant partners and sons. To be a servant is to be one whom the Lord is protecting, guiding, loving, and caring for. Matthew recalls the Old Testament covenant background when he affirms that Christ is the Lord of the New Covenant (26:28). Christ's "Follow me" expresses both his offer and his expectation of covenant love, loyalty, and ready action. The "good and faithful" servant lives up to his expectation in accepting the Lord's offer. His acceptance is the condition for the actualization of the Lord-servant relationship; it permits the Lord's covenant love, loyalty, and ready action to become effective in him.

Although Christ is the Lord with all authority and power in heaven and on earth (28:18), he does not come in power, the way the Gentile rulers do (20:25). He does not coerce men to respond to his "Follow me," nor does he coerce those who have responded. Rather, the evidence of his coming is his service. Where the Lord acts, he serves; *he gives his life* for others. When and where the Lord acts, it is *"to give his life* as a ransom for many" (20:28). When a man accepts the lordship of Christ, he does not accept the tyranny of one who domineers; rather, he accepts the lordship of one who ". . . has not come to be served, but to serve, and to give his life" (20:28). His lordship is for man's welfare, not his. Thus, Matthew's way of saying "God is love" (1 Jn 4:8) might be paraphrased as "The Lord is a servant." The Lord serves those whom he rules; he ministers to those whom he leads; he takes care of those whom he governs: "This is my blood of the New Covenant, which is poured out for many for the forgiveness of sins" (26:28).

The Lord is where he acts. And the quality of his action is service. Therefore, the Lord is where he serves. The Lord is in communion with his "good and faithful" servant in the very act of service: ". . . as long as you did it to one of the least of these my brethren, you did it to me" (25:40). The servant's life is the Lord's life of service, and therefore credible evidence of the Lord's existence and activity among men. Together with his servants, "He will save his people from their sins" (1:21).

Théo Preiss, in his monograph, "Life in Christ" (London: SCM Press, 1957, 46), underscores the significance of service in his translation of "As you did it to one of the least of these my brethren, you did it to me" (25:40) by "as you *served* one of the least . . . you *served* me." Preiss explains that in Aramaic Jesus could only have used the verb *abad,* which means both to "do" and to "serve." He argues convincingly that in this text the essential meaning is to "serve."

Matthew's understanding of the Lord as a servant has its roots in the Old Testament. He sees the Lord as the Servant of God prophesied by Isaiah: "my servant whom I have chosen" (12:18) and "my servant . . . my beloved with whom my soul is well pleased" (3:17). J. Jeremias, in his monograph, "The Servant of God" (London: SCM Press, 1957, 79–104), compares correlative texts in Matthew and Isaiah in which the Lord is regarded as the fulfillment of Isaiah's prophecy concerning the Servant of God: 8:17 (Is 53:4); 12:18–21 (Is 42:1–4); 20:28 (Is 53:10, 12); 26:63 and 27:12 (Is 53:12); 11:5 and 5:3 (Is 40). The Lord is himself the prototype of the "good and faithful" servant.

The Lord-servant relationship is one which Matthew understands from personal experience. It was not coercion that forced Matthew to leave his tax-collector's table and follow the Lord for the rest of his life; it was rather the experience of the Lord's overwhelming love for him that "compelled" his following. Christ's power to lead men as their Lord is not based on the power to coerce. Christ has his own way of being Lord that does not resemble man's. His power and authority are based on his overwhelming love for persons. His effective lordship is established by the power of his creative love; it is in response to this that a man becomes his "servant." Thus, the love of Christ for men is creating the kingdom of God, the actualization of the Lord-servant relationship among men. The personal inspiration of the Lord creates the servant.

John L. McKenzie, in his article, "Authority and Power in the New Testament" (*The Catholic Biblical Quarterly* 25 [1964], 421), considers the nature of Christ's lordship in the context of the Church and implicitly suggests the context within which those with charisms may have been condemned. McKenzie remarks that, when the officers of the Church dominate the faithful rather than become examples for the flock (1 Pt 5:3), the Church takes on a secular character. He notes that in the New Testament description of ecclesiastical leadership one person does not impose his will on another. If the members of the Church are not united in that love which makes all seek to serve each other, then coercion and control are no substitute for what is missing. The Lord does not dominate his servants like the rulers of a police state.

Despite the Church's failure in individual members to achieve the perfection of Christ's lordship (i.e., love), she retains her identity; individual failures do not destroy her identity and continuity as the community which the Lord has called into existence by the power of his love. It remains the community of the Servant of God through which he continues to come to serve, to save, to give his life for the ransom of many (20:28).

Matthew's Hebrew concept of knowledge is related to his understanding of the dynamic Lord-servant relationship. For the Hebrews, knowing someone meant far more than being able to identify him. It implied a personal knowledge that could be even as intimate as the relationship of husband and wife; it indicated a vital relationship in which persons had entered into one another's private history. Thus, the Lord knew Israel as intimately as one person can know another (Amos 3:2; Osee 5:3).

The Lord's judgment, "I never knew you" (7:23), must be understood in the context of Hebrew thought. This precludes any interpretation of the judgment which might possibly hint at a divine vendetta provoked by man's ingratitude. In its Hebrew context, "I never knew you" means that there was never any intimate personal reciprocity between the Lord and his potential servant. Neither had really entered into the other's life, despite the Lord's initiative. Neither, therefore, really knew the other.

If the Lord comes as one who serves, then he is known and experienced as one who serves. Matthew's theology of the Lord-servant relationship implies that those who cried "Lord, Lord" had never really known him, because they had never had any experience of him and his life of service for others. Consequently, their "Lord, Lord" was a false, reprehensible claim to a knowledge they had never had, and to a life they had never shared.

Those who had possessed the charisms are responsible for their own alienation, because the Lord comes as one who serves. When and where the Lord acts, he serves, *he gives his life* and this is the way he loves and saves. The Lord could not and would not cause their alienation, because this is not the way he acts. He comes as a servant because "He will save his people from their sins" (1:21). He does not come to separate men from him; rather, he invites with his "Follow me." Therefore, his judgment, "I never knew you," expresses something the Lord has never willed, and that is the meaning of sin. Because the Lord had wanted to know them, because he had come as a servant and had given his life for many, because he had invited them with his "Follow me," their failure to respond appropriately was a sin, a resistance to and failure to do his will, a refusal to accept him.

The human tragedy is the rejection of the Servant of God in the refusal to know the Lord. "I never knew you" expresses man's rejection of the Lord, rather than the Lord's rejection of man.

16
Love in the Message of Paul

St. Paul had a clear and deep awareness of the primacy of love in Christian life. He saw it, first of all, as a gift of the Father, who made himself known and manifested his love in Jesus: "For I am convinced that neither death nor life nor angels nor their hierarchies nor the present nor the future nor any supernatural forces either of height or depth nor anything else in creation will be able to separate us from the love God has shown in Christ Jesus our Lord!" (Rom 8:38f).

Through his own beloved Son, God saves the world: "He has rescued us from the dominion of darkness, and has transferred us into the realm of his dear Son, by whom we have been ransomed from captivity through having our sins forgiven" (Col 1:13).

God's love is boundless: "For, through the Holy Spirit that has been given us, God's love has *flooded* our hearts. For when we were still helpless, at the decisive moment Christ died for us godless men. Why, a man will hardly give his life for an upright person, though perhaps for a really good man some may be brave enough to die. But God proves his love for us by the fact that

Christ died for us when we were still sinners" (Rom 5:6ff). It is a superabundant, merciful love: "But when the goodness and kindness of God our Saviour were revealed, he saved us, not for any upright actions we had performed, but from his own mercy, through the bath of regeneration and renewal by the Holy Spirit, which he has poured out upon us abundantly through Jesus Christ our Saviour, so that we might be made upright through his mercy and become possessors of eternal life in fulfillment of our hope" (Tit 3:4–8).

The Father's love goes to the extreme of permitting his Son's death that we may obtain the gift of eternal life: "But God proves his love for us by the fact that Christ died for us when we were still sinners" (Rom 5:8); "Will not he who did not spare his own Son, but gave him up for us all, with that gift give us everything?" (Rom 8:32).

The Father's gift of love, Jesus Christ, enables us to become sons of God: "God sent his Son, born of a woman, and made subject to law, to ransom those who were made subject to law, so that we might receive adoption. And because you are sons, God has sent into our hearts the Spirit of his Son, with the cry, 'Abba!' that is, Father. So you are no longer a slave, but a son; and if a son, then an heir, made so by God" (Gal 4:4–7).

Perfect Love Revealed in Jesus

In Jesus we love God and are loved by God. Jesus is love itself and, as love incarnate, dwells among men as God's concrete human appeal for us. Through him the filial dialogue with God is realized among mankind.

The love of Jesus calls for reciprocity: "We know that in everything God works with those who love him, whom he has called in accordance with his purpose, to bring about what is good. For those whom he had marked out from the first he predestined to be made like his Son, so that he should be the eldest of many brothers; and those whom he has predestined he calls, and those whom he calls he makes upright, and those whom he makes upright he glorifies. Then what shall we conclude from this? If God is for us, who can be against us? Will not he who did not spare his own Son, but gave him up for us all, with that gift give us everything? Who can bring any accusation against those whom God has chosen? God pronounces them upright; who can condemn them? Christ Jesus who died, or rather who was raised from the dead, is at God's right hand, and actually pleads for us. Who can separate us from Christ's love?" (Rom 8:28–33). Again: "But if one loves God, one is known by him" (1 Cor 8:3).

The *cross* reveals the overwhelming intensity of God's love. It was necessary that love should suffer: "When he had assumed human form, he still further humbled himself and carried his obedience so far as to die, and to die upon the cross. That is why God has so greatly exalted him, and given him the name above all others, so that in the name of Jesus everyone should kneel, in heaven and on earth and in the underworld, and everyone should acknowledge Jesus Christ as Lord, and thus glorify God the Father" (Phil 2:8–11). Thus the cross manifests the love of obedience.

The cross is the reason why Jesus is "crowned with glory and honor" (Heb 2:9). Love motivated his suffering: ". . . he suffered death, so that by the favor of God he might taste the bitterness of death on behalf of every human being. For it was appropriate that he who is the great first cause of the universe should, in guiding his many children to his glorious salvation, make their lead in it fully qualified through what he suffered. For both he who purifies them and they who are purified spring from one source. That is why he is not ashamed to call them brothers" (Heb 2:9–11). Only a suffering saviour of a suffering humanity could truly claim solidarity with the human race.

Jesus's free acceptance of suffering assures us of his love, that ". . . our high priest is not one who is incapable of sympathy with our weaknesses, but he has been tempted in every way just as we have, without committing any sin. So let us come with courage to God's throne of grace to receive his forgiveness and find him responsive when we need his help" (Heb 4:15–16).

The love of Jesus is without reserve. Jesus gives himself entirely to the Father and to all men, without exception: "It is Christ's love that controls me, for I have become convinced that as one has died for all, all have died, and he died for all that those who live might no longer live for themselves, but for him who died for them and rose again" (2 Cor 5:14–15).

Through the cross God is fully glorified (Jn 17:4); and the man Christ Jesus, and with him all humanity, becomes capable of God's unreserved love: "For there is but one God, and one intermediary between God and men—the man Christ Jesus, who gave himself as a ransom for *all* men. That is what was testified to at the proper times, and I was appointed a herald and apostle of it— I am telling the truth, I am not lying—to teach the heathen faith and truth" (Tim 2:5–7).

The scandal of the cross is the scandal of divine love. This becomes the prototype of love which Paul holds up as a model for married people: "You who are husbands must love your wives just as Christ loved the church and gave himself for her" (Eph 5:25ff).

The love of Christ is the ultimate motive for the Christian life: laws are not observed for their own sake. "I have been crucified with Christ, and it is no longer I that live, but Christ that lives in me. The life I am now living in the body I am living by faith in the Son of God who loved me and gave himself for me. I refuse to nullify the mercy of God. For if uprightness could be secured through law, then Christ died for nothing!" (Gal 2:20–1).

The Role of the Spirit

The universality of love in the Spirit is stressed in Paul's message. If Calvary is the place where the perfection of love was manifested, the way in which it was manifested was a decisive test: Christ's friends had abandoned him. Adhesion to Christ's love is not a question of a physical encounter or human reasoning: "I have estimated nobody at what he seemed to be outwardly; even though I once estimated Christ in that way, I no longer do so. So if anyone is in union with Christ, he is a new being" (2 Cor 5:16). With the gift of the Spirit at Pentecost (Acts 2:1–36), God created in man that "new heart" of which the prophets had spoken (Jer 31:33ff; Ezek 36:25ff), and which Christ had promised (Jn 14:16ff). The Spirit is now present in the world through the Church: "You are built upon the apostles and prophets as your foundation, and Christ Jesus himself is the cornerstone. Through him every part of the building is closely united and grows into a temple sacred through its relation to the Lord, and you are yourselves built up into a dwelling for God through the Spirit" (Eph 2:20–22). The Spirit teaches men what Jesus had taught them, helping them to understand the deep inner meaning of his instruction and mission. Whether or not men have been eyewitnesses of Jesus's terrestrial mission, there is an equality transcending time and race. Every man needs the spirit before he can say "Father" (Rom 8:15) and glorify Christ (Jn 16:14). Thus the Spirit has poured forth his love (Rom 5:5) and urges us on (2 Cor 5:14), motivating us with a love that makes us inseparable from Christ (Rom 8:33–39) and prepares us for the final encounter with love in which "We shall know as we are known" (1 Cor 13:12).

"*God is love*" (1 Jn 4:8, 16) characterizes Pauline theology, although he does not state this fact as concisely and poignantly as does St. John. The eternal love of the Father and Son is the source of all love between God and man. The love of the Spirit —in short, of the Trinity—is the ultimate source of our every blessing: "The blessing of the Lord Jesus Christ, the love of God, and the participation in the Holy Spirit be with you all" (2 Cor 13:13).

Paul's strong assurance of God's love for us in Christ rests on three facts. God has sent his own son (Rom 8:32), and this act of love was perfected on the cross in the perfect self-surrender of the Son "who loved us." God has called the apostle and continues drawing those whom he has chosen; his love radiates upon them and they are "beloved" (1 Thess 1:4; Rom 9:11ff). God's love is poured into our hearts and becomes the decisive reality of our existence. God's loving work is revealed and realized in the life and work of Jesus (Rom 5:8). A world-transforming event takes place when eternal love becomes human love. The sanctification of man becomes possible through the agency of Jesus: "Blessed be the God and Father of our Lord Jesus Christ, who through Christ has blessed us with every spiritual blessing in the heavenly realm. Through him he chose us before the creation of the world, to be consecrated and above reproach in his sight in love. He fore-ordained us to become his sons through Jesus Christ, in fulfillment of his generous purpose, so that we might praise the splendid blessing which he has given us through his beloved Son" (Eph 1:3–6).

The idea that *love is the work of the Spirit,* which sets men free, finds classical expression in Paul's message: "But what the Spirit produces is love" (Gal 5:6); "the love of the Spirit" (Rom 15:30); "love in the Spirit" (Col 1:8). God's love comes through the Spirit: "We always have to thank God for you, brothers whom the Lord so loves, because God chose you from the beginning to be saved through consecration by the Spirit and through faith in the truth, and called you to it through our preaching of the good news, so that you may share in the glory of our Lord Jesus Christ" (2 Thess 2:13).

Paul sees the love of God revealed in a *historic event,* the coming of Jesus. The cross and resurrection of Christ are the unique
and sufficient revelation of God's love (Rom 5:8; 8:28). The
"historic" love of God is also creative and elective. Paul stresses
the sovereignty of God in choosing and calling whom he will to
constitute his Church on earth (Rom 9:13): the elect are the
beloved of God, which comes to the same thing (Rom 1:7; Col
3:12; 2 Thess 2:13; Eph 1:4; 2:4). Finally, the love of God in
historic action in the person of Jesus is a love which shows mercy
and pardon. Paul declares the merciful love of God with a precision which leaves nothing to be desired. Paul speaks of God's
justifying of man through his sovereign, free, reconciling love
which is supremely concretized on the cross. The love of God is
an objective fact, the permanent reality by which the Church lives.
Knowledge of this love is the root and foundation of the Christian
life (i.e., communion as well as comprehension) as its goal and
fulfillment: it "fills" the Christian with the fulness of God: "Your
roots must be deep and your foundations strong, so that you and
all God's people may be strong enough to grasp what breadth,
length, height, and depth mean, and to understand Christ's love,
so far beyond our understanding, so that you may be filled with
the very fulness of God" (Eph 3:17–18). Thus the love of God
for man is shown in his interventions in history on behalf of his
people; it is elective and creative, constituting the people of Israel
and, later, the universal Church; finally, it is a merciful love
which saves, helps, consoles, restores, and pardons.

Love of Neighbor

Two loves are taught in Pauline theology which are never
dissociated in the New Testament: love of God and neighbor.
Paul insists that we must "bear one another's burdens, and in
that way carry out the law of Christ" (Gal 6:2); "You must bear

with one another and forgive one another, if anyone has reason to be offended with anyone else. Just as the Lord has forgiven you, so you must forgive. And over all these put on love, which completes them and fastens them together" (Col 3:14).

Fraternal charity is the aim of all law: "Owe nobody anything —except the duty of mutual love, for whoever loves his fellow men has fully satisfied the law. . . . all [the commandments] are summed up in one saying, 'You must love your neighbor as you do yourself.' Love never wrongs a neighbor, and so love fully satisfied the law" (Rom 13:8–10). God is our model, we imitate his love in loving our fellow men: "You must be kind to one another, you must be tenderhearted, and forgive one another just as God through Christ has forgiven you. So follow God's example, like his dear children, and lead loving lives, just as Christ loved you and gave himself for you, as a fragrant offering and sacrifice to God" (Eph 5:1–2). If we sin against our neighbor, we offend the Holy Spirit of love: "You must not offend God's Holy Spirit, with which you have been marked for the day of redemption. You must give up all bitterness, rage, anger, and loud, abusive talk, and all spite" (Eph 4:30–31). Love for others is presumed as an evident hallmark of Christian life: "You do not need to have anyone write to you about brotherly love, for you have yourselves been taught by God to love one another, and you are doing it to all the brothers all over Macedonia" (1 Thess 4:9–10). Love of God and neighbor has the same origin as "the love that the Spirit inspires" (Rom 15:30); "For through the Holy Spirit that has been given us, God's love has flooded our hearts" (Rom 5:5). In loving our brothers, we love the Lord, because we all form the body of Christ (Rom 12:5–10; 1 Cor 12:12–27).

Love is a gift. Paul sees Christian charity as imaging God's boundless love for all men (Rom 5:5ff). Its universality allows no racial or social barrier (Gal 3:28). As the love of Christ for the Church has two essential features (he gave himself for her, and desires her to be perfect and glorious in his presence), so a man will love his wife with a love which surrenders itself and which provides for her true destiny (for the "glory" of her spouse). Conjugal love receives its ultimate significance and intensity from the love of God for mankind, of Christ for his Church (Eph 5:25, 28, 33; Col 3:19).

The Spirit's Presence in Fraternal Love

Sin, as illustrated in the Babel story of man's defiance of God, divides men. That love which indicates the presence of the Spirit of God unites us with others: "Your love must be genuine. Hate what is wrong, and hold to what is right. Be affectionate in your love for the brotherhood, eager to show one another honor, not wanting in devotion, but on fire with the Spirit. Serve the Lord. Be happy in your hope, steadfast in time of trouble, persistent in prayer. Supply the needs of God's people, be unfailing in hospitality. Bless your persecutors; bless them; do not curse them. Rejoice with those who rejoice, weep with those who weep. Live in peace with one another. Do not be ambitious, but accept humble tasks. Do not be conceited. Do not pay anyone back with evil for evil. . . . Do not be conquered by evil, but conquer evil with good" (Rom 12:9–21). Fraternal charity obliges the Christian with many daily exigencies: ". . . each must tell his neighbor the truth, for we are parts of one another. Be angry, but do not sin. The sun must not go down upon your anger; you must not give the devil a chance" (Eph 4:25).

Paul's famous "hymn of love" is perhaps the most concrete and eloquent passage on fraternal love in Scripture: "I will show you a far better way. If I can speak the languages of men and even of angels, but have no love, I am only a noisy gong or a clashing cymbal. If I am inspired to preach and know all the secret truths and possess all knowledge, and if I have such perfect faith that I can move mountains, but have no love, I am nothing. Even if I give away everything I own, and give myself up, but do it in pride, not love, it does me no good. Love is patient and kind. Love is not envious or boastful. It does not put on airs. It is not rude. It does not insist on its rights. It does not become angry. It is not resentful. It is not happy over injustice, it is only happy with truth. It will bear anything, believe anything, hope for anything, endure anything. Love will never die out. If there is inspired preaching, it will pass away. If there is ecstatic speaking, it will cease. If there is knowledge, it will pass away. For our knowledge is imperfect and our preaching is imperfect. But when perfection comes, what is imperfect will pass away. When I was a child, I talked like a child, I thought like a child, I reasoned like a child. When I became a man, I put aside my childish ways. For now we are looking at a dim reflection in a mirror, but then we shall see face to face. Now my knowledge is imperfect, but then I shall know as fully as God knows me. So faith, hope, and love endure. These are the great three, and the greatest of them is love" (1 Cor 13).

The Church is built through love (1 Cor 8:1; Eph 4:16). Through love man achieves the necessary perfection for the day of the Lord (Phil 1:9). The requirement of love appears at the end of all the epistles (especially Romans and Galatians), as a consequence of the salvation of God described in the body of the letter. This love is the "fruit of the Spirit" (Gal 5:22; Rom 15:30). Christ is where his Spirit is, and the Spirit is where love is. The faith that has assented to the truths of salvation becomes active and productive through love alone (Gal 5:6). Fraternal love in suffering and joy belongs to the kingdom of God (Philem 5; Col 1:4; 1 Thess 4:9).

Paul's teaching on love implies that truth must go in beauty or she will go unregarded. The beauty of Christian love led the early Romans to the truths of the Gospel: "Look how they love one another." Paul realized that all Christian love of neighbor takes its origin and strength from the intimate union of God and man. Such love of others does not live on human strength alone, but on the wondrous power of the Holy Spirit through whom "the love of God has been poured out in our hearts" (Rom 5:5). It is this same power, this gift of divine love, which, according to St. John, makes man's life an opportunity to become a son of God. Without the power of this love, St. Paul wisely concluded that we are nothing. The Pauline enumeration of love's signs offers excellent material for the Christian's examination of conscience.

INDEX OF AUTHORS

L. Alonso-Schökel, vii
B. W. Anderson, 69
T. Barrosse, 116
Calvin, 166, 182
B. Childs, 134
J. Daniélou, 167, 182
J. D'Aragon, vii, viii, 117ff., 121–125.
I. de la Potterie, vii
H. de Lubac, 182
C. H. Dodd, 89
B. Gehardsson, 167, 182
A. Gelin, 68
A. M. Henry, 76
E. C. Hoskyns, 167, 182
J. Jeremias, 166
John XXIII, 75
A. Jones, 67
L. Legrand, 69
Luther, 166, 182

R. A. F. MacKenzie, vii
F. McCool, vii
J. L. McKenzie, 150, 201, 224
Maldonatus, 166, 182
G. Marcel, 77
D. Mollat, vii
K. Rahner, 164
H. W. Robinson, 68
C. A. Simpson, 184
J. Skinner, 67f.
J. D. Smart, 40
D. M. Stanley, vii, 167
K. Stern, 76
St Thomas, 75
R. C. Trench, 182
C. Tresmontant, 155
P. van den Eynde, 182
B. Vawter, 69
F. Werfel, 67
T. Wilder, 69

SUBJECT INDEX

Anamnesis, 129

Benedictus, 81

Celibacy, 59ff., 67, 69
Chaos, 57, 185–188, 190–194, 196
Charity, universal, 79, 81f., 84, 86
Contemplation, 61
Conversion: becoming like a child, 161; a commitment, 148; through community, 155; through the compassion of Christ, 157; through creation and nature, 150f.; formulas expressing, 146; in freedom, 146; through history, 152; through law, 149; the creation-through-order, 156; the process of "putting on" Christ, 163; through prophets, 149; a relationship, 159; a response, 147f.; through revelation, 149; through sacrifice, 159; the Will of God:

238

through wisdom, 149f.; through the Word of God, 149
Covenant commitment, 148
Covenant love, 149

Didactic unity, 177
Diptych development, 80f.
Dominion, 27–31, *passim.*

Evidence, 99–112, *passim.*

Glory: apparition of, 43f.; as the Church, 51; eschatological, 46; in St. John, 96, 116; in the liturgy, 48ff.; man's reaction to, 45f.; as the theophany, 49

Happiness: messianic, 88; theology of, 87
History: the continuing act of divine loving kindness, 189; begins with meaning, 186; creation continued, 193f.; depends on the wisdom and power of Yahweh, 188; the emer-

gence of Yahweh's plan, 200ff.; a gift of God, 189; incomprehensible because of sin, 192; meaningful because of Yahweh, 190, 192f.; the order imposed on creation, 189; personal, because determined by a Person, 202
Hope, 65, 136

Image of God: through the agency of the Holy Spirit, 40; dominates lower creation, 31; through the effects of wisdom, 34; Jesus, the perfect image, 39; renewed in Christ, 36; represents God among creatures, 32; shares in divine sovereignty, 32
Insight, 61, 63, 65

Judgment: in St. John, 96; Matthew's eschatology of the, 204ff., 210, 214f.

Kerygma, 179
Knowledge of God, 92f.

Life: eternal, 65, 91, 171f., 174; a gift, 67
Literalism, 71
Liturgy for Advent and Lent, 145
Logos, 98

Magnalia Dei, 132f.
Magnificat, 81
Mercy, gospel of, 182n.
Messiah, 79, 87f.

Natural virtues, 71

Parallelism, 77
Peace, 25, 31f., 111

"Reintegrating" action, 25
Remembering: an attitude of joy and gratitude, 130; evokes trust, 134; God's, 130–133; Israel's, 133–141; in Luke's Gospel, 142f.; of specific saving events, 130
Responsiveness, 114, 212f.
"The Returned," 163

"Salvation," 173
Self-righteousness, 79
Signs: casting out devils, 100f.; contingent upon persons, 113; disciples empowered to give them, 104; evidence for faith, 102; faith and obedience, 102; humiliation, 109; indicate sonship, 103; love of enemies, 103; mercifulness, 103; point beyond themselves, 103; preaching, 100f.; service, 105, 108; a *skandalon,* 110; a social obligation, 107; suffering, 109; transmit Christian revelation, 112; unity of mutual love, 106
Solidarity, 38, 155
Solitude, 63
Son of God, 98
Son of Man, 97
Suffering, 56
Symbolism, 89f.

"Temple Sermon," 66
Theology: banquet, 83f., 87; happiness, 87; poverty, 84–87
Truth, 93f., 96

Vocation, 53f., 56